A Shifting Shore

A Shifting Shore

LOCALS, OUTSIDERS, AND THE TRANSFORMATION
OF A FRENCH FISHING TOWN,
1823–2000

Alice Garner

CORNELL UNIVERSITY PRESS

ITHACA AND LONDON

This publication is supported by a grant from the Research and Graduate Studies Committee, Faculty of Arts, The University of Melbourne.

First published 2005 by Cornell University Press

Printed in the United States of America

Design by Scott Levine

Library of Congress Cataloging-in-Publication Data

Garner, Alice, 1969–
    A shifting shore : locals, outsiders, and the transformation of a French fishing town, 1823–2000 / Alice Garner.
        p.   cm.
    Includes bibliographical references and index.
    ISBN 0-8014-4282-6 (cloth : alk. paper)
    1. Arcachon (France)—History—19th century.   2. Arcachon (France)—History—20th century.   3. Arcachon (France)—Economic conditions—19th century.   4. Arcachon (France)—Economic conditions—20th century.   5. Arcachon Basin (France). I. Title.
    DC801.A675G37   2005
    944'.714—dc22   2004015588

Cornell University Press strives to use environmentally responsible suppliers and materials to the fullest extent possible in the publishing of its books. Such materials include vegetable-based, low-VOC inks and acid-free papers that are recycled, totally chlorine-free, or partly composed of nonwood fibers. For further information, visit our website at www.cornellpress.cornell.edu.

Cloth printing   10 9 8 7 6 5 4 3 2 1

One cannot help but recall a wonderful, paradisiacal description
of Fénelon's with which he delighted his royal pupil, when admiring
the sun-kissed freshness of Arcachon, its jaunty, smiling villas, its chilly
chalets nestled under the pine trees, the liveliness of its little provincial
streets, the feeling of calm which emanates like a fragrance of forgetting,
the richness of its caravanserai, the fertility of its hothouse plants, the
soothing quality [*lénitude*] of its enchanting climate, and the poor
little sick ones who will soon be angels, and the rugged
mariners of the Atlantic who wish to tame the sea.

—P. A. de Lannoy, *Guide aux plages girondines*, 1900

CONTENTS

MAPS

A Shifting Shore

Heri solitudo, hodie vicus, cras civitas.
Yesterday solitude, today a town, tomorrow a city.

—Lamarque de Plaisance, mayor of Arcachon, 1860

INTRODUCTION

In August 1844, a well-to-do family takes a two-hour train trip from Bordeaux to the Arcachon bay, for a seaside cure. At the La Teste railway station—at the end of the line—they are surrounded by local women who compete to offer them a boat ride to the desirable Eyrac beach, where the best hotels are situated. They choose a guide, who leads the visitors to the foreshore, wades fully dressed through the shallows to deposit their luggage in a rowing boat, and returns for each family member. She heaves the tourists one by one onto her back and carries them to her vessel, so that they may keep their shoes, skirts, and trousers dry. She then rows the family westward toward Eyrac, a quiet, sandy beach that will eventually become the center of a new town, Arcachon.[1]

Today, Arcachon is a popular, highly developed seaside resort with its own railway station and freeway connection. The bay, or Bassin d'Arcachon, a large, triangular body of water, lies some sixty kilometers (thirty-seven miles) west-southwest of Bordeaux, in France's Gironde department. The Bassin's capacity alters dramatically with the tides, its surface area dropping from 155 to 40 square kilometers (about 60 to 15 square miles) as the water ebbs out through treacherous narrows, or *passes,* into the Atlantic Ocean. Bordered by shifting sand dunes, and fed by the Leyre River, this is a constantly changing environment, whose edges have nevertheless become home to a permanent population of oyster farmers and fishing families, a seasonal population of vacationers, and, more recently, retirees from the Bordeaux area. The oblong hump of the town of Arcachon juts up from the southern shore of the Bassin. Situated at the eastern end of its beach is one of Europe's largest marinas, built in 1964: a floating city of pleasure craft jostling a fishing fleet whose foothold is gradually being pried away by the combined forces of tourism, declining fish stocks, environmental degradation, and European regulations governing every aspect of their work. This book tells the story of that prying away.

Arcachon is now only forty-five minutes from Bordeaux by train, making daily commuting a possibility. It is often recommended as a day trip to tourists staying in the Girondin capital. In summer Parisians can make the trip on the Train à Grande Vitesse (TGV), or High Speed Train, in less than four hours. They are advised to sample the Bassin's oysters, visit the Dune du Pyla, the tallest dune in Europe at 114 meters (374 feet), and stroll through pine forests that meet the town's edges. Guides recommend a ferry trip to Cap Ferret, the peninsula opposite Arcachon, beaten by the Atlantic on one side and lapped by the Bassin on the other, and a boat tour of the Bassin reveals the Ile aux Oiseaux (Bird Island), where houses on stilts hover over the water, as well as a front-row view of Arcachon's most impressive shorefront villas.[2] Visitors can stay in one of the many hotels or serviced apartment buildings, or—for those seeking a more "picturesque" experience—in one of the mansions in the Ville d'hiver (Winter City), perched among the pines high above the town center.

Arcachon is a young town by French standards. It became a municipality only in 1857. For an Australian historian like me, there is something familiar and comforting about its mid-nineteenth-century beginnings, its mixture of fanciful holiday architecture and more recent—and mostly ugly—overdevelopment. Stepping out of the small railway station at the end of the line from Bordeaux, the visitor has little immediate sense of Arcachon's past. Arcachon trades on nearby natural beauties—the sea, the dunes, the pine forest—rather than on historic atmosphere. The streets leading from the station to the water are recently paved, their storefronts revealing little of what the place might once have been like. Holiday apartment blocks built in the 1980s overshadow the few pretty villas remaining in the commercial center.

FIG. 1. France, showing Paris, La Teste, and Bordeaux.

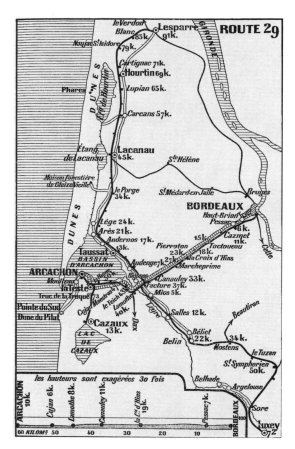

FIG. 2. Bassin d'Arcachon. From Paul Joanne, *De la Loire aux Pyrénées* (Paris: Librairie Hachette et Cie, 1908), 365.

Before Arcachon was made a municipality in its own right, it was a subsection of La Teste-de-Buch, the most populous community on the shores of the Bassin d'Arcachon. The name *Arcachon* was taken by the new town's founders from this body of water that lapped at the feet of at least eight other, well-established villages. To claim the name for itself, suggesting that it was the principal settlement on the Bassin, despite being new, was a bold act, guaranteed to annoy Arcachon's older neighbors. The town's first mayor, Jacques-Thomas-Alphonse Lamarque de Plaisance (with a surname which, in a nice twist, can be translated as "The Mark of Pleasure," or even as "the Yachting Brand"), and other property owners and investors, who held high hopes for Arcachon's future as a seaside retreat for wealthy families, evidently believed it would not do for Arcachon's history to be subsumed within that of the humbler, more rustic La Teste.[3] A new identity must be forged, a separate founding story, a way of differentiating the new town from the old.

In 1860, Lamarque de Plaisance designed a coat of arms for the newly minted village. In this way he could communicate Arcachon's significance, its links to the past, and his vision of its future in one tidy, legitimizing graphic. A pine tree, torn from the earth, floats beside a golden beehive and six bees over an azure background. The tree represents the pure air emitted by the extensive pine forests, one of the new town's claims to fame, as well as the timber and resin industries so essential to the local economy. The beehive, according to one explanation, symbolizes "the first source of wealth for Arcachon"—honey.[4]

A golden Virgin Mary and guiding star, set against a red background, hover on a silver cloud over a sailing vessel in a storm-tossed sea: this refers to the local sailors' veneration of Mary, to whom they appealed when in trouble, as well as to the monk Thomas Illyricus's discovery of an alabaster statue of the Virgin on a deserted beach in 1520—a moment considered by many to mark the beginning of Arcachon, despite the fact that fishing and forest communities already inhabited the area and had since Roman times.

Floating above these images is a band of black, silver, and gold, representing respectively sand (the past), new light (the present), and the envisaged "apotheosis and the beneficial rays of the sun" (the future).[5] The band is in turn crowned by a wreath of sailing ships, while the arms are supported by two angry, sharp-toothed, and scaly dolphins, intertwined with a black anchor that provides a frame for the banner.

This coat of arms is one among many attempts to represent the space—or place—of Arcachon, in a quickly readable vocabulary of figures, colors, and lines. We can read Lamarque's design as part of his strategy for the promotion and development of Arcachon as a place where the forest meets the sea, and where both are tamed by a pious and industrious people. Although some potentially frightening elements (the angry dolphins, the storm-tossed sea) appear within this graphic space, they are under control, their wildness harnessed, hemmed in by the curling scroll of text and held down by the anchor.

The coat of arms, of course, tells only a truncated story about the new town's origins. That is as Lamarque de Plaisance would have wanted it. It is not difficult to find out more about the history of Arcachon if one is interested, but it is easily read representations like the arms that tend to speak loudest and have an immediacy most appealing to visitors. A few moments from the town's past are repeatedly recounted, and they come to represent the whole history of the place. A statue of the Virgin Mary, the cultivation of oysters, the highest dune in Europe, and an extensive pine forest planted (singlehandedly, one is led to believe) by the engineer Nicolas Brémontier: these have become the key symbols of Arcachon. When I told French people that I was working on the history of this place, they inevitably mentioned oysters, which have become the principal sign of Arcachon.

But where is a richer history of the place? And why did I, an Australian historian, want to investigate it? My interest in this region grew out of a general question that had possessed me during vacations on other shores in Europe. Postcards, guide books, and interior design magazines dwell on gaily painted boats, rusted metal, whitewashed cottages, wizened faces of fishermen and -women—in other words, they aestheticize fishing communities and their paraphernalia, the material of their working and domestic lives. I wanted to know when and how this romanticization had begun, and what it was like for the people pictured to become the object of tourists' fascination.

This called for an investigation into one particular town—necessarily a fishing port turned bathing resort—leading into a broader questioning of how the sea and shore were represented by different groups, and what relationship these representations had with the space as lived by local and visiting people. The French town of La Teste (and its "daughter" Arcachon) beckoned for a number of reasons: its situation on a bay and its connection to the Atlantic Ocean, two very different bodies of water; its rapid transformation from remote outpost to popular tourist destination; its proximity to a regional capital (Bordeaux); and the fact that the region's history had not been overfished!

When I began looking for early signs of a tourist mentality in the first part of the nineteenth century, in national, departmental, and municipal archives, I found that my questioning needed to expand to consider visions and developments predating tourism. It was necessary to move well beyond the beach and the Bassin's protected waters, in both directions, to take into account the history of the interior, the *landes* between Bordeaux and the Bassin, as well as the troublesome foreshore zone and the Atlantic Ocean beyond the heads. The Bassin and its beaches could not be separated from these connected spaces, and the language that developed over the nineteenth century, in particular around new conceptions of property and ownership, affected them all equally powerfully.

I eventually came to ask how various floating worlds understood each other and the sea and shore that supported or lured them: the fishing community on its work vessels, investors and engineers with their dreams of a bountiful future, invalids floating between life and death in their forest villas overlooking the sea, and vacationers temporarily moving in and through, not anchored to the place by responsibility or obligation.[6]

While the work of local historians and geographers was indispensable to my project, in particular for empirical contributions, my overall approach has been somewhat different from theirs.[7] My interest in the coastline—a zone that resists all attempts at definition—has shaped this book. Rather than attempt to write a chronological history of the settlement and evolution of Arcachon, I have undertaken an investigation into aspects of the development of the Bassin's southern shores over the nineteenth and (in somewhat less detail) twentieth centuries, in an attempt to recover something of what the social theorist Henri Lefebvre calls "lived space," people's bodily experiences of a place undergoing transformation, experiences that cannot easily be communicated or preserved beyond the moment of their happening. This complex, multilayered lived space can be lost in representations like Lamarque de Plaisance's coat of arms, in maps and photographs, because the fixing of one moment, invented or real, obscures the exchanges and confrontations, the sounds and the silences, that are part of the "production of space." And yet we must rely on these arrested images, along with written reports, to gain an understanding of times past. This means that, if we wish to get beneath the glossy image of a tourist resort that has, according to a nineteenth-century observer, seemingly sprung up "as if by magic," a critical analysis of documents that might otherwise have the last word (or view) is necessary.[8]

This approach to the history required a familiarity with a broad body of literature, including geography and spatial theory, cartography, maritime history, fine arts, French literature, anthropology, sociology (incorporating leisure and tourism theory), architecture, planning, and the history of medicine.[9] Each has its own vocabulary and system of thought, of course, and this

wide reading provoked an expansion of my notion of what a history of Arcachon might look like. But certain texts proved to be particularly influential:
Henri Lefebvre, Alain Corbin, and Jean-Didier Urbain formed a core trio of
reference and inspiration.

In his *La production de l'espace,* Henri Lefebvre offered a set of useful ana-
lytical tools as part of his theorization of "social space," in particular, what he
called "representations of space" and "lived space."[10] Lefebvre conceives of social space as one of those delicious French multilayered pastries, the *mille-
feuilles*—that is, as a coexistence of differently produced spaces. People actively create networks of spatial practice through living; they do not simply
move through an abstract, inert space. This book responds to Lefebvre in its
attempt to make sense of the nature-space of the Bassin as it has been lived
and represented and transformed and fragmented by people, in and through
their bodies. My central question, using Lefebvrian terms, is this: How did
representations of space (conceptions, systems, forms of knowledge about
space, with a strategic objective) created by engineers, property developers
and investors, and, later, vacationers, who became interested in the Bassin, in-
tersect or conflict with the lived space of the local inhabitants? What kinds of
difficulties faced those who wished to reinvent the shores and hinterland of
the Bassin, zones that were never empty, either of people or of meaning?

While Lefebvre's formulations could be applied to all the connected spatial
experiences this book traverses, Corbin's and Urbain's focus on the coastline
sharpened my understanding of the particularities and challenges of the shifting point where sea meets land. In *The Lure of the Sea,* Alain Corbin delves
into almost every aspect of the ways the European sea and shore were experienced in the eighteenth and early nineteenth centuries, tracing how European
attitudes toward this "territory of emptiness" changed over two centuries,
from a profound horror before the deeps, to a desire to experience a bodily
communion with the water, initially for therapeutic purposes, later for pleasure. While he offers many localized examples of changing relationships to
the sea throughout his book, his broad European focus—ranging from Hol-
land's dikes to the Mediterranean, Channel, and Atlantic coasts—and long
time span mean that he cannot afford to dwell for too long on any one place.
His study stops in the early 1800s, just where I pick up the story of La Teste
and Arcachon.[11]

Urbain, in his *Sur la plage: mœurs et coûtumes balnéaires (XIXe–XXe siècles),*
addresses the changing social, moral, and aesthetic identity of the (mainly European) beach, zooming in on the microcosm of the sand or strand. His contention is that the beach as we know it today is an invented, decontextualized

space, reflecting an idealized image of a desert island. Emptied of indigenous peoples and of any signs of labor, the beach has been re-created as a neutralized edge upon which people can fantasize about their own renewal and act out their regeneration. While his main focus is on this twentieth-century "polynesianisation" of the shore, he takes care to analyze the steps leading to this moment, from the early nineteenth century onward. His work also makes it clear that a close examination of the ways humans use and imagine the beach can contribute to a broader understanding of behaviors and desires that are by no means confined to the hiatus of the holiday period. It is "one of these privileged places," he argues, "where society enacts itself."[12]

Urbain argues that the beach seems to offer the possibility of stripping back the complexities of urban life to an elemental simplicity and truthfulness. If the sea is a site of renewal, of death (submersion) and revival (reemergence), the beach, as its threshold, must be emptied of contaminating associations, cleared of old meanings. For this reason, the locals—usually a fishing population—must be removed from sight, or at least "sweetened" (*édulcorés*) so that they become part of the decor but have no claim to the stretch of sand that must be neutral, untainted.

Although Urbain acknowledges that the beach becomes the "theatre of a conflict between bathers and fishermen from which the former emerged victorious, despite, on occasions, some resistance, and from which the latter withdrew and disappeared," he does not investigate these resistances in any detail.[13] How does the fishing community resist, and why do they withdraw, if indeed they do? This is where I hope my study can offer something different. I intend to look at the way in which the emptying and "taming" of the Arcachon beach was carried out and actively resisted.

What is lacking in the historiography of the world of the beach is a strong body of work offering close analysis of particular seaside communities and their evolution. John K. Walton has tried single-handedly to fill this gap; he has done extensive, locally focused work on the history of British seaside resorts, as well as on San Sebastian. He notes that the dearth of local studies in other countries has led historians to make unfounded generalizations about the social history of the beach. A more nuanced, comparative understanding could emerge if local experiences, shaped by different topography, climate, patterns of demand, and moral and governmental frameworks, were explored more thoroughly.[14] This book responds to Walton's call. It is firmly anchored in the place known as Arcachon, but it also looks outside the town's edges, taking into account ideas and approaches that have been formulated in broader terms by scholars writing about other shores.

There are, naturally, some gaps and challenges in this history, which I wish to acknowledge here. First, I do not claim to offer a comprehensive, chronological account of Arcachon's history. For example, the story of the stabilization of the dunes and the planting of the vast pine forests has been so well told by other historians that I allude to it only briefly.[15] My focus is the nineteenth century, when the conflicts over the maritime zone heightened and to some extent dictated the shape and tenor of later developments. The last chapter covers in one sweep the twentieth-century Bassin and points the way toward exciting possibilities for further research. The advent of mass tourism and the impact of war on the sea and shore in this region, which I discuss briefly, deserve their own book.[16]

Second, the sources I rely on could never give me the unmediated voice of fishermen and -women, most of whom were illiterate. Alain Cabantous, who has written extensively about France's seafaring communities, calls the mariner "l'homme de l'oralité," or man of the spoken word—and the fisherwoman's voice was even less likely to be recorded than his.[17] Petitions, council minutes, and reports can offer only a filtered version of their perspective. But their voices are, of course, still worth seeking out. If we listen hard enough, if we scrape away at the prejudices and vested interests in their spokespeople's (or opponents') version of events, something of their worldview becomes apparent, without which we cannot appreciate the full meaning or impact of the remaking of the shore.

Third, definitions are of great importance in the struggles that take place between the fishing community and outsiders over the nineteenth century. Terms for features of the land and seascape are hotly contested when appropriation or transformation is proposed. I faced a similar problem in the translation of words for coast, beach, shore, and synonyms. In fact they are not quite synonyms, and this is where translation becomes a delicate matter, particularly when legal arguments arise. In French, there seem to be more terms for shore than there are in English: *lais et relais, rivage, grève, plage, littoral,* and *côte*.[18] I have tried to be faithful to nuances of meaning, but given that these words were the subject of violent disagreement in the period covered by this book, I cannot claim to have arrived at a definitive position. I have translated all quotes in the body of the book (unless otherwise indicated), and where I have felt my translation to be in any way inadequate, or where English could not convey the subtleties of the original, I have offered the original in the endnotes.

And finally, a note on currency during the period. A meaningful conversion of French franc amounts into American dollars is virtually impossible due to regional differences and fluctuations over time in French wages and purchasing power. Instead, I offer the following figures as a rough guide to monetary value in the period covered. Under the July Monarchy (1830–48), the average daily wage for a working man was estimated by one statistician at 2 francs, 1 franc for a woman and 0 f. 45 to 0 f. 75 for a child.[19] Note that, because provincial workers usually earned a good deal less than Parisian laborers, any averages are skewed by the Paris figures. In his 1927 *Histoire de la classe ouvrière en France de la Révolution à nos jours,* Paul Louis provides a table of average daily wages between 1853 and 1911, based on 34 trades. In the Gironde department in 1853 the average male wage was 2 f. 92; in 1896, 4 f. 79; in 1911, 4 f. 96. The corresponding figures for women were: 1853, 1 f. 15; 1896, 2 f. 10; 1911, 2 f.[20]

Let us now go forth and dip our toes into the Bassin's rich history.

PART ONE

The Colonizing Impulse

CHAPTER ONE

Hideous Virginity, or Beautiful Maps on Annonay Paper

*In an era of progress of every kind . . . civilized France cannot
keep within its breast another, uncultivated France; immense deserts will
progressively be overcome by a philanthropic and intelligent activity.*

—Compagnie Agricole et Industrielle d'Arcachon, 1839

Arcachon today feels a little like an outer seaside suburb of Bordeaux. It was not always like this. Until the railway arrived in 1841—one of the earliest lines in France—few Bordelais, let alone people from other parts of France, visited the area. It was a rough journey of up to three days by ox cart, with an overnight stop in the humble (and, to some, seedy) village of Croix d'Hins. "O. D." (probably Testerin councillor Oscar Dejean), author of an 1845 *Guide du voyageur à La Teste,* depicted the pre-railway traveler arriving in La Teste at six in the morning "broken, bruised, exhausted, crushed, worn out, aching all over as far as is legally possible since torture has been abolished and there is no longer such thing as an official torturer [*tourmenteur-juré*]."[1] Only those with an established personal or commercial connection to the Bassin, or government officials, would bother to make the trip on a regular basis. So, although the distance (fifty-two kilometers, or thirty-two miles from Bordeaux) was not great by modern standards, before the age of rapid and reliable transport, La Teste seemed far away, inaccessible, and therefore alien. Compounding the sense of distance was the fact that between Bordeaux and the Bassin lay what was considered to be an ugly, featureless, and depressing expanse of *landes* (moors).[2]

We cannot consider the Bassin d'Arcachon separately from this hinterland, whose flat expanse struck horror into the hearts of men who saw value and beauty only in tamed, tilled, fertile, enclosed fields. The landes were not unlike the ocean: they had an elusive and terrifying quality. In summer they were scorched, in winter great swathes lay under water. For outsiders the landes were the epitome of emptiness, a view endlessly repeated in reports about the region in the early nineteenth century, drawing on a vocabulary developed in the mid-eighteenth century by physiocrats who preached the benefits of dividing up communal lands.[3] In 1839, for example, the Baron Mortemart de Boisse described the landes as this "space without borders, this horizon without limits," a blot on the French landscape. Now was the time, he argued, to solve the problem of France's seven million hectares of "unproductive land." Something must be made of this "nothingness," this "depressing nudity" that "expands ad infinitum."[4]

In fact, the landes played an essential role in the agricultural economy of the region, as pasture for sheep whose manure ensured the survival of subsistence crops in poor soils. The landes' open spaces, while seeming endless to the physiocrats, were in fact already strained by the region's growing population, which demanded larger grain yields, and in consequence more livestock to provide the essential fertilizer. As arable land encroached on the *vacants,* or untilled and unenclosed land, more sheep and goats fought over diminishing pasture. Adding to this squeeze on resources was the creation of pine forests, which competed directly with the pastoral economy, given that on no account could livestock be allowed through the young plantations, for they ate the saplings.[5]

To urban bourgeois traveling through, the shepherds who traversed the flatness appeared to be "savage beings" wandering about on their stilts, achieving little and making no effort to transform or "improve" their environment.[6] This apparent emptiness fed reformers' fantasies of a neglected land awaiting renewal. There were strong mythical resonances in the obsession with colonizing and improving the region around the Bassin. Writers often made reference to ancient, mystical places, promised lands, in their descriptions of the area. Mortemart de Boisse, for example, spoke of the landes as "the mysterious Thule, or the Atlantis of the ancients."[7] All imagined an ideal version of this space, a filling up of the void. "For outsiders," writes Marie-Dominique Ribereau-Gayon, "emptiness allowed for experiments of every kind: royal, revolutionary, republican or imperial governments treated the landes in identical fashion—as an internal colony."[8] The plans for the development of the landes offer a classic example of the way in which representations of space failed to take account of the "lived space." That is, by imagining, describing, and mapping them as empty, the reformers overlooked the ways they were known and understood by those already there, those who passed across them daily. This was, of course, the same approach that colonial empires took in their appropriation of more remote territories.

The 1830s were an intense period of colonization, both inside and outside France. Legitimist nobles alienated by the Orléanist regime returned to the land full of plans to regenerate their class through a renewed engagement with agriculture. They embraced grand projects for the rehabilitation of the landes alongside Saint-Simonian technocrats, who believed in social and economic progress through technological development and agricultural modernization. While this was not the first time the region had attracted reforming minds—indeed, canal projects had been proposed in the 1600s and again in the years leading up to the Great Revolution—the 1830s ushered in passionate interest and, perhaps more important, concerted action from investors.[9]

Projects under consideration and in some cases already under way that would affect the Bassin included the construction of canals and, later, a railway line crossing the landes, improvement of the channels (*passes*) leading from the Bassin d'Arcachon to the Atlantic, dune stabilization by means of extensive pine plantations, and transformation of communal pasture into privately owned arable land and of naturally occurring salt pans into fish farms. All of these were interrelated in various ways. For example, the channel-fixing could not work without first stabilizing the dunes, and the financial viability of the canal system would depend on cargo ships' easy passage through the heads to the Bassin, ensuring the safe transport of timber and resin from the forests and anticipated produce from the rehabilitated moors. While this book is above all concerned with the projects for the development of the Bassin and its shores, rather than with the landes, the way reformers of the 1830s spoke about the area between Bordeaux and the Bassin in their company reports indicates the ways in which they and their followers would then represent the "little sea" of Arcachon—as an oasis in the desert.

In the 1830s, two private investment companies, the Compagnie d'Exploitation et Colonisation des Landes de Bordeaux, and the Compagnie Agricole et Industrielle d'Arcachon, bought up large tracts of land in an area close to the Bassin.[10] The Compagnie des Landes, formed on 1 June 1834, planned to import laborers from other parts of Europe to drain the landes and build a canal between the Bassin and Lake Mimizan to the south, via the intermediary lakes of Cazaux, Biscarrosse, and Parentis. The promoter of the canal project was Jean-François-Bernard Boyer-Fonfrède, a Bordeaux lawyer who had made a handsome marriage in La Teste and whose uncle had been a Girondin deputy to the National Convention (1792–95). His father François-Bernard helped him to obtain the necessary authorizations and financial support, outstripping the Ponts et Chaussées engineer Claude Deschamps and financier Pierre Balguerie-Stuttenberg, who had been working for many years on a more ambitious canal plan. Legitimist nobles joined Boyer-Fonfrède's cause, including Ambroise de La Rochefoucauld, duke of Doudeauville, who was named president of the Compagnie.[11]

The Compagnie d'Arcachon, founded three years later, in February 1837, proposed to undertake "the exploitation of lands, woods, swamps, waterfalls, mines and irrigable plains which make up the vast domains belonging to it in the communes of La Teste, Gujan and Le Teich . . . which [together] contain a population of 8,000 souls."[12] These projects would benefit from Boyer-Fonfrède's canal. The directors were two Saint-Simonians and a legitimist aristocrat: Paul-Emile Wissocq, a former marine engineer who was to write an optimistic report in 1839 on how best to improve the Bassin d'Arcachon *passes* (a project dear to the hearts of all those sinking money into the region); Pierre-Euryale Cazeaux, a polytechnician who founded the didactic magazine *Le magasin pittoresque;* and Count de Blacas-Carros, president of the Compagnie, who brought with him an impressive group of nobles, enlisted as subdirectors.

These men and their families were expected to live on the land they were to administer and "improve," and their willingness to forsake the conveniences of an urban lifestyle points to the power of the discourse of moral and social regeneration that surrounded the legitimist return to the land during this period.[13] In a document outlining the "considerations" leading to the creation of a "colonization committee" within the Compagnie d'Arcachon, the landes were characterized as "immense uncultivated lands, [which] await the powers of the agricultural arts to subjugate this wild nature which it will be so beautiful to conquer." The project would, the directors argued, help slow down the rural exodus which "troubles the peace and existence of so many families."[14] The promise of social regeneration in the face of rampant urbanization thus lay in the hitherto untapped landes. This masculinist vocabulary of domination—"subjugate," "conquer"—highlights their conception of nature as something to be overcome and transformed.

Both Compagnies published accounts of visits to the region, describing for

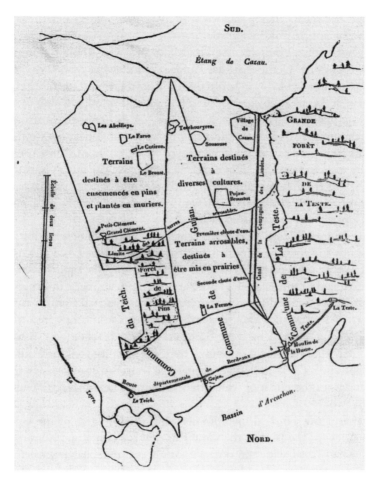

FIG. 3. Compagnie Agricole holdings. From Hennequin, *Notice sur la Compagnie d'Arcachon* (Paris: Imprimerie de Bourgogne et Martinet, 1838), 3. Bibliothèque municipale d'Arcachon.

publicity purposes their plans and work already undertaken, texts that illustrate the way the Bassin and its hinterland were seen by these outsiders. All observers dwelt on the potential richness of a barren and underutilized region, and the future they imagined was an agriculturalist's paradise. Seaside tourism was not part of their vision.

In October 1833, Louis-Henry-Jules Mareschal, who would become one of the founders of the Compagnie des Landes the following year, visited the landes in the company of Boyer-Fonfrède and a geometer-engineer, M. Herbage, to observe and explore the area to be colonized and through which their canal would eventually pass. The trio left Bordeaux on 24 October "furnished with all the relevant maps, plans and documents," representations that would direct their gaze and guide their movements and their responses. They traveled to Gujan by road, via the villages of Croix de Hins (now known as Croix d'Hins), Marche-Prins (Marcheprime), Les Argentières, and Le Teich. Mareschal wrote his report on the day following their return to Bordeaux, and it was published in the Compagnie prospectus in 1834.[15]

What is most striking about Mareschal's rich, detailed observations on the landscape is his continual comparison between the actual and the potential state of the area he visited. Mareschal always sought out signs of fertility, of productivity, of promise. He had little appreciation, aesthetic or otherwise, of the place in its "natural" or original state.[16] What excited him most was the discovery of successful plantations, crops of any kind "conquered from the desert."[17] About halfway between Bordeaux and the Bassin, he was astonished to find that "these beautiful meadows, these lovely cultivated fields, these vigorous pine and oak plantations, are separated from the immense desert of untilled landes, in the midst of which they drown, by an interval no wider than a foot or two."[18]

His use of the word "drown" (*noyer*) indicated his fear of the emptiness and openness of the landes: the same fear that his contemporaries often expressed when faced with the ocean.[19] Any space that had not been clearly marked out with boundary lines and signs of occupation threatened the reformer's sense of control over the environment. For Mareschal, the two-foot interval between beauty and sterility served only to remind the farmer of the precariousness of his hold, as though the emptiness might at any moment leap over the divide and engulf that which had been painstakingly wrested from its empire. In the same way, along the coast, the ocean and its representatives, the dunes, always threatened to encroach on territory pegged out by communities of men and women.

When the travelers came to Le Teich, on the banks of the Leyre River that flows into the Bassin, they found it to be, to an even greater extent than Croix d'Hins, "like a great oasis in the middle of the desert." Mareschal was once again impressed with its richness of vegetation after the barrenness of the landes from which he had just emerged. But his first view of the Bassin was to eclipse all that had come before. He thought it deserved the name "Sea of Arcachon." He saw it from Mestras, part of the commune of Gujan, when the tide had just began to ebb. He and his companions were "seized with admiration, the eye losing itself before the marvelous spectacle of the immense stretch of water criss-crossed in every direction by light fishing vessels from the surrounding coast."[20]

From an aesthetic point of view, Mareschal had arrived at the right moment, when, as "O. D." (probably Oscar Dejean) would express it later in his 1845 guide book, "this magnificent Bassin offers to the traveler's gaze the most grandiose and appealing sight"; had Mareschal first glimpsed it at low tide, he may well have experienced it as "a saddening sight, which leaves an unpleasant impression on the mind"—O. D.'s description of the wrong moment.[21] The Bassin, with its dramatic tidal regime, would prove a difficult subject for improvement, as reformers were to discover.

On the day after their arrival in October 1833, the group visited La Hume, the proposed outlet for the canal, and La Teste. At the La Hume water mill, where the canal was to meet the Bassin, they followed Boyer-Fonfrède's plans, "maps in hand," Mareschal describing this as an "application to the terrain." They came to the conclusion that the plans "were of the simplest, easiest execution and that the site presented all the conditions for a sure and quick success."[22] They then moved on, without so much as mentioning the fact that there had been major disagreements between Boyer-Fonfrède and the La Teste council over his choice of La Hume for the canal mouth. Boyer-Fonfrède's representation of the terrain was thus considered by the Compagnie's representatives to be the correct one, the one to be applied.

Given the promotional nature of the document he was writing, Mareschal's failure to note the locals' opposition to the canal's outlet is hardly surprising: any sign of conflict might deter investors. But this decision to wipe the battle between Boyer-Fonfrède and the Testerins from the record must have rankled with the latter. In the March 1833 council minutes, seven months before Mareschal's trip, we are given a taste of the depth of enmity that already existed between the canal planner and the Bassin notables. In a report with the title: "On the insults written by M. Fonfrède against the Commune and the municipal council of La Teste, and the purpose of these insults," the councillors complained that Boyer-Fonfrède had ignored their advice concerning the best site for the canal outlet, and accused him of engaging in "base and gross insults, as much against us members of the council, as against the rest of the population of this commune."

They were appalled at Boyer-Fonfrède's description of their commune as a "miserable village [*bourgade*] . . . destined to vegetate," and they stated their determination to "lift [their] Commune from the kind of debasement with which it has pleased Sieur Fonfrède to present it." The councillors then listed all the commune's features and statistics under the heading "On the importance of the commune, port and commerce of La Teste," and ended with the claim that Boyer-Fonfrède had "truly, systematically slandered the commune of La Teste, all the better to promote his private interests [*vues d'intérêt*], which he pretends are simply those of a citizen imbued with love for his country."[23] Here was a new slant on the rhetoric of the reformers, who couched the worthiness of their projects in terms of the greater good and the future of "la belle France."

Boyer-Fonfrède had seriously wounded the Testerins' pride by dismissing their claim to greater knowledge of local geography and the needs of the community. Given the personal fortune he was sinking into the region, it seems unlikely that he really thought La Teste "destined to vegetate." Perhaps he made his comment in a fit of pique provoked by Testerin criticism of his plans. Then again, when we discover that the Compagnie hoped eventually to create a town called Doudauville at the point where the canal met the Bassin, alongside an imagined port, to be named *Larochefoucauld*—thereby immortalizing the Compagnie's noble president—it may well be that La Teste would struggle to compete with the new settlement.[24]

At this time, though, Doudauville was still a figment of the canal-builders' imaginations (as it would forever remain), and Boyer-Fonfrède's alienation of local notables placed the whole venture at risk. This kind of disagreement would plague many a project for the "improvement" of the region. Enthusiastic but blinkered investors rarely took much note of local knowledge or resistance, and in some cases this contributed to their eventual failure.[25]

The resonances of these conflicts could also permeate daily life in surprising ways. In 1839—by which time Boyer-Fonfrède had been dismissed by the Compagnie des Landes for mismanagement and poor relations with his workers and colleagues—Mistress Manuelle Gazaillan took a man called Jean Cazenave before the Justice of the Peace in La Teste. One of her witnesses, a midwife from Gujan, testified that Cazenave had called Gazaillan "a snob [*puante*], that she was a slut of that bastard Monsieur Fonfrède," while another recalled hearing Cazenave say to her, "I'll send you to find your Fonfrède; La Teste justice won't do; [only] the green carpet in Bordeaux will; I want to see you die of starvation, you and your filthy mother." While Mistress Gazaillan may well have had an affair with Fonfrède, it is equally possible that this was the worst insult Cazenave could come up with when she prevented him from passing with his oxen (presumably over her land). In other words, Fonfrède's name was mud.[26]

Returning to Mareschal's 1833 account, the visitors gained another view of the Bassin, this time from the top of a dune, the Pic de l'Oreille: this filled Mareschal with "great thoughts," thoughts that remained with him when he saw the ocean from the Moulleau beach (southwest of present-day Arcachon). "The sea rolled its waves majestically," he wrote, "with nothing to break the uniformity of the swell." For him, the ocean was a "terrifying element, where man's strength and care are so useless in the face of danger."[27] But this was no aimless expression of the sublime. Mareschal was on a scientific mission: his reverie was for a purpose. His oceanically inspired "great thoughts" dwelt on what these "wild" places—at least their edges—might become, once in the right hands.

From Moulleau, the visitors went on to see the Arcachon chapel, so central to the religious lives of local fishermen and women, and then the monument erected in 1818 to Brémontier, the Ponts et Chaussées engineer given sole credit (quite unfairly) for saving the region from the invading sands by stabilizing the dunes with pine plantations from the 1780s onward.[28] The following day they took a boat to Cap Ferret and observed the *passes*. Sunday to Wednesday were spent exploring the landes and lagoons south of the Bassin, and on the eighth day they returned to the Bassin to visit the *prés salés* (salt pastures). The visitors sought out marks of civilization in the wilderness, evidence of the presence and achievements of other humans in this alien environment. This was the basis for the development of an itinerary of sites and views, which tourists would later (and still do today) follow closely.

Although tourism—or more accurately, the therapeutic bathing trip—was already in its nascent stages at this time, with one or two bathing establishments having already appeared on the Bassin's shores, the Compagnies did not consider tourism a key to the region's prosperity. Agricultural produce, timber, pine resin, and fish were their main concerns. Mareschal's vision of the region's future made no reference to tourism: "[A] greater development of ideas and agricultural industry," he wrote, "is the only thing required in this land to make a rich, blooming and productive countryside out of an uncultivated and almost uninhabited desert, in a matter of years."[29]

The "port" of La Teste was a misnomer, he thought, for it was nothing but "a deserted and sandy beach, upon which boats lie high and dry," which convinced him of "the extreme utility of the execution of the canal, whose opening would create a real port."[30] Like the landes, the Bassin and the ocean must be brought under control and made useful and productive. The creation of a "real" port would place La Teste on the map and would, of course, underpin the success of the canal and other landes improvement projects. Transport was the key to enrichment: waterways were seen as arteries bringing life to the region.

While observers agreed that an improved transport network was the key to the region's revival, they did not necessarily agree on the form it should take. Competing with Boyer-Fonfrède's canal were Deschamps' Grandes Landes canal and Goury's Petites Landes waterway. There were also the early proposals for a railway line, still considered an untried, risky proposition at the time. In mid-1834, when the Compagnie des Landes was constituted, a correspondence was published in the royalist newspaper *La Guienne* between the Testerin notable Lalesque *père* (probably former mayor Jean-Baptiste Marsillon) and a "Peasant of the Landes"—a highly literate detractor of Boyer-Fonfrède's canal project whose choice of pen name reflected not his socioeconomic position but his claim to an intimate knowledge of the area—a correspondence that illustrates aspects of the debate that raged over the transport issue. The Peasant declared that it was folly to attempt to develop industry "in these sad lands, which will be the tomb [of all such endeavors] until rapid and economical transport has been established between Bordeaux and La Teste."[31] Boyer-Fonfrède's project would fail because it was not ambitious enough: produce would not accrue in value until it reached the metropolis.

The Peasant preferred the engineer Deschamps' more ambitious Grandes Landes canal model, which traced a route between Bayonne and Bordeaux. He considered Boyer-Fonfrède's canal useless "precisely because it would begin at the already isolated point of La Teste, and move adventurously in the direction of a sterile desert." Boyer-Fonfrède was, in his estimation, a "schemer" (*faiseur*) who cared little for the real needs of the region, a claim with which many Testerins probably agreed.[32] It was "with the help of beautiful maps on Annonay paper" (vellum or superior parchment) that such types managed to convince the Chamber of Deputies of the public utility of projects like this. In fact, the Peasant claimed, they were nothing but "pompous speculation schemes whose uselessness ruins the present."[33] He counted the proposal for a railway line from Bordeaux to La Teste among these schemes, calling it a "second chimera as vaporous, as elusive as the canal."[34] This skepticism might seem surprising in light of what we know the railway's impact to have been, but when the Peasant was writing, France had not yet seen its first passenger train and debate raged over the profitability of canals as compared to the newfangled railway.

Opponents might well accuse the Peasant and Deschamps' own vision of being a vaporous chimera. As Jacques Sargos points out, the Grandes Landes canal does exist, but only in the archives: "There, it stretches across several hundred meters of maps. One can follow its sinuous course across beautiful canvas maps where its blue waters run between gouache forests."[35] The way maps, with their sweeping lines on white paper, permit the draftsman to dream unfettered by the complications and obstacles found on the ground— in the "lived space"—only makes the eventual difficulties of execution the more painful.

Lalesque, a longtime resident and former mayor of La Teste who owned property at the heart of what would become Arcachon, responded to the Peasant's barbs with a different vision. While he acknowledged the need to lift the area out of its lethargy, he defended the landes against accusations of sterility. Not only did he foresee rising property values as a result of the canal, but he believed that canals built to the north and south would supply the Bassin with more water and thereby deepen the channels, allowing large vessels to move freely through the *passes*. Indeed, he predicted Boyer-Fonfrède would succeed brilliantly, giving new life to "the native agony of our countryside." In another letter he referred to the area's "hideous virginity," demonstrating his sympathy with the Compagnie directors who looked at the landes as a place showing no sign of being possessed, a place whose "treasures" awaited discovery.[36] The land was figured as female, passive, and promising.

In his 1838 report on the Compagnie d'Arcachon, Joseph-François-Gabriel Hennequin, former head of the office of the ministry for the navy, carried on the rhetoric of transformation that Mareschal, the Peasant, and Lalesque employed. He too spoke of "treasures," of "vast deserts" and the "wild state" of the countryside, and of the utility of "fertilizing an important part of France, a virgin land situated in the middle of one of our most beautiful provinces, and which blamed civilization for having left it in oblivion for so many centuries."[37] Coming several years after Mareschal and the Peasant, Hennequin knew about the coming of the railway line, "which will make of the small town of La Teste a suburb of Bordeaux." He imagined the railway as a force for change: "it will bring about the creation of new agricultural products, it will fertilize the country it crosses, and generally activate all the proposed improvements in the Landes."[38] Like Mareschal he did not seem interested in the railway line as a stimulus to tourism. As he pointed out, the managing directors "above all want the company to remain principally *agricultural*," and although he was making this point with reference to industrial developments and the Compagnie d'Arcachon's decision to establish only those factories deemed "indispensable," it appears that encouraging tourism was still not on the agenda.[39]

Hennequin's main concern seemed to be the quality of the young noblemen the Compagnie would recruit as managers. He played on age-old notions of the aristocracy's links to the land and their responsibility to improve the soil and inspire others to follow in their steps. He claimed that candidates for the subdirectorships were "coming forth in droves" to join the campaign to "bring to life a vast countryside which seemed destined to the death of the desert."[40] Only men of a certain caliber, already blessed with wealth, education, and hereditary links to land, Hennequin argued, could reveal the hidden treasures of the soil.[41] Count de Bonneval, who reported to the Compagnie d'Arcachon's agricultural committee in November 1837, agreed. "Ordinary colonists" were to be avoided, for they possessed "limited intelligence" and were lazy, careless, and attached to routine.[42]

Although it was rarely stated explicitly, it is clear that the local population was deemed unfit for the Compagnie's work. They were considered responsible for neglecting the region and failing to appreciate its promise. They had not realized that "there is in effect some glory to be acquired in fertilizing uncultivated lands which are, so to speak, a stain on France's beautiful soil."[43] In their address to the shareholders of the Compagnie in February 1839, the directors declared that the results of their agricultural experiments would prove

> that the landes' unproductive state is not always due to the nature of the soil, but to neglect, to their abandonment by man. In an era of progress of every kind, such a state cannot endure; civilized France cannot keep within its breast another, uncultivated France; immense deserts will progressively be overcome by a philanthropic and intelligent activity.[44]

These observers held the geographically deterministic view that the character of the local people reflected the land they inhabited. Differences were regularly drawn between the "puny" *landais* (inhabitant of the landes) and the robust Testerin, but both types were seen as unformed (to different degrees), requiring the guiding hand of the enlightened Compagnie directors. Colonizers were frustrated by the locals' tendency to reject their advice; Mortemart de Boisse commented on the Testerins' independence and suspicion of newcomers, their fear of innovation, and their desire to "stay as they were."[45]

Back in 1833, Mareschal, while admiring plots of land successfully cultivated by the locals, said that they had managed this feat despite their "carefree
character and unenlightened minds." He claimed many had unwittingly chosen plots of land less favorable than pieces close by. This observation only
confirmed the Compagnie directors' preference for managers and workers
brought in from other countries and regions. Mareschal also expressed the
conviction that the importation of foreign workers, who would move up the
hierarchy from day-laborers to sharecroppers to small landowners, would encourage the "indigenous population" to emulate them and accept these new
ideas about land use.[46] Once again we see the connections between the discourse of internal and external colonization, based on the notion of the "civilizing mission."[47]

The institution of new kinds of land use meant that local grazing practices
would have to be eliminated or confined to limited areas. The Compagnie
observers were confident that they could overcome the resistance of shepherds
to the elimination of their pasture. They would be "civilized" as part of the
process of reclaiming the land, and brought under the tutelage of enlightened
aristocrats who claimed to have their best interests at heart. No longer would
the shepherds be the "despots of these vast plains." These "fantastic shadows"
that "float between sky and earth" on their stilts would make way for flourishing, enclosed fields of maize or neatly planted forests.[48] Their practice of
grazing sheep on privately owned land after the harvest, known as *vaine pâ-
ture*—seen as "a wound in our countryside" by investors—would no longer
be tolerated.[49]

The colonizers, however, were *not* able to make a clean sweep of existing
people and their practices. These "empty" spaces were already known by heart
and in daily use, and they would be defended—with violence if necessary.
There were cases of Compagnie crops and young pine trees being burned by
shepherds angry at the expropriation of their pasture; more common were
cases of simple trespass by flocks and their keepers.[50] The municipal councils
often defended their inhabitants' right to graze on Compagnie holdings—a
right recognized by the local seigneur in 1550—but councillors were inevitably
confronted with the difficult balancing act of promoting agricultural development and investment in the region while defending the rights of those members of the community—both owners and carers of livestock—for whom the
continued existence of adequate and accessible pasture was essential.[51]

In 1839, the La Teste council reported that local owners of livestock were
being deprived of pasture in a section of the landes being cleared by the Compagnie d'Arcachon. The council argued, with proof, that the seigneur had ac-

knowledged the inhabitants' grazing rights in this section in 1766, and so, in exchange for exclusive use of the 2,463 *journaux* (about 1,000 hectares, or 2,470 acres) in question, the Compagnie d'Arcachon offered the inhabitants of La Teste and Gujan usage rights to several pieces making up 3,000 *journaux,* situated in other parts of its holdings. But the Testerins rejected this offer, arguing that they would have to travel much farther to reach the grazing land, crossing property owned by the Compagnie, for which they would be fined.

The Compagnie's offer implied that an exchange of 3,000 *journaux* for a piece measuring 2,463 *journaux* would be a good deal for the communes. But as both parties knew well, there was much more at stake than bald measurements. Proximity and accessibility were essential, as were knowledge of the terrain and an established sense of belonging, that is, ownership through usage.[52] This conception of land as an exchangeable commodity, disconnected from its past use and meanings, would reemerge when development took off on the Arcachon foreshore—and would again cause conflict.

Unlike Deschamps' Grandes Landes canal, which Sargos describes as existing only in the archives, Boyer-Fonfrède's canal was taking shape. Workers were digging deep into the earth between the Bassin and Lake Cazaux: they were changing the landscape, turning a spatial representation (plans, maps) into lived space. An eighty-room headquarters for the ambitious Compagnie administrators was built, and by 1838, the canal bed, 14.5 kilometers (9 miles) in length, had been dug, but the locks, of which they proposed eight, were yet to be constructed. On 10 July 1838, an impressive ceremony was held to celebrate the laying of the first stone, an honor given to the archbishop of Bordeaux, Monseigneur Donnet. He was escorted to the site of the planned third lock by a cortege of two hundred people on horseback. Locals in their Sunday best looked on as he placed a time capsule containing various medals and Compagnie coins beneath the stone, which, once lowered, was repeatedly hit with an ebony-handled mallet by a queue of officials.[53]

While Monseigneur Donnet declared on this occasion that the Compagnie was encouraging "a new spirit of fraternity" in the local population by opening up the region to the outside world, events surrounding the building of the canal told another story. The introduction of hundreds of foreign workers, mostly Basques fleeing the civil war in Spain, proved a sore point with the Testerin community. This was not the aristocratic colonization of which the directors spoke so glowingly in their reports. This was an occupation by men who camped out in the landes in "miserable cabins" with their families, men whose poverty led them occasionally to commit theft and trespass.[54] Single foreign men in particular were often implicated in drunken fights and threats to locals. The La Teste council in March 1835 reported that the reopening of the Fonfrède canal works in April would attract "a considerable number of foreign workers to this area; that it is to be feared that among them might be found criminals and people with bad intentions." The council moved to prohibit locals from providing lodging to any foreigner without first notifying the town hall of their boarder's name and usual address.[55]

In July 1839 the council reported that a police inspection of the canal work site had uncovered twenty-seven "individuals" without passports. "For some time," they claimed, "thefts, offenses, violent acts, have been committed against several inhabitants of this commune and especially at . . . Cazeaux [sic], where the police cannot keep watch given that they are stationed three leagues from the administration's residence." In view of this, the directors of the canal were prohibited from employing any workers who had not handed in their passport.[56]

One incident near Lake Cazaux involved eight canal workers who visited a M. Varan in search of wine. According to one report, Varan refused to let them inside, saying that his bar (débit de boissons) was no longer operational. When he offered to give them some alcohol to take away—in other words, not allowing them to drink inside—they entered the house forcibly and attempted to break open a wine barrel. A fight ensued, and a detachment of the local National Guard was called in to defend Varan and his friends. It was alleged that a National Guardsman and his son were struck repeatedly with a shovel.[57]

The other side of this story is the extreme hardship reportedly experienced by underpaid and undernourished foreign canal workers, shivering in their huts. Health regulations drawn up in 1834 were routinely overlooked by the administrators, and workers who fell ill were frequently dismissed. According to reports by Testerin councillors during a tumultuous meeting in September 1835, workers' bodies could sometimes be found along the road to Bordeaux. The Testerins requested an ambulance, but were thwarted by Boyer-Fonfrède. He convinced the prefect this was an unnecessary expense and that the commune's charitable fund should cover the expense of those who died penniless.[58]

The Compagnie des Landes managed to complete only seven of the eight planned locks, and the waterway never lived up to its promise. It operated at a loss for many years, and in 1845 it was opened to tourism in a vain attempt to keep it viable, while the eighty-room mansion built in anticipation of a flourishing Doudauville was advertised to those now visiting the Bassin for therapeutic bathing at 15 francs a room per month—an indication that agriculture was making way for a different kind of economic development, one centered on the seaside as a curative destination.[59] The Compagnie des Landes was liquidated in 1857.[60] The Compagnie d'Arcachon had folded ten years earlier.

There were many reasons for the Compagnies' failure, aside from significant local resistance: the arid soil that pushed up fertilizer and labor costs, the lack of experience of some of the directors who were chosen for their family name rather than their knowledge of farming, and disagreements between the two companies over water levels in the proposed canals that affected irrigation plans.[61] The Compagnie des Landes also had the railway engineers to contend with, who, in a blatant attempt to frustrate their canal-building competitors, built a bridge over the canal so low as to prevent the passage of the barges. As if this weren't enough, the land itself seemed to reject their enterprise. Sand was building up; by 1856 dredging was necessary, but was never carried out, no doubt due to prohibitive expense.[62]

The Compagnies' desire to "create a new country" had come up against the existing country, a country of shifting borders, which was nevertheless anchored in the minds and bodies of Testerins.[63] But the desire to make something rich out of something seen to be poor or bereft, the urge to fill the emptiness, would live on, taking many other forms through the nineteenth century. Whether it was the improvement of the *passes* and of navigational safety, or the appropriation of the tidal zone for fish farms and the beach for bathers, the Bassin and hinterland were characterized as requiring remodeling, renewal, taming, cleaning up. The language of the canal companies lived on well past their demise, although its meaning changed in subtle ways. And each "civilizing mission" met the resistance of local people who had their own, entrenched ideas about the meaning and use of the places targeted.

CHAPTER TWO

A Site of Contention

THE *PRÉS SALÉS* OF LA TESTE

*"We are prohibited from fishing in the places where the fish
spawn, we are banned from catching immature fish, we, the poor,
who have no other livelihood but fishing and who buy the right with
our [naval] service, and rich landowners unjustly claim the right
to place their nets in places forbidden to us."*

—Mortemard [*sic*] de Boisse quoting fishermen, in "Extrait d'un rapport adressé
le 4 juin 1849 au Ministre de la Marine," 4 June 1849.

On Tuesday, 28 January 1834, two men stood before La Teste's justice of the
peace and swore to carry out faithfully the mission entrusted to them: the de-
marcation of the boundaries of the so-called *prés salés* (salt pastures), bought
by M. Antoine de Sauvage three and a half years earlier.[1] This was the pro-
logue to a performance of property ownership, a performance that entailed
walking across the land in question, marking its edges, and recording in writing the repeated actions of the participants.

Though I have translated *prés salés* as "salt pastures," this is not entirely
satisfactory.[2] This is partly because the term in French was, and still is,
controversial, at least in the case of La Teste. The liminality or in-be-
tween-ness of this zone made definition difficult: situated between sea and
dry land, it belonged to either or both areas at different times. While
under water, it was part of the Bassin. When uncovered by the retreating
tide, its salty grasses provided pasture for livestock and fertilizer for farmers. It defied definition because it was ever changing. Only by removing it

from the sea's incursions by the construction of dikes could it be considered dry land.

The story of the prés salés of La Teste illuminates the challenge that the sea poses to humans who seek to identify where territories begin and end, and also the changing nature of property over the nineteenth century: a shift from usage-based communal ownership to outright, unencumbered possession by private property.

The two men who stood before the justice of the peace described themselves as "experts" in their report of the boundary-marking exercise (*bornage*) of the prés salés. Their names were Martin Jules Cameleyre, mayor of Gujan, and Jean Ronveau junior (*fils*), a landowner from Bordeaux.[3] Cameleyre had been named expert by the State domain administration, while Ronveau was there to represent Antoine de Sauvage, the owner of the property in question.

The object of the exercise was to plant markers identifying the boundaries between the prés salés belonging to M. de Sauvage in the commune of La Teste, and the shores of the Bassin d'Arcachon that lay within the State domain.[4] In other words, they were expected to determine the point at which the shore met dry land. One might have expected them to approach members of the local community with a sound knowledge of the area and request their help in ascertaining the highest point reached by the tides in the prés salés zone, for this could be determined only by regular and close observation. But the experts' failure to consult the locals reveals the real purpose of their visit: they were there not to learn about actual conditions but to reinforce a representation of space contained in titles going back some fifty years or more.

Their first step was therefore a perusal of the titles submitted to them by the domain administration and Sauvage. The first title was an enfeoffment contract from 1780, whereby the seigneur of La Teste (known as the Captal de Buch) made a grant to a Bordelais merchant, Henri Giers, of "all the lands and prés salés belonging to the said Seigneur situated within the parish of La Teste, taken *from the La Hume Mill Stream as far as the sand dunes and the Arcachon mountain* [dune]." The contract stipulated that only upon the enclosure of the territory by dikes could its true area be determined.[5]

The widow of Henri Giers had sold the *prés* to Pierre Dumora, whose heirs sold them to Pierre Fleury and Joseph Oxéda. The second document that the experts reviewed recorded that sale in 1813 (along with another piece of prés salés called "Truc de Baillon"), and the third contract, dated 9 October 1830, recorded Fleury and Oxéda's sale of the prés to M. de Sauvage and his late father-in-law.[6] Ronveau and Cameleyre simply listed these three documents in their report; they provided no commentary. But their next step indicated that they did not dispute their validity. "We visited M. de Sauvage's prés salés," they reported, thereby recognizing his ownership from the start. Upon their arrival, they met two other men, both residents of La Teste: Pierre Antoine Silvain, property registry officer, present "in the interests of the domain," and Pierre Fleury—probably the very Fleury who had sold the prés to Sauvage— who had been summoned on 27 January by Sauvage to provide any necessary information.[7] Silvain and Fleury were to accompany the experts on their de-marcation expedition.

Before they could proceed with the demarcation, they realized that they needed a "figurative map," so they retired to the Hôtel d'Arcachon where they worked on their map until late in the evening, when they agreed to stop and meet again the following morning. All this preparation was considered necessary before they could look properly at the land. Not only were their ac-tions dictated by the wording of the sale documents, but they needed to pic-ture their plan of attack—literally. They were creating a script according to which they would act. There were to be no spontaneous improvisations: everything must be figured out in advance.[8]

A curious thing happened at the end of that first day. After drawing up their map and agreeing to continue their work in the morning, they all signed *except for Fleury,* "who declared he did not want to [sign] because of his rela-tionship with the inhabitants of La Teste." Why this refusal to put his name to what appeared to be a harmless document? Why should his relationship with the Testerins prevent him from signing?

The reason lies in Cameleyre and Ronveau's failure to acknowledge that a long-running conflict of interests lay behind the call for a bornage. Their au-tomatic acceptance of Sauvage's ownership of the prés flew in the face of the local community's repeated attempts to prevent Sauvage from appropriating them. Fleury's refusal to sign indicated that he could not acknowledge Sauvage as the legitimate owner of the prés without jeopardizing his relations with his own community.

Despite this noncompliance, which we might read as a rejection of the basis upon which the bornage was to proceed, Fleury met the experts and Sil-vain on the prés the next morning, Wednesday, as arranged. Having com-pleted the necessary groundwork—or rather paperwork—the experts and their companions could now begin their boundary marking. First, they noted that the prés were divided naturally into two parts by the port and the road leading into the village. They proceeded to record the boundaries of the two sections.

The team decided to begin their marking at the eastern limit of the first section; that is, beside the La Hume stream. They consulted the 1780 contract and "after having determined with some certainty that in this section nothing has changed, we proceeded with the delimitation of the said prés salés from the Bassin d'Arcachon by means of placement of the following markers." We might well ask how they came to the conclusion that nothing had changed since 1780. Did Fleury or Silvain provide this information? How could such a thing be determined in a tidal zone? They also gave no indication of how they decided on the point where the Bassin stopped and the prés salés began. The first marker, "A," they placed "*on the beach*" ("sur le rivage") 459 meters (just over a quarter of a mile) from a seawall belonging to a M. Pétro. According to the *Robert* dictionary, the *rivage* is a "zone subject to the action of waves and, in some cases, of tides"; thus, the experts were including part of the maritime domain within the bounds of Sauvage's property.[9] If Fleury made any protest at this point, it was not recorded. Only his silence—the gap where his signature should have gone—was deemed worthy of comment.

They followed the shoreline, planting two more stone markers that rose fifteen centimeters (about 6 inches) from the ground. These markers would probably be difficult to see from a distance, particularly where the grassy expanse was undulating. It would only be in retracing the steps of the experts that one could locate them. In other words, this performance of possession would require a reenactment for its traces to be recognized.

At six o'clock that afternoon, Fleury, Silvain, and the experts agreed to meet again the following day. Once again, they all signed the report except Fleury, who when asked why gave the same reason as on the first day.

The next day, Thursday, the same process was repeated. Silvain, the property registration officer, left for Bordeaux, but his absence did not seem to trouble the experts. They began by "recognizing" the previous day's marker "C" before going on to plant one last marker, "D," for the first section of the prés. Once again, they made no attempt to explain how they identified the point where the shore stopped and the prés began. They followed the dimensions recorded in the sale documents, which had been calculated in relation to permanent structures inland from the shore. The experts' mission was to make concrete the measurements from a document that was over fifty years old—not to ascertain whether the original estimates were valid or to take account of changing conditions.

After positioning "D," the three men moved onto the second part of the prés, on the other side of the channel leading to the port. Ronveau noted that pine plantations from neighboring properties belonging to the heirs of Testerin notable Pierre Cravey and the government extended into Sauvage's property.[10] The experts acknowledged Sauvage's right to investigate the possibility of recognizing the original limits, but they were not in a position to do this themselves, "given how difficult it would be to bring together the inhabitants of La Teste who, we might add, are *little disposed to help us in this undertaking.*"[11] Here we are given a tantalizing hint of the Testerins' feelings about this issue. The "experts" phrase it so that the locals' lack of cooperation reads as apathy. While it may be true that they were not keen to *help*—that is, to approve the positioning of the markers as recorded—we will see that they would willingly have been present at the bornage.

What, then, was Pierre Fleury's status? While he professed to care about the opinion of his fellow inhabitants, it seems he did not inform them of the boundary marking, otherwise we can assume they would have turned out to observe the proceedings. Fleury simply looked on, mute. As the vendor and brother of the mayor, his position was delicate. Perhaps silence was his only defense against pressure or accusations from both parties. When six o'clock struck, Fleury once again refused to sign the report.

There was one day left to complete the bornage. The experts met Fleury again, "recognized" all the positioned markers and undertook to determine the dimensions of the two halves of the prés salés. The resulting figures included land occupied by paths that Henri Giers had been obliged (by the 1780 contract) to keep open to La Teste's inhabitants for the purpose of "allowing out the produce of [their] existing establishments" and for the passage of water. Cameleyre and Ronveau were required to respect the terms of that enfeoffment. Once again we see the acknowledgment in earlier documents of usage rights that would come to be seen as an unacceptable burden. At quarter past six their work was done. Ronveau wrote up the report, which he and Cameleyre, but not Fleury, signed.

In December—nearly a year after the report was finished—the prefect of the Gironde, Charles de Lacoste, authorized Cameleyre and Ronveau's report, without even mentioning Fleury's repeated refusal to sign it. For the historian, though, Fleury's silence resounds, inviting a closer look at the history of the prés salés. The history of this zone is a complicated one, involving a huge cast of characters and conflicts at all levels of government over property definitions. We begin our passage through this maze by analyzing the effects of one man's effort to appropriate this space.

Antoine de Sauvage, nephew of the powerful minister Duc Decazes, had bought the chateau and domain of Arès (a Bassin commune) in 1811.[12] Even though Sauvage had been living on the Bassin for over twenty years by the time of the bornage and had even become mayor of Arès, he was still considered an outsider—or *estrangey* in Gascon, the local dialect. He was also much richer than most of the notables on the Bassin, so he wielded considerable political power in the area.

In 1828, he proposed to build a port and canal in La Teste in return for a toll on fishing and maritime commerce. It was a long-held dream of Testerin notables that their natural harbor would one day be developed as a reliable commercial port. On 12 March 1828 the councillors agreed in principle to Sauvage's proposal and drew up terms and conditions that modified some of his demands. When Sauvage came back with new proposals, they renegotiated certain clauses and—according to some accounts—accepted his claim to perpetual ownership of the prés salés in return for two payments of 4,000 francs. It seems, though, that the council was divided over his appropriation of the prés salés. The sticking point was Sauvage's intention to create fish farms on the prés salés and on the Ile aux Oiseaux, situated in the Bassin, for which he had obtained a lease in 1829 from the domain administration.

Once the community knew about Sauvage's fish farm plans, it was clear that there would be strong opposition to his arrangement with the council. Jean-Baptiste Taffart, the deputy mayor of La Teste, thought the question of such importance that, in 1831, he resigned from his municipal position to devote his undivided attention to the matter of the prés. In a letter to the prefect on 5 July 1831, he declared his intention to unveil to the superior authorities

> all the intrigues to which this affair had given rise, such as the promises and threats made in the name of a peer of France, prospective prime minister; [certain] abuses of authority with regard to the municipal council, supposed minutes, false reports, secret inquiries, servile letters and other documents of a similar nature, which Edifying collection I have managed to assemble, and with which they have succeeded in deceiving you.[13]

Taffart pulled no punches, accusing Sauvage of "convincing all the department administrators, engineers etc etc, and . . . making them testify unanimously that the leasing of the Isle des Oiseaux [*sic*] would be neither prejudicial to fishing nor to navigation, and that nothing opposed it." Fortunately the navy and finance ministers remained impervious to the "seductive atmosphere that surrounds Sauvage." The minister for the navy—the fishermen's protector—ordered an inquiry into the matter to be carried out by the deputy commissioner of naval classes in La Teste, Guillaume Verrière.

Taffart launched into a sordid tale of deception and intrigue surrounding the lease of the Ile aux Oiseaux. In 1828, when Sauvage proposed a port and canal for La Teste and offered what Taffart considered to be a 4,000-franc bribe "in the hope of dazzling the municipal council," he had the support of the prefect. A council meeting was held on 12 March, at which four members expressed their disapproval of the project. Another meeting, on the 31st, was attended by the subprefect "to use his influence to ensure the acceptance of Sauvage's offers." The assembly of eight, presided by the subprefect, was evenly divided, but somehow, "despite the fact that not one signature confirmed its passage, the prefect [*sic*], in an operation that one would rather not characterize, went back to Bordeaux carrying a copy of a resolution which accepted all of Sauvage's proposals."[14]

Sauvage had useful connections; he knew how to work the system. And for this reason, he came to be seen by Testerins in the same light as the canal-building "schemer" Boyer-Fonfrède. Taffart went so far as to characterize Sauvage as one of those "professional adulators, who circumvent . . . and mislead the authorities whenever it is to their advantage to do so." In contrast, Taffart described himself as a "a frank and loyal man . . . a real friend." Sauvage, the smooth talker with connections in the capital, was pitted against the "rough shell" of Taffart, an impassioned local—though a local who had spent his career with the domain administration.[15]

Fortunately for Taffart and La Teste, the minister never signed off on Sauvage's arrangement with the council because of the Revolution of 1830, which brought about a purge in national and local administrations. The change of regime opened up a space for Taffart to make strong accusations against an influential figure like Sauvage. When Sauvage made known his intention to pursue his projects despite this political setback, a petition opposing the fisheries and signed by 127 "cargo and fishing boat owners, captains, pilots and other notables" was sent to the navy minister, who then sent it on to the finance minister. He called on the domain administration to assemble all the documents. It was in response to this appeal that Taffart wrote his report in 1832.

Whether or not Taffart's allegations of corruption against Sauvage and others were founded, they indicate the depth of animosity and the intricate maneuvers that surrounded the prés salés conflict. This was no small local matter, he implied. Even politicians at the highest level had an interest in its outcome. The 1830s saw intense discussion at the national level about the future of communal lands (*communaux*). In 1836 the State launched a national inquiry into the possibility of leasing and exploiting communaux, and their management was handed over to municipal councils in 1837, opening up fresh possibilities for local power brokers.[16] In this light, Taffart's claims concerning the political machinations surrounding this issue seem plausible.

In his lengthy 1832 report on the prés salés and Sauvage's intentions, Taffart's arguments revolved around the definition of the prés and the ways he believed Sauvage and previous purchasers had circumvented the authorities. The defining of the disputed space was an essential part of his battle against Sauvage's appropriation. Before we unravel Taffart's report, though, and in order to understand the Testerins' opposition to the bornage of 1834, we need to consider what the prés salés meant to them.

The prés salés and the saltwater channels that snaked through them were an integral part of the Testerins' subsistence activities. To lose them to an individual proprietor would threaten their livelihood. The commune's usage rights were acknowledged in the 23 May 1550 *baillette,* an agreement between Frédéric de Foix, Captal de Buch (seigneur of La Teste, Gujan, and Cazaux), and the inhabitants of the Captalat (seigneurie) granting the inhabitants his "padouens et vacants" in return for a one-off payment of 800 *livres* and an annual rent of 80 *livres.*[17] Jean Hameau, mayor of La Teste between 1844 and 1848, considered this *baillette* to have been an important element in the Captal's strategy to encourage population growth and agricultural development in the Bassin area after the ravages of war in the twelfth and thirteenth centuries. According to his version, the Testerins were named "true seigneurs, through usage [*utiles*], peaceful possessors, as though of their own thing" of 14,000 hectares (34,595 acres) of *vacants* or landes.[18]

The Captal Amanieu de Ruat's subsequent enfeoffment of prés salés to the absentee bourgeois Giers in 1780 appears not to have prevented the locals from gaining access to the zone, even if it did take away their control on paper. Indeed, this kind of grant was still associated with a feudal property regime that acknowledged usage rights—a conditional ownership different from the unencumbered concept of property that would take root over the nineteenth century, particularly under the July Monarchy (1830–48).

Given the Testerins' conception of property as anchored in usage and repetitive actions of appropriation, it was only when their *practices* were threatened that they took action. Antoine de Sauvage's purchase of the prés in 1830 and his acquisition of the lease for the Ile aux Oiseaux in 1831 were the turning point. When it was discovered that he intended to enclose the prés and convert them into fish farms, the community reacted strongly. The La Teste council expressed its concern at a meeting on 9 October 1831. It argued that the enclosure and transformation of the prés salés would deprive the Testerins of their only source of fertilizer for their "sandy properties," fertilizer that they had been removing "for centuries" from the surface of the prés; Sauvage would thereby "deal a mortal blow to agriculture" in the commune. The creation of fish farms, "whose enormous productivity would profit only Mr. Sauvage to the detriment of more than a thousand families," and which would result in a decline in fish stocks more generally, would "plunge the entire maritime population of the eight communes on the Bassin d'Arcachon into the most terrible destitution."[19] These were serious claims, which illustrate the extent to which the sea and local agriculture were intertwined.

The fishing community had detailed the way they used the Bassin's channels and sandbanks back in 1806, during a battle with state and municipal authorities over the appropriation of the Ile aux Oiseaux—an island that had much in common with the prés salés. Petitioners against the island's leasing out argued that "duck hunting, eel fishing, and the collection of oysters and other shellfish" occupied an "infinite number of mariners" as well as providing a training ground for children "who in this way become apprentices to the seagoing profession." The product of these activities formed "all their patrimony and the only resource providing for their needs and those of their large families."[20]

In the battle over the prés salés in the 1830s, arguments based on *usage* continued to be invoked against Sauvage and others' claims to the prés salés, but Taffart, the Testerins' main spokesman, realized that this would not suffice. His careful analysis of documents led him to a more radical conclusion: that the prés salés were not prés salés at all. His 1832 report contained a "Preliminary and Indispensable Digression" in which he discussed the nature of the prés salés. He began by defining two kinds of prés salés:

1. Land *totally and freely* abandoned by withdrawing sea water, long enough in the past that it can have acquired the degree of dryness necessary for the growth of Grasses.

2. The shore [*Grèves et rivage*] whose *Conquest* (it is the proper term) has been achieved over the sea itself by means of dikes which have forced the water to retreat from its natural limits, and created an obstacle against any new eruptions.[21]

He claimed that none of the first type existed around the Bassin, but that several of the second did. If anything, the sea was encroaching increasingly upon rather than abandoning the shores of the Bassin.

In other words, what everyone was calling prés salés or salt pastures were in fact the "edge, strand and shore of the bay, covered and uncovered to a greater or lesser degree according to the waxing and waning of the moon." He rejected the claim by Fleury, Oxéda, and Sauvage that the land was composed of small hillocks of sand similar to dunes. Rather it constituted "a vast, flat and unified beach, predominantly of clay, divided by a multitude of shallow openings [or channels], and so saturated by water for the most part, that impracticable and even dangerous muddy holes have formed there."

The prés should not be equated with the sandy part of the beach alone. Taffart claimed that even the area where sea grasses grew, which might resemble dry land, must not be mistaken for prés salés, for the waves deposited refuse there and the surface was "annually raked and stripped by the inhabitants to the depth of an inch, and carried to the land destined to be sown with wheat, being the best fertilizer and the only one available to Farmers."[22]

These distinctions were essential to his case because by claiming that the so-called prés salés were part of the shore, Taffart was situating them within the public domain, the alienation of which was illegal. Taffart based his definition on Jean-Baptiste Colbert's 1681 Naval Decree, which declared the *seashore* to be "that which the sea covers and uncovers during new and full moons, and up to the point on the beach reached by the great March tide."[23] Some six months earlier, the council had also defined the prés salés as part of the maritime domain, contradicting advice given by Mayor Fleury, whose private interests had led him to understate the extent of tidal incursions. The councillors emphasized that they had "a perfect knowledge" of the localities concerned and that "even in the calmest weather, and at each new and full moon, that is *every fortnight,* the salty pastures in question are covered by the sea, for over eight days."[24] The prés, *according to the council,* must therefore be seen as an extension of the Bassin.

The representation of this zone in official documents could affect the daily lives of the inhabitants profoundly. This is brought home by Taffart's report, a large section of which offered an analysis of the titles by which Sauvage, Fleury, and Oxéda asserted their ownership of the prés. Article by article he dissected their claims, entering difficult legal territory—territory he must have had to traverse often during his career in the domain administration. He dismissed his opponents' argument that the prés salés were included in the *vacans et padouans* mentioned in King Louis XI's letters patent of 1462 (granting the Captalat or seigneurie to Jean de Foix) by using his knowledge of local terminology describing variations in terrain. He noted that the 1550 agreement between the seigneur and the inhabitants (*baillette*) made no explicit mention of prés salés, and argued that the 1780 enfeoffment contract in which the term first appeared was invalid. He discussed different kinds of State ownership, or *domaine* (*petit, casuel,* and *fixe*); fearlessly demolished his opponents' recourse to the ten-year prescription; and reminded them of the King's Council commissioners' warning in 1742 against then seigneur Amanieu de Ruat's "claiming for himself any stretch of sea" on pain of a 1,500-franc fine and legal proceedings.

Taffart declared that Henri Giers and his successors had not shown signs of possession of the prés salés for over thirty years, unlike the Testerins, who had used the public domain since time immemorial. Communities seeking recognition of their usage rights in eighteenth- and nineteenth-century France frequently used the term "time immemorial." It expressed their sense of having established a relationship with the land that went beyond titles and laws.

The prés salés' self-proclaimed owners, Sauvage, Fleury, and Oxéda, sought to show that Dumora, the first leaseholder after Giers, had established his occupation and thus ownership of the prés by building a windmill and sea baths on the property.[25] They claimed, moreover, that they had paid land tax since 1809. Taffart dismissed these claims by remarking that Dumora's constructions did not fulfill the requirements of the 1780 contract (which called for the planting of wheat and building of mills) and that, in any case, there was no sign of them now: "The construction of a mill that has never turned and sea baths that have never been used, in no way fulfilled the conditions they had agreed to." Whether or not Dumora actually built the sea baths, it is worth noting that they were being planned so early in the Bassin's history. Consider that the Duchess of Berry's famous and (supposedly) pioneering swims at Dieppe began in 1824.[26]

The purchasers' final claim that they would suffer "complete ruin" should the 1780 contract be annulled was dismissed out of hand by Taffart. They would lose nothing, he argued: not one coin had changed hands between the various "buyers." Their loss was nothing compared to the loss they would impose on the local community should their fish farms go ahead. Taffart's defense of the Testerins was passionate. Unfortunately he would have to confront the colder argumentation of people with no personal link to the region.

Taffart's emphasis on a careful definition of the prés makes sense when we look at a report written the following year by Gairal, a lawyer and spokesman for the litigation committee that had been given the brief of determining whether the domain administration should claim the prés salés—that is, declare them part of the public domain and thereby annul any private ownership.[27]

Gairal acknowledged that the prés were regularly covered by the tides and therefore lay within the public domain as it is usually understood, but he argued that the letters patent of 1462 confirmed that the king had abandoned this part of the domain to the Captal de Buch. The prés salés, even though not specifically named until the enfeoffment of 1780, were necessarily part of the lands and seigniories granted. So, while recognizing that according to ancient law and the Civil Code, the prés were part of the public domain, Gairal argued that this did not mean they had always been considered inalienable. He claimed that they were part of the *petit domaine* and that lands in this category could be alienated permanently, "given the utility and the necessity of cultivating and working the empty wastelands, pasturage, and empty marshes [*marais*] belonging to the King," according to the Edict of 1566.

The law of 1 December 1790, which declared "any misappropriation of the public domain . . . essentially null or revocable" did not apply to grants, sales, enfeoffments, and the like from before 1566, and it confirmed any alienations after that date of "empty wastelands, landes, pasturage, marshes, and uncultivated lands, other than those situated in forests or up to one hundred *perches* from them" as long as they had not involved theft or fraud and were executed according to the law of the day.[28]

Gairal did not care that *rivages* (shores) and prés salés were not named in these documents: he considered them to be covered by other terms. He rode roughshod over Taffart's careful distinctions between real prés salés and the tidal flats around La Teste. He referred to seigniorial documents concerning the *dunes* as proof of the Captal's right to dispose of the tidal zone despite the fact that the prés salés were *not* dunes. He thought the Testerins' differentiation between dunes and the area in dispute was in bad faith. He supplied a definition of *dunes* that he found in the dictionary of the Academy: "sandy hills which stretch the length of the seashore." He considered this to be an accurate description of the property. He did not care for local particularities, for the subtle differences between land formations and their uses. One wonders whether he even visited the Bassin.

Generalizing definitions are like maps in their imperfect translation of lived, local experience. In 1846, Hameau, mayor of La Teste, noted that the map attached to the 1834 bornage report represented the channels in the prés salés as being "So small, So small, that the frailest skiff could not pass through them; but fortunately they have retained their actual breadth in nature."[29] Gairal's remoteness from the scene of the battle meant that he was working from this kind of reduced, simplified, and abstracted representation of the prés salés.

Gairal's conclusion was that Sauvage must be acknowledged as the proprietor of the disputed land and that there was no point in the Domain seeking to appropriate the prés salés. He was loath to get mired in the conflict and stuck fast to his brief, arguing that the domain administration "should take no part in the debate that may arise between the owners and the commune."[30] Gairal wrote his report in Paris: we sense his distance, both physical and mental, from the epicenter of the struggle.

Gairal's understanding of the prés was shaped by his reading of reams of paper, by his training in law. As James C. Scott puts it in *Seeing Like a State,* "[S]tate officials . . . cannot be expected to decipher and then apply a new set of property hieroglyphs for each jurisdiction" because they seek to develop a simplified property regime, one that can be read and manipulated from the center.[31] The Testerins, on the other hand, were talking about a space full of meaning, Lefebvre's "lived space": their bodies had left traces there and had been shaped by this space between sea and land. The *baillette* of 1550, in which they had been recognized as "true seigneurs, through usage, peaceful possessors, as though of their own thing," had become an important story about the land. It was reenacted each time they worked on the prés, grazed their livestock there, scraped off the marine and manure deposits and heaved them onto their fields and vegetable patches. For this reason, Gairal's conclusion that Sauvage was indeed the legitimate owner could not hold with the Testerins on the ground.[32]

In 1837, Sauvage sold the prés salés to the Marquis de Castéja. Perhaps Sauvage had tired of the ongoing battle over the status of the prés salés. In September that year, the Marquis' private guard reported sixteen inhabitants for taking fertilizer from the prés, which they had done (the council argued) "according to custom." In February 1838, the council agreed to defend the Testerins' usage rights.[33]

A month later, La Teste's justice of the peace, Louis-Auguste-Frédéric Turgan, recorded a visit to the "site of contention," commonly known as the prés salés, where he found "a large number" of inhabitants assembled, as well as the naval commissioner. His report makes clear the extent to which the prés were still subject to the tidal regime. Even with an offshore breeze, the seawater rose as far as the wall enclosing the cultivated land adjoining the prés salés "not only in one place, but . . . over a distance of nearly half a myriametre [five kilometers or 3.1 miles]." The water traveled down the road leading to the port and commune of La Teste, past the first residence, and entered the customs officer's hut. "The entire plain known as the prés salés was covered," Turgan reported, and "several vessels came onto our prés salés to let people off onto the sea walls."[34] Similar observations were made in another report in March 1839.[35] The prés were, according to these accounts, very much part of the maritime domain.

This raised the thorny issue of the ownership of fish stocks. The investors who attempted to prove their ownership of the prés expressed interest in creating fish farms, and this posed a direct threat to the fishing community's sole source of income. Any appropriation of the sea's resources challenged the community's most basic assumption—that fishing was free. This assumption had been confirmed in 1742 when the Testerins' refusal to give the seigneur the second-best fish out of every catch and three *sous* per vessel each week had led to a debate in the courts and a victory for the fishing community. The Naval Decree of 1681 had been upheld and the seigneur's pretensions destroyed.[36]

The community held that no individual should have the right to herd the fish, which belonged to everyone, into his own private reservoirs. This would be to deprive poor fishing families of their rightful share. The fish farmer—already a rich man—would profit enormously with little or no risk of failure. The work of the fishermen and their families, on the other hand, was life-threatening. The seafarers had also proved their loyalty to their king and nation by faithfully carrying out naval service, which often lasted years. Unlike the seagoing fishermen, the reservoir's owners and workers would not be required to enroll for naval service because they were not navigating on the open sea. They would use the sea, steal its riches, but suffer none of the associated obligations.

Commander Mortemart de Boisse, who publicized the canal companies' efforts in 1840, was later named president of a commission of inquiry into oyster stocks in the Bassin. In June 1849, he sent a report to the minister for the navy, a section of which dealt with the creation of fish farms and their effect on the local fishing community. He argued for the rights of local fishermen who were registered with the navy. He noted that the fish farmers had placed fine-mesh nets at the openings of sixty-two locks, by which they captured "all the immature fish carried there naturally by the incoming tide." The commissioner could not fail to be moved by the complaints of local fishermen who cried:

> We are prohibited from fishing in the places where the fish spawn, we are banned from catching immature fish, we, the poor, who have no other livelihood but fishing and *who buy the right with our [naval] service,* and rich landowners unjustly claim the right to place their nets in places forbidden to us and to capture fish of all sizes!![37]

The fishing community and their defenders often dwelt on the importance of experienced sailors to the State. Naval conscription, introduced in the late seventeenth century and reorganized during the Revolution, required the services of sailors (*gens de mer*) for up to a year out of every three or four to man the king's vessels. This applied even in peacetime, so fishermen had heavier obligations than did other French citizens. The continued reproduction of this population of sailors was of great concern to governments. Between 1670 and the Revolution of 1789 the male seagoing population was estimated at between fifty thousand and sixty thousand. *Cahiers de doléance* (Registers of grievances) often referred to this "precious" and "indispensable" class of men.[38]

While naval service was a heavy burden, seasonal fishing also took its toll. Mortemart de Boisse emphasized the kinds of sacrifices made by the fishermen and -women, in contrast with the fish farmers' relatively risk-free undertaking. Sixty-two nets benefited large landowners who employed neither boats nor sailors, and when Mortemart drew up a balance sheet there was no doubt as to the losers. He counted 1,043 registered sailors—"not counting women," who, though they took part in fishing, were not eligible for naval registration—who maintained 373 boats "of all sizes," and who earned in total between 200 and 250,000 francs each year. This had to be weighed against an annual loss of "1 *Chaloupe* [ocean-going fishing vessel], 10 Drowned sailors, 7 Widows, 16 Orphans." In comparison, fourteen reservoir owners rented out their farms for about 50,000 francs, that is roughly 300 francs per hectare (2.47 acres), "while the best cultivated lands bring, in this region, 75 franc per hectare at the most."[39] These figures help us to understand why Sauvage and his successors went to such lengths to have their ownership of the prés salés recognized, why local opposition was so ferocious, and why the battle continued for so long.

Taffart's campaign during the 1830s culminated in a decision in 1839 by the Tribunal de Première Instance de Bordeaux which found in favor of the Testerins' usage rights, though not their proprietorial status: they could continue to use the area but only until the prés were enclosed.[40] Taffart's efforts had not been in vain. But the story was far from over; the status of the property had not been definitively decided.

In the 1840s, Etienne de Verneuil and then Germain René de la Forest, Count d'Armaillé, acquired the prés, and the same arguments continued. Gairal's 1833 advice, based on the erroneous definition of the prés, formed the basis of several administrative decisions that favored the purchasers over the commune.[41]

In 1846, Mayor Hameau, in a letter opposing d'Armaillé's proposal to enclose and transform the prés, claimed the Count had used the 1834 bornage report to support his claims. According to Hameau, the 1834 report had been carried out "in secret without the commune being called upon, even though by rights it should have been. Thus the commune has not been party to any engagement; its rights are still the same, and this document is null where the commune is concerned."[42] Later, the council repeated the accusation that in 1834 it had been denied the chance to "express its feelings about the point where the boundary was placed" and that the markers placed by the experts "advanced too far into the Bassin d'Arcachon, which remained part of the public domain."[43] The legitimacy of the bornage, whose itinerary we traced with some suspicion, was again called into question.

Count d'Armaillé's case for ownership of this contested zone was aided by the fact that in 1845, the new road from La Teste to Eyrac (the future Arcachon) was completed by the government, effectively cutting off part of the western half of the prés salés from the sea—against the wishes of Testerins who had requested a bridge allowing the seawater to remain in contact with the prés.[44] By enclosing this section, which d'Armaillé claimed as his own, the government had fulfilled one of the conditions of the enfeoffment of 1780, thereby strengthening the Count's proprietorial claims and his intentions to farm the land.

The next few decades saw incremental changes in favor of those claiming the prés salés as private property, despite the occasional reminder that the unenclosed parts were still subject to regular tidal incursion and thus, in theory, inalienable.[45] Disagreement between the ministries of public works and the navy led to conflicting decisions concerning the legality of d'Armaillé's fish-farm proposals, but in 1865, despite two imperial decrees in 1859 that declared the unenclosed sections of prés salés part of the public domain, the State chose not to claim the zone for itself. D'Armaillé's widow proceeded with the planned enclosure in 1868, after the boundaries delimited in 1834 were confirmed.[46]

In 1875, the issue was thrashed out yet again before the Première Chambre du Tribunal de Première Instance. The most recent buyer of the prés salés, Bordelais merchant Harry Scott Johnston, won the case when the judges accepted the fish farms as a legitimate usage in a generous reading of the word "etcetera" in the 1780 baillette's clause requiring the planting of wheat. This would not be the last time Johnston sparred with the fishing community.

In 1872, upon acquiring the eastern section of the prés, Johnston, like the widow d'Armaillé before him, had requested the official confirmation of his boundaries with another delimitation, as the 1834 and the 1866 markers had disappeared—further evidence of the shifting, elusive quality of this zone.

This new bornage eventually took place after Johnston's possession had been confirmed, in 1876. Thus, his ownership was acted out, just as Sauvage's had been forty-one years earlier. In an echo of the 1834 bornage, the mayor of La Teste, Joseph Bissérié, who was named to the committee tasked with replacing the markers, withdrew from the operation, citing his disagreement with the other members.[47]

This 1876 bornage would change the local people's patterns of movement and their working relationship with this liminal zone. Definitions, words, could affect the way the land's edge was lived; even if markers were washed away or buried in sand, the notion of property they represented was well entrenched. According to Franck Bouscau, the eastern prés salés were indeed converted into fish farms, except for a small strip along the port wall, which became the La Teste oyster farmers' workshop zone. The western section of the prés was enclosed in the 1930s.

CHAPTER THREE

To Suspend the Ocean

It is because the destructive work of the ocean appalls us, that it is useful, that it is great, that it is of national importance to suspend it, if we cannot stop it.

—Mortemart de Boisse, *Voyage dans les Landes de Gascogne*, 1840

The Bassin d'Arcachon provided a welcome respite for those who traveled across the "desert" of the landes. Here the eye was refreshed by the sight of boats plying the seawater, the mind restored by (relatively) civilized company, and the appetite satisfied with fresh fish or oysters. The Bassin was a stretch of water the mind and oar and foot could grasp: it was triangular, its edges visible from the center. It was also a haven for those coming from the open ocean—if they were lucky or skilled enough to make it through the heads.

The Bassin is the only refuge for sailors along a two-hundred-kilometer (124-mile) stretch of the Atlantic coast, between the Pointe de Grave to the north (where the Gironde River meets the ocean) and Bayonne to the south. The harbor of Arcachon is deep enough for large vessels to drop anchor, but the channels (*passes*) leading into the Bassin are infamous for their treacherous sandbanks and changeable conditions, preventing easy entry to the protected waters, not only for sailors unfamiliar with the region but also for locals who cannot always be sure how the banks have changed. According to a local ship's captain in 1810, the opening was "two Leagues wide" and "the space between these two points . . . almost totally filled by a chain of sandbanks, which are covered and partially uncovered with every tide."[1]

A comparison of maps of the Bassin drawn during the eighteenth and nineteenth centuries illustrates how changeable this environment was: Cap Ferret, the tip of the peninsula jutting southward from Lège, and forming a narrow barrier between the waters of the Bassin and the huge swell of the Atlantic Ocean, advanced by approximately 4,800 meters (2.98 miles) in a south–southeasterly direction between 1768 and 1826. [2] For the fishing community, up-to-date knowledge of the current position of the sandbanks and the depth of the channels was essential, especially in winter when they left the protected waters of the Bassin to fish in the ocean.

If it were not for this fickle and difficult entry, the Bassin might have become a great naval and commercial port. Many investors and engineers tried to achieve this. When Mareschal toured the Bassin in 1833, he pronounced on the "extreme utility of the execution of the canal, whose opening would create a real port," and he was by no means the first to dream of a great harbor so close to Bordeaux.[3] Engineers proposed ingenious channel-dredging or redirecting works from the mid-eighteenth century on, and although none of these projects eventuated, the regularity with which they appeared, in slightly different forms, says much about the preoccupations of administrators and investors at the time.[4] Above all, the planners expressed a desire to outwit nature, bring it into line, and mold it to their needs.

We cannot fully appreciate their way of seeing without considering the power—and the limitations—of the map. The creation of a map entails the abstraction and fixing of particular elements from "lived space" onto a two-dimensional surface, allowing planners to draw sweeping lines across a page and to envisage huge engineering works without acknowledging what effect these might have on the space as it is experienced on the ground, from below, or inside.[5]

When we stand in a forest, the trees dwarf us. They obscure what lies in the distance, and we are hemmed in, our actions limited. We look up and get a glimpse of the sky: a distant patch of blue. But when we look at a map of a forest, we lose the sense of what it is to stand among the trees: now, we tower over them. Essential to the cartographic perspective is the reader's sense of elevation, of having a bird's eye view. Michel de Certeau, commenting on the heady experience of looking over New York from the top of the World Trade Center (sadly no longer existent), writes: "It transforms the bewitching world by which one was 'possessed' into a text that lies before one's eyes. It allows one to read it, to be a solar Eye, looking down like a God."[6] Maps provide the

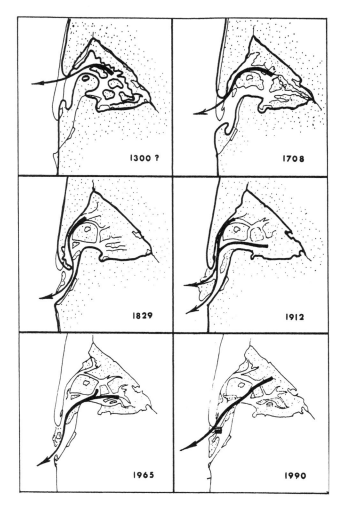

Fig. 4. Evolution of the morphology of the Bassin d'Arcachon and its hydraulic axes. From Jean-Marie Bouchet, "Evolution du Bassin d'Arcachon et des conditions de navigation," in *Le littoral gascon et son arrière-pays* (Arcachon: Graphica, 1990), 70. By permission Société Historique et Archéologique d'Arcachon.

same satisfaction: a city or a forest made small, unified and reduced to some pen marks on a page, appears to be a dominated space. It seems possible to make an impression, change things, and even destroy what once overwhelmed us.

Similarly, the experience of being at sea—bluish-green, brown, pink sea—rocked by the swell and hanging on for dear life to the rails or the mast when strong winds come up, searching through the fog for signs of land or another vessel, is transformed by the hydrographer. A moving, buoyant element becomes a series of pen strokes, a flat, transparent expanse of blue littered with tiny numbers.

How does the cartographer move from the deep and varied world in which we live to the lines and colors of a chart? What I want to articulate here is the difference between the mapmaker's representation of a place and the experience of living in that place. Clearly the mapmaker gained a sense of what it was to live in the area under scrutiny because he had to spend enough time there to do the required survey work. His mission—the transformation of lived space into a two-dimensional representation—demanded a certain way of approaching the environment in which he moved. He was there with the intention of mapmaking, and making a map requires selecting (and creating) certain kinds of information and shaping them into a form that bears little resemblance to the world as we perceive it through our five senses.[7]

When it came to measuring distances and angles, depths and heights, the surveyor used instruments through which he analyzed the landscape. It is as though he *projected* accuracy onto the landscape: accuracy emanated from his protractors, squares, height gauges, compasses, and levels.[8] But this was mathematical accuracy, applying only to the moment and the particular site of his measurements. Cartographers necessarily choose certain points from which to measure the area they are mapping: they are, in effect, generalizing about the surrounding areas by leaping over them. Geographer Peter Gould argues that, "as we take bigger and bigger geographic chunks as our building blocks, we will get smoother and smoother representations: 'smoother' in the literal sense that all the rough spikes and edges are rubbed off."[9] The generalization effected is both temporal and physical: what is represented becomes fixed in space and time, and yet claims to speak for more than that moment of its creation.[10]

Of course we recognize the necessity for the suppression of some information in a map for the sake of clarity and utility; a map is a tool, after all. As Mark Monmonier argues, "a good map tells a multitude of little white lies; it suppresses truth to help the user see what needs to be seen."[11] But we can also take up de Certeau's challenge: to remember that which the map kills. "These

fixations," he argues, "constitute procedures for forgetting. The trace left behind is substituted for the practice. It exhibits the (voracious) property that
the geographical system has of being able to transform action into legibility,
but in doing so it causes a way of being in the world to be forgotten."[12]

When we look at nineteenth-century hydrographic maps with this in mind,
the gaps—the uncharted spaces in between the cartographer's chosen points—
stand out. The sea floor was measured blindly by sounding the depths with a
lead at (more or less) regular distances; the configuration of the in-between
spaces had to be imagined. Monnier's 1835 map of the Bassin features what
looks like a swarm of flies over the contours of the sandbanks and channels:
swirls and lines of tiny numbers showing the depths at various points.[13] This is
where the map reader's imagination comes in: we must fill the gaps by believing in this as a representation of water. We must make this conceptual leap to
use the map as a tool.

The hydrographic engineers who mapped the Bassin often appealed to
locals for information on weather patterns, sandbank movements, and the
like, with the aim of using their accumulated knowledge for the benefit of
investors and government. This must have saved engineers much time and
effort during their extensive reconnaissance missions. And yet obtaining
this help was not always easy, particularly when the locals were out fishing.
A letter written by an engineer surveying the Bassin in 1868 illustrates the
difficulty of the undertaking. The locals informed his team that in 1825,
the hydrographer Raoul had cut short his survey after two months because
the sea was "difficult." Charles-François Beautemps-Beaupré, the engineer
who replaced Raoul in 1826, arrived with a personnel of 150 men and 17
boats of all sizes, and took another two months to finish the job. These
boats had to be "strong enough to hold their anchors in the *passes* or beyond." The local vessels, which he described as "flimsy rowboats," were
not up to the task.[14]

A Monsieur Sauveroche, sent to the Bassin in 1830 to report on the state of
the *passes,* confirmed the difficulty of obtaining accurate measurements. "It
will not be possible," he informed Jean-Baptiste-Bazile Billaudel, the chief engineer of the Ponts et Chaussées in Bordeaux, "to place a scale beside the sea,
due to the difficulty of finding capable people, the sea moreover being very
agitated and the beach, which is alternately covered and uncovered, too long
to allow us to determine the degrees of the scale with the incoming tide."[15]
What an impressive feat of abstraction it was, then, to translate this chaotic,
interrupted, watery experience into a legible and portable document.

Plans to improve the *passes* to facilitate the development of a large-scale commercial port were proposed from the mid-eighteenth century on. The engineers' main concern was to ensure access to a reliable and deep channel for large vessels. Planners envisaged a time when La Teste could provide a refuge for naval ships in times of conflict. Before 1816, they focused on the Bassin's defenses and facility of access to the sea in times of war, while later projects demonstrated a growing interest in rural development.[16]

Defense concerns were foremost in Kearney's 1768 report on Arcachon coastal navigation, which followed d'Hérouville's 1755 evaluation of security along the Atlantic coast.[17] He sought to determine whether it would be possible to "deepen the so-called Bar" to improve access to the Bassin, whether naval dockyards could be established there, and whether warships, "once ready to go to sea, should fear being blockaded as in most of our ports." He also investigated whether cultivation of "the immense plains that separate Arcasson [sic] from the fertile banks of the Gironde, from the Garonne to the Adour" was possible, and whether the soil "might not offer a crop of particular interest to the Navy."[18]

Kearney's answer to the first question was to propose the damming of the northern channel, between the Banc du Matoc and Cap-Ferret, in order to create a stronger outgoing current in the remaining channel; he believed that the concentrated ebb tide would then force a passage through the bar and deposit any sand it carried farther out to sea. A dune-stabilizing program would contribute to this process by limiting the amount of sand blown into the Bassin. To reduce costs, the dam could be constructed with local pine, which Kearney claimed was "incorruptible in sea water."[19]

He thought the establishment of naval dockyards in the Bassin desirable, and emphasized the inlet's strategic advantages. "The Enemy" would be prevented from blocking the port because of the prevailing westerly winds that would "force him toward a coast without resources," while the northerly and northwesterly winds would push him toward Bayonne and the Spanish coast. "There lies the advantage of this position over all others in the Gulf of Gascony," he concluded.

Kearney also saw agricultural promise in the fallow plains surrounding the Bassin. Resources for the proposed dockyards could be obtained from the planting of pine and oak trees, from the existing iron mines, and from salt pastures, which he thought could be turned into abundant fish farms, "so favorable to the seafaring population"—an assumption we know to be deeply flawed. Kearney concluded by saying that his project for the improvement of the *passes* was neither difficult nor extravagant, and yet it never came to fruition. As one who has passed through the narrows in a fishing boat, I wonder at Kearney's confidence. This is where we see the power of the map—a project that seems preposterous on the ground (or water) becomes feasible when we look at a chart.

Kearney's way of seeing the Bassin was shaped by strategic concerns, so that the mouth of the bay came to represent an escape route, or, for the enemy, a trap. The agricultural potential of the hinterland had value only as it served defense needs, and the same could be said for the local men, four to five hundred of whom were eligible to serve in the navy. Any benefits to the local population—such as their being saved from being engulfed by sand from the encroaching dunes—were worth noting, but incidental to Kearney's main concern. It was possible, then, for an observer to find objective value in the Arcachon seascape: military requirements provided a framework through which the Bassin and its surroundings could be evaluated.

How does this compare to the fishermen's perspective, and how can we determine this from Kearney's report? On the second page he refers to the locals' estimate of the width of a sandbank, the "Banc d'Arcasson," so he must have sought their advice. He also notes their observations on the prevailing currents, which they judged according to the movement of their fishing nets, and on seasonal patterns: "in winter the gusts of wind are more frequent, the tides, the local people say, are more abundant than in Summer; and it appears to be so."[20] Their accumulated knowledge was valued, but not necessarily their wishes: Kearney did not ask them what they thought of his proposed changes, or if he did, he chose not to record their answers.[21]

At one point, he used the experience of the local fishermen to prove that anchors could hold along the Arcachon coast even in the worst conditions. Kearney claimed that the Bassin fishermen resisted the winter westerly winds in their anchored *chaloupes* (rowboats). "It is true," he conceded, "that the wind has little grip on these kinds of boats, whose masts are lowered, but they too would be engulfed if the sea were as big as general prejudice concerning the navigation of this coast suggests. . . . It is a question of having good cables and good anchors."[22] Here we glimpse the daily buffeting the fishermen endured and their resignation or adaptation to their working conditions. This is what Lefebvre would call "lived space" and de Certeau "operational" space—a "practiced place . . . composed of intersections of mobile elements"—in contrast to the abstracted and stilled space of visual constructions or representations.[23] The fishermen's every act was a negotiation with the elements, a grappling with the unpredictable. Their strategies for passing in and out of the Bassin varied according to the conditions of the day, and this was only possible because their boats were small and maneuverable, unlike the unwieldy vessels that Kearney and his successors hoped one day to see anchoring in the port of La Teste.

Another way into imagining the fisherman's perspective, given that we cannot find an unmediated expression of their way of seeing, is by reading the second section of Kearney's *Mémoire,* "Manoeuvre to execute to enter the Port of Arcasson." This takes the form of a portolan book (or *routier*), the model for which originated in the Mediterranean in the sixteenth century. The portolan book contained navigational instructions for sailors, written "in a direct style, using the familiar form of verbs," and was usually accompanied by a chart.[24] It is here that the horizontal experience, the view 'from below,' from the thick of the waves, is articulated. Kearney moves between descriptive passages and map references in his directions to navigators; he switches between vertical and horizontal modes. The direct, descriptive approach conveys a much better idea of the lived space of the sea than any two-dimensional diagram could hope to do. These *routier*-style instructions were to be taken up by Jules Taffard forty-two years later.

Kearney's was only the first of a series of proposals for the fixing of the narrows. Jules Taffard put forward his project in 1810. He was a local who had served in the navy, and who, "possessing a heart full of fire for the prosperity of the place where [he] was born," requested the navy minister's permission to survey the Bassin and "draw up a maritime chart, noting all the dangers, the narrows, the soundings and generally, all that can contribute to the exact knowledge of a port."[25] In his *Mémoire sur la navigation du Bassin d'Arcachon,* he describes all the landmarks that can be used by the sailor to negotiate the narrows, and rather than using abstract, numerical reference points, he paints a vivid picture of the coastline. He claims that any sailor who follows his directions can navigate the *passes.* "Sailors who combine prudence with the knowledge of their craft," he writes, "can approach our bay without fear . . . If some have been shipwrecked along our coast, most owe it to their inexperience and their lack of courage."[26] His portolan-style instructions, similar to but more detailed than those offered by Kearney, convey a strong sense of what it was to approach the Arcachon coast in a boat.

Taffard describes a series of landmarks that the sailor should identify at certain points along the way to the Bassin. Remaining "one League out" from the coast, approaching from the direction of Bayonne, the seafarer is told to look out for features including the Mimizan pine forest, the tops of the Biscarosse pines—with indications as to the different aspect of these two forests—then fishing huts, "which you must bring to the corrected Northeast of you." After this, Arcachon's "little forest" and more pine plantations, each clump separately named, and finally "the Southern Battery [sandbank] and the markers." Once the sailor has accosted the narrows, following Taffard's bearings, he describes sand dunes according to their color—those of the north shore being "slightly red" and the southern dunes "white."

The spatial awareness this navigation involved would have become second nature to those who had to navigate the *passes* regularly. Keep in mind the fact that those using the portolan were floating on water: the horizon was constantly dipping and rising. The weather conditions changed constantly. Taffard notes that in bad weather one would have to be close to the coast to make out the dune grasses that were one of the signs he listed for recognizing Cap Ferret. Jean-Marie Bouchet points out that an appreciation of distances and indentations is difficult when sailing off a flat rectilinear coast and trying to land. Whereas today "the forest gives relief to the pale ochre band of the sandy beaches, and the very recent Dune du Pilat helps us recognize, without any possible doubt, the entry to the Bassin," this was not the case in Taffard's time. And only an "experienced eye" could spot the *passes,* "by the color of the water and the camber of the swell, . . . the general roll of the waves and breakers."[27] These were the visual cues that a chart—a fixed, graphic representation—could not communicate.

Once we take into account the experience of those who worked on the sea, adapting to its constantly changing conditions, the engineers' maps and projects seem all the more removed from reality: they seek to impose order on a moving world that resists definition and boundary making. Taffard appeared to straddle the two ways of seeing. On the one hand, he seemed to know the local waters well enough to compile a full set of instructions in the horizontal mode, in other words, from below, looking across the surface toward the hard-to-distinguish features of the mainland. On the other hand, like Kearney, he wished to address the question of how the *passes* might be improved; he embraced the perspective from on high. He too was focused on the Bassin's usefulness for the navy: he carried out his survey when the British naval blockade was in force.

Taffard noted that the *passes'* unpredictability made it possible to undermine the blockade: when the port of Bordeaux was under siege, goods were transported via La Teste, and even large ships managed to negotiate the *passes.* He had seen how English warships off the ocean coast were unable to prevent vessels from leaving the Bassin, "for, upon the smallest storm in summer, upon the least appearance of a westerly wind in winter," the enemy was forced to move thirty to forty leagues out to sea, at which point the local merchants slipped out and sailed to Bayonne or Bordeaux. He had witnessed

France's enemies unleashing their "devastating fury" in other ports where conditions favored the establishment of a blockade, and so his eyes "were naturally drawn to the Arcachon coast": he was determined to prove the utility of La Teste as a safe port for naval and commercial ships.

Taffard's suggestions for the improvement of the narrows were not as grandiose as those of Kearney. He believed in the benefits of stabilizing the dunes of Piquey on the northwest shore of the Bassin, which, once immobilized, would prevent the transfer of sand into the Bassin: "the sandbanks, no longer receiving nourishment would then take an invariable position; the *passe* would be fixed and the current would dig itself a deeper bed." The plantations would also shield those sheltering within the Bassin from enemy eyes.

Taffard's belief in the possibility of finding an "invariable position" for the *passes* supports Catherine Bousquet-Bressolier's assertion that until the 1870s, engineers believed it was possible to halt coastal changes permanently around the Bassin.[28] Taffard assumed that differences between his and Kearney's surveys were due to miscalculation on Kearney's part: he overlooked the possibility that work carried out since 1768, in particular the planting of pine trees, might have changed the Bassin environment. He doubted "that clayey soil covered in grasses and exposed to weak currents could experience great changes over a 42 year period."

Beautemps-Beaupré's 1826 survey of Arcachon showed that the Bassin's interior regime had changed enormously since the Kearney report.[29] But curiously enough, when Taffard asked old sailors from the region whether they had observed any alteration in the position of the channels and the exposed banks, they informed him that they had remained the same since their childhood.[30] Bousquet-Bressolier attributes this to their daily use of the space: when in constant contact with something that changes, people tend not to register transformation. This suggests, then, that their adaptation to the shifting *passes,* because so gradual, was an unconscious, automatic process.

The validity of hydrographic projects like Taffard's centered on their authors' claims to geometrical accuracy. Taffard was at pains to distinguish his surveying method from that of Kearney. "I do not claim to value my work over that of any other; but I took precautions such that I can ensure its exactitude. I made an exact triangulation, in order to place each visible point according to its real position; everything was subject to calculation; next I did the perimeter. The trigonometric points served to establish the position of all the channels in an invariable manner."[31] This was the surest method of carrying out such an operation, he argued. This way he could produce a true representation of the land and seascape.

In this respect, Taffard could be likened to Lefebvre's draftsman, who, looking at a blank sheet of paper, "believes that this neutral space which passively receives the marks of his pencil corresponds to the neutral space outside, which receives things, point by point, place by place. . . . He thinks he is reproducing while in fact he produces!" If we think of a drawing or design as a representation full of holes, "a filter selective towards contents, eliminating this or that part of the 'real,'" as Lefebvre puts it, then claims to objectivity and accuracy like Taffard's lose much of their power.[32]

Taffard's desire to overcome the unpredictable and chaotic nature of the *passes* was shared by later planners. Engineers' proposals throughout the nineteenth century swung between modest dune-stabilizing programs like that suggested by Taffard and more ambitious transformations, harking back to Kearney's bold brushstrokes. Rather than dwell on military requirements, they saw the development of the port of La Teste primarily in commercial terms, as part of a larger program of regional development.

Unlike local seafarers, whose lives were tuned to the rhythm of changing conditions, planners were not happy to float with the current: they were desperate to assert their control over a threatening land- and seascape. They feared that the surrounding communities would be engulfed in sand or even water. In May 1830, a member of the commission appointed by the Baron d'Haussez to investigate the possibility of improving the *passes* reported that they had agreed unanimously "that the current *passes* of the bay of Arcachon are bad, that their situation worsens daily, that we can even fear and predict a disastrous event which, with a violent storm, would close the bay's outlets and cause the submersion of the region and the ruin of its inhabitants."[33]

D'Haussez, who had developed a radical proposal for the improvement of the *passes* in 1829 when he was prefect of the Gironde, was named minister for the navy soon after. His *Notice* on the Bassin appeared in the same year as the publication of the hydrographer Beautemps-Beaupré's new map of the area. D'Haussez believed the Bassin to be vast and deep enough to hold "all the fleets of Europe," the only obstacle to the creation of a port being its lack of an "easy entry." He proposed the construction of a brand new channel, to be cut through the Cap Ferret peninsula. For the new channel to operate effectively, the old *passes* would need to be closed, thus giving greater force to the water moving through the man-made channel. The Baron imagined that the existing channels could be blocked off with the shells of sunken ships![34]

The essentials of the project, if not the sunken ship idea, were taken seriously by the commission's members. In the résumé of the commission's findings, Billaudel, president of the commission, recognized "that the existing *passes* are not susceptible to real or durable improvements, that nature herself indicates the only possible way to remedy the present evil and to warn of the dangers envisaged, by leaving man with the possibility of re-establishing a channel to the north in the very same place where, according to a recent tradition, the waters of the Bassin once had an outlet to the sea."[35]

The plan to build a new *passe* found support: starting afresh, creating a new passage, was an appealing plan. In this way the engineers could maintain control over the land and seascape. They would not have to submit to the unpredictable, changeable regime of the existing *passes:* they could combat the "evil" and "dangers" they saw in this natural environment. They would try to overcome the incursions of sand "vomited by the sea," "whose inexhaustible source is a plague for our countryside," to use commission member Sauvage's words—the same Sauvage who was at that time trying to appropriate La Teste's prés salés (salt pastures) in the hope of wresting them from the sea's (and the Testerins') control.[36]

Individual commission members' responses to the Baron's proposals varied, especially regarding the blocking of the old *passes.* Sauvage suggested blocking off the northern *passe* to improve the depth and force of the southern *passe,* as well as opening up the new channel, although he was concerned about the division and consequent weakening of the outward flow of water. Beautemps-Beaupré, whose map had probably inspired the Baron's sweeping proposal, was pessimistic about the proposal's chances of success. He argued that it would be difficult to dam a wide and deep channel with a strong current and banks of moving sand. Even if it were possible to block the *passe,* a sandbar would form at the mouth of the new channel, and the interior regime of the Bassin would be seriously affected.[37] Note the interesting difference in attitude between Beautemps-Beaupré, who mapped the Bassin in 1826, and the Baron, who used that same map in his grandiose imaginings. For the man who effected the translation from lived space to two-dimensional representation, the project seemed impossible; one presumes he remembered what it was really like to carry out the soundings from a rocking boat. The Baron, safely ensconced in his Bordeaux or Paris rooms, was free to let his mind run wild as he slid his finger across the lines and numbers of the hydrographic chart.

Despite the commission members' differences of opinion, they must have come to an understanding because, in their findings, they were unanimous in concluding that the closing of the old *passes* was impracticable. They feared "that the quantity of water that the Bassin receives would be considerably diminished and that the fish which are so important to the fishing activities within the Bassin would no longer arrive in such abundance." They agreed,

though, that a new channel through Cap Ferret was desirable, and proposed
that it be reinforced by two breakwaters of approximately 100 meters (328
feet) in length to the north and south of the channel's opening into the Atlantic, and another breakwater inside the Bassin "to attract a greater mass of
water at ebb tide."[38]

It is in these reports from 1830 that we finally catch a glimpse of the locals'
attitude to the improvement projects. Sauvage, to whom the president of the
commission addressed certain questions relating to the likely success of the
project, wrote: "The two channels, by dividing the water [flowing in and out
of the Bassin] are mutually harmful; the local sailors, who are *merely* fishermen and coastal navigators, would prefer to conserve them because of the
possibility of using whichever channel they find themselves closest to upon
their return."[39] The fishermen saw advantages in the flexibility that the existence of two channels provided: they could read the conditions and make a
choice. Their concern about the project was based on observation and practice going back centuries: Sauvage's dismissal of their response thus seems extremely shortsighted. His attitude toward the locals is an illustration of the
distance that lay between those who came from outside, seeking to impose
order on the Bassin, and those who knew its ways and had learned to make
the most of them. The fishermen were, one imagines, naturally suspicious of
such newcomers: how could they be sure what effects d'Haussez's "improvements" would have on a space they knew so well?

Billaudel acknowledged in 1831 that the fishermen considered the correct
placement of beacons (*balises*) to be of prime importance. "Each day," he reported to the prefect, "their eyes are fixed on them, and only they know the
dangers and directions of the *passes* and in consequence it is from their indications that the position of the signals and their usage should depend."[40] He
hoped to institute a reliable and regular system of notification of changes by
the sailors, to be recorded monthly and acted on by the naval commissioner.
But the harbormaster (Chef Maritime), while agreeing on the importance of
accurately placed beacons, concurred with the local captains, head fishermen
(*maîtres*), and boat owners that it made more sense to report changes as soon
as they occurred rather than adhering to a monthly reporting system. He also
noted the navigators' concern that the current beacons, "while quite tall, are
not visible enough and that it would be good if they were a little larger."[41]
This observation brings home once again the sensorial experience and precariousness of working at sea.

The locals' focus on correct signposting indicates their wishes with respect
to the *passes*. Most references to the locals in engineers' reports concern advice

they gave on prevailing winds, changing positions of sandbars, and similar questions—or on the difficulty in finding local sailors who could read and write, especially when they were all out fishing.[42] Their knowledge of the area was regularly sought out, but not their opinion on the proposed "improvements." They were considered to be courageous, healthy specimens of manhood, but certainly not progressive in their attitudes. When we see Sauvage refer to them as "merely" fishermen, it is not hard to understand why the citizens of La Teste should have fiercely opposed his attempts around the same time to create fish farms on the Ile aux Oiseaux and the prés salés.

The 1830 *passes* project, like the projects before it, was never executed. In 1831, the Baron d'Haussez, already in exile in London, was condemned by the new Orleanist regime. This put an end to his ambitions for Arcachon.[43] But in May 1835 the new minister for the navy sent M. P. Monnier, a hydrographic engineer, to Arcachon, to undertake another survey of the Bassin and express his opinion "on the importance attributed to it as a maritime position by Messrs. Boyer-Fonfrède and Mareschal, director and inspector of the enterprise for the exploitation and colonization of the landes of Bordeaux"—that is, the Compagnie des Landes, whose fortunes we followed in chapter 1.[44] Boyer-Fonfrède and Mareschal were no doubt determined to convince the minister of the utility of their canal scheme. Perhaps they hoped a new survey would encourage the minister to take up the Baron d'Haussez's plans of five years earlier, for the opening up of La Teste port would contribute enormously to the viability of their project. If so, they were to be sorely disappointed.

Monnier carefully compared his survey results to the observations of his precursors, going back as far as the early 1600s. He was taken aback by the extent of the changes to the Bassin's form, noting Cap Ferret's 4,800-meter (3-mile) advancement toward the south-southeast over the fifty-eight years since Kearney's survey (see fig. 4). His observations led him to conclude that "no work of art, no matter how well-conceived, could result in the creation of a *passe* permitting easy access to the La Teste harbor at all times, and even less the creation of a permanent state for the *passe* and the interior regime of the bay, conditions which it would, however, be necessary to fulfill before thinking of forming great maritime establishments in these waters."[45]

He argued against the possibility of closing off the southern *passe*, citing the impact of the "violent" currents of the ebb tide on the wall of sunken ship shells proposed by d'Haussez, and the likelihood of the Bassin waters "ploughing" through the Banc de Matoc and creating a new passage. The "extreme mobility of the sands" would militate against any permanent reinforcement of the shores on either side of the narrows.[46] Monnier considered the close monitoring and regular repositioning of landmarks on the two points to be the only feasible solution to the navigational problems posed by the shallow *passes*. Despite dismissing the feasibility of the grandiose improvement schemes of d'Haussez and others, he recognized that "the Bassin d'Arcachon's position is extremely useful to commerce and would be of great help in times of war, because it cannot be blockaded." He was concerned, though, to discourage sailors from coming too close to the entry to the Bassin when a strong onshore wind was blowing. To emphasize the dangers posed by the narrows, he noted that even the "hardy fishermen of La Teste," who had suffered many "disastrous events" over the years, dreaded them.[47]

Monnier showed a greater interest in the experience of the local seafarers than had any of his predecessors. He claimed that his "first thought" on arriving in La Teste was "to interrogate the local people on the diverse circumstances which must have accompanied these great changes"—that is, to the positions of the sandbank and the points. He was particularly interested in their observations on the improved northern, or Canonnière, channel, which had been "impracticable" in 1826 but was now "the only one in use." He also listened to "fishermen who observe daily what happens at the Bassin's entry," whose advice convinced him that the opening of the northern channel had been caused by a narrowing of the southern channel due to the "sudden displacement" of the Banc de Matoc, one of the largest sandbanks in the Bassin. This had come about "under the prolonged action of the impetuous Westerly and North-westerly winds."[48]

It seems likely that his consultation with the fishermen contributed to his pessimistic view of the feasibility of altering the *passes*. We can only assume that the account they gave of their observations indicated their wishes: their knowledge gave them some power in this situation. The La Teste councillors were not on good terms with Boyer-Fonfrède, who had ignored their advice concerning the canal outlet, and who described their town as a "miserable village [*bourgade*]" back in 1833.[49] It is possible that others from within the fishing community shared the councillors' ill feeling. Why should they lend support to his profit-making venture? If Monnier's report was to influence the outcome of the canal project, this was a good opportunity for them to flex some muscle.

Monnier was to be strongly criticized for his pessimism by Paul-Emile Wissocq, an ex-naval hydrographer and legitimist noble who presented a report on the *passes* to the director-general of the Ponts et Chaussées four years later.[50] Wissocq was also one of the founders of the Compagnie Agricole et Industrielle d'Arcachon (discussed in chapter 1), so he had a vested interest in the future prosperity of the region. A beautifully executed map of the Bassin accompanied Wissocq's *Mémoire*. He was convinced that the Bassin's entry could be improved, and he developed a detailed and carefully justified project that involved damming the Chenal de Leige, a channel within the Bassin, and opening up a new *passe* through the Cap Ferret peninsula in the place where the northern channel had run in 1786 (before natural deposits of sand extended the tip by thousands of meters). His submission came at a time when the Bordeaux-La Teste railway line was only two years away from completion, which no doubt influenced his opinion of the importance of the region.[51] He also considered the *passes'* improvement essential to the eventual construction of a waterway between Arès (on the northern shores of the Bassin) and the Gironde River, leading to the port of Bordeaux—yet another canal project.

Wissocq criticized Monnier for not trusting enough in "science and the power of art." He thought Monnier defeatist, for he had cut short "the solution of the gravest questions by declaring it impossible." By "giving substance to erroneous opinion"—perhaps Wissocq was referring to the fishermen's advice here?—he had directed the government away from an area deserving of its attention and caused "the postponement, for centuries, of work of the first necessity."[52] Wissocq implied that Monnier had argued against the viability of the d'Haussez project because he was not prepared to see it through: he was lazy or lacked courage. Wissocq, by comparison, was ready to embark on an enormous undertaking.

His answer to the problem of blocking off the old *passes* was ingenious. "It is not by sinking ship shells, as has frequently been proposed, that a dam such as this can be executed," he claimed. He pointed out the extreme difficulty and expense in building a dam "almost level with the coastline of the Gulf of Gascony, where the sea beats the coast with such prodigious power, a dam more than 2,000 meters [1.25 miles] long, resting on a bed of moving sand in a place where we find up to 50 and 60 feet of water at low tide and where the currents move at up to 12,000 meters [39,370 feet] per hour."[53] Instead, Wissocq proposed stopping the Leige channel well inside the heads, and therefore in calmer waters, with rows of wooden cases 50 meters (55 yards) long, whose sand-weighted canvas bases, once sunk, would take on the form of the sea floor. The Bassin waters, meeting this obstacle, would then naturally follow the remaining Teich channel and be directed toward the new, man-made opening. The old *passes* would eventually silt up until only the new one was left, and the force of the outgoing current would create a much deeper passage, permitting large vessels to enter the Bassin and

FIG. 5. The *passes,* mapped by Wissocq, 1839. Map accompanying Wissocq, *Mémoire sur les travaux à exécuter pour améliorer l'entrée du Bassin d'Arcachon* (Paris: Imprimerie Porthmann, 1839). Bibliothèque Municipale d'Arcachon.

reducing the roughness of the breakers, thereby improving conditions for smaller boats as well.[54]

At no stage does Wissocq report having sought the advice of local mariners, and indeed his *Mémoire* is theoretical: he uses diagrams of generalized situations, relating to the formation of sandbanks and the like, and regularly refers back to his map of the Bassin, using letters to indicate positions: "dam XY," "point A," and so on. His map is beautiful but more general than earlier ones; there are fewer figures indicating depth because the scale is smaller. This is an example of the smoothing effect of choosing to represent a larger geographical chunk. Bousquet-Bressolier considers Wissocq's work as indicative of a movement toward greater abstraction and reasoning, based on mathematical principles rather than on observation, which developed in the mid-1820s and marked the rest of the century. The growing tendency to favor deductive thought meant that engineers like Wissocq were taught to assume that one could plan major works on the basis of laws of nature. "Reality" and local knowledge were pushed aside, as theoretical reasoning and its mathematical basis took precedence.[55]

This helps to explain Wissocq's lack of interest in local experience. His approach had something in common with the canal builders, who ignored the advice of people who lived in the area and drew lines in the soil that seemed ridiculous to Testerins. The new *passe* proposed by Wissocq (and d'Haussez) satisfied the aesthetic of the straight line, an aesthetic that also guided the canal and railway builders, but the enormity of the project meant it was shelved yet again, and there were no more hydrographic proposals until the Second Empire.

The only changes made to the Arcachon channels in the wake of this series of improvement proposals were to marking (*balisage*) the entry with wooden poles, buoys, and eventually a lighthouse. So Monnier the skeptic saw his suggestions acted on. Indeed, when I went out through the *passes* in 1996 on a fishing trawler, tall buoys still played an essential role alongside the sophisticated navigational instruments on board.

Testerins were not necessarily hostile to the idea of the "improvements" proposed for their coastline, but it appears that they frequently took offense at the planners' behavior and assumptions. They gained a reputation for stubbornness and an apparent lack of interest in progress. In 1844, councillor Johnston claimed that "the inhabitants of La Teste have seized every opportunity to fight enterprises useful to their region," and in 1850, a Ponts et Chaussées engineer declared in a letter to his superior that "the population of La Teste which has profited so greatly from the new creations resulting from the opening of the railway, has always been hostile to all improvements and establishments which contribute to the prosperity of this commune."[56]

Of course it would be in the fishing community's interest to ease navigation through a stabilization of the *passes,* but their lifetime of seagoing experience must have suggested to them that these ambitious engineers could not possibly succeed, and if anything they were likely to make things worse by altering the flow of water and affecting the fish stocks and the depth of the channels the locals had come to know so well. They had spent their lives rolling with the swell, making do, and they probably couldn't believe that men with bits of paper rolled under their arms were going to change things for the better after all this time. They had only to think of Taffard, the local-born navigator who had dreamed of altering the *passes:* he failed spectacularly in his attempt to rise above the chaos and impose order. In January 1811, he made a trip to the *passes* to note changes that had occurred there since his 1810 survey: his boat, the *Emilie,* was wrecked, and he drowned.[57]

CHAPTER FOUR

We came to save the population from shipwreck and we found them united against us.

—Captain David Allègre, *De la pêche dans le Bassin et sur la côte extérieure d'Arcachon,* 1841

The winter of 1836 was a hard one for the people of the Gironde department. Strong winds, rain, and frost caused great losses to farmers; agricultural work had to be put on hold.[1] The end of Lent was usually a productive time for ocean fishing, but the fishermen of La Teste and neighboring communes found themselves confined to land for a month because rough seas prevented them from tackling the *passes.* When the weather finally improved in late March, they planned a fishing expedition, which they hoped would help cover their equipment and maintenance costs for the season.[2]

Jean Fleury (*fils aîné*), the mayor of La Teste, wrote to the prefect of the Gironde on 1 April 1836, to inform him of the results of this expedition. "It is with a heart overcome by grief," he began, "and surrounded by agonizing cries echoing throughout this commune today, that I take up my pen to announce the deplorable misfortune causing this general desolation, plunging a considerable number of families into grief and distress." On March 23, eight fishing boats had left the Bassin, expecting to return with their catch the next day, but only two made it back. The others had been caught by a rough sea and, the weather continuing to deteriorate, were unable to confront the *passes.* On Palm Sunday, March 27, "they were seen off Cap Ferret and close to the *passe,*" but were still unable to reenter, so they headed north for the mouth of the Gironde River, "or any other port." They were too late: "before they could reach shelter, the terrible storm of the 27th and 28th took them by surprise and today, after having spent several painful and anxious days, we learn the sad news that they all perished." There was a crew of thirteen on each boat, which meant that seventy-eight men were lost.[3]

Fifty-six of these men were fathers, so they left behind the same number of wives, one hundred and sixty children, and numerous dependent, elderly parents. The mayor of Mios called them "the elite of the sailors of the quarter of La Teste" in his report to the prefect. The shipwreck came to be known by locals as "Lou Gran Malhour" (The Great Sorrow).[4] It appears to be one of the few historical events from the Bassin region to have survived in popular memory.

What must it have been like to watch the men struggle on their pitching, flimsy wooden boats from the safety of the Cap Ferret shore? They were not far away, but out of reach: the sea was another world. These fishermen lived a dual life, attached both to the land where their families lived and to the unpredictable, dangerous, but eternally promising ocean. Ocean fishing was surely a very different experience from fishing within the Bassin where land and sea seemed to exchange places with every tide.

In the 1800s, the frequency of drownings in and near the *passes* was of great concern to the local fishing community as well as to the administrators and investors who dreamed of creating a great port in the Bassin. In a report to his superior in Bordeaux, La Teste's naval commissioner claimed in 1818 to have lost thirty-four of his "best sailors" that year and estimated that a quarter of the enlisted sailors in his administrative section drowned annually, leaving destitute wives and children.[5] In 1842, Captain David Allègre made a telling comparison: between 1793 and 1814, some thirty to forty sailors from La Teste were killed during naval service, whereas between 1836 and 1842, one hundred and twenty men drowned locally.[6] In response to this appalling toll, close scrutiny of local fishing practices and boat design accompanied proposals for the improvement of the *passes.* But, just as the hydrographic schemes failed to ignite the fishermen's enthusiasm, the attempted introduction of a new design for fishing vessels met resistance from people who, one might have thought, stood to benefit from larger, sturdier boats.

Despite the frequency of shipwrecks and drownings, local fishing practices remained essentially unchanged. There was financial risk involved in building new boats or making expensive changes to existing vessels. Added to this was a fatalism among the seafarers. They were not foolhardy, but risks had to be taken. Their lives depended on fish, and fishing sometimes took away life. Lists of dependents of sailors who perished in 1831 (five years before the Grand Malheur) included "Parents," who were nearly all widowed mothers. Alain Cabantous calculates thirty-five as the average age at death for seagoing men in the eighteenth century.[7] Perhaps the Testerin fishermen's fathers had drowned at sea before they could become "dependents."

One might expect this grieving community to welcome any improvements to safety. But what would the proposed changes mean for people who worked their bodies in the shell of a boat riding the waves, people whose daily activities were dictated by the tides and weather patterns? To understand why they resisted change, we must begin by looking at the seasonal rhythms and established work rituals of the Bassin's inhabitants.

Cereal crops, the staple product in most rural communities, did not thrive in the poor soil of the landes. Although subsistence crops were grown, the economic base of the region lay in the Bassin's produce and the exploitation of the surrounding pine forests. Trade with Bordeaux and other Atlantic ports was essential to the locals' livelihood: the Testerins were the main suppliers of fresh fish and shellfish to Bordeaux. Before the opening of the Bordeaux–La Teste railway line in 1841, fishmongers and women selling their husband's catch made the trip by cart along a poorly maintained road, usually flooded in winter and scorched dry in summer.[8] According to the geographer Elisée Reclus, writing in 1863: "Only the women and the professional fishmongers knew the city and they recounted marvels to the fishermen and resin collectors of La Teste, who were enclosed on all sides by desertous moors"—once again an image, so popular with the canal planners, of empty landes contrasting with the oasis of the Bassin. Note that although women worked as carters, fish sellers, and fisherwomen, they were not considered "professional."[9] Reclus did, however, acknowledge that the Testerin women's work, inside and outside the home, was essential to their families' survival.[10]

The Bassin people, according to their means and the season, practiced various fishing methods. Between April and October, fishing families caught sardines, gray and red mullet, bass, sole, and sea bream from their *pinasses,* flat-bottomed rowboats made with local pine.[11] Both men and women used these vessels, which challenges the commonly held belief that women in traditional fishing communities were forbidden to set foot on fishing vessels because they were thought to bring bad luck (or similar tales). In fact, the Bassin women's active involvement in fishing had been a matter of some concern as early as

1768, to naval hydrographer Kearney, in his treatise on the Arcachon coast. In the margins of a paragraph in which he noted the number of sailors eligible for naval service in La Teste, he observed: "the number of sailors in this department would be greater, if women were not permitted to fish in the Bassin[;] there are a great many of them, and they would be better occupied clearing the moors."[12] In other words, even though women's work was essential to the local economy, the government considered their navigational skills of little use because they could not serve in the navy.

Different kinds of nets were used for different types of fish. There were also different methods of using the nets, including *la pêche aux palets* (*palet* fishing), which involved placing sticks in the exposed banks with nets attached, forming an enclosure in which to trap fish as the tide came in. On the other side of the *passes,* along the ocean beaches, *la pêche à la senne* (seine net fishing) demanded two crews, one on foot and another afloat, working at either end of a long, vertical net, to encircle shoals of fish on the signal of a leader skilled in recognizing the glint of scales. Nets were also used to catch ducks and other migratory birds during the winter months. Throughout the year, shellfish including oysters, mussels, pippies, and clams could be collected on foot at low tide from the *crassats* (exposed mud banks).

Between November and March, the fish migrated out into the Atlantic, and crews of fishermen followed them, weather permitting, in their vessels known as *chaloupes.* Women were not usually involved in this deep-sea fishing, or, in Gascon, *pêche au péougue*—at least, their numbers had probably diminished since 1793, when the La Teste council declared that it was "against good morals" for women to join ocean fishing crews (*pariadges*) and threatened those who did not return to agricultural work with the epithet "debauched women" (*femmes de mauvaise vie*).[13] The ocean-going *chaloupes,* more solid than the flat-bottomed *pinasses* that were used in the Bassin, were built so that they could make it through the heads, although according to Jules Mareschal's 1833 description, the canal builder Boyer-Fonfrède's *chaloupe* offered its passengers little security. Mareschal and his companions "saw not without some surprise and emotion, the life of all entrusted to some planks hardly six *lignes* (half an inch) thick, joined by nothing but wooden nails, and moreover whose greatly dilapidated state meant that they nearly succumbed to the beating of the waves."[14]

Chaloupes were without decks, equipped with twelve oars and two or three sails, the nets operating as ballast. Teams of thirteen men—twelve fishermen and a *pilote* (helmsman)—left the Bassin on these vessels. Each outing, called a *traite,* usually lasted twenty-four hours. The men would go out only in calm seas, the helmsman determining whether the crew should venture through the heads. If he decided the conditions were unfavorable, the men had to row back to La Teste. In bad weather, the breakers over the infamous sandbar were to be avoided at all costs, but judging the sea was a challenge. Over a twenty-four-hour period, the weather could turn more than once, as it did in March 1836, causing the shipwreck described at the beginning of this chapter.

Shortly after this tragedy, Captain Allègre, a retired naval officer living on the Bassin in Arès, wrote a pamphlet entitled *De la pêche dans le Bassin et sur les côtes d'Arcachon: Moyen de la pratiquer sans danger et avec profit* (On fishing in the Bassin and on the Arcachon coast: How to practice it safely and profitably). He was a member of a commission of inquiry set up to investigate the causes of the shipwreck "with the object of preventing further misfortunes."[15] A group of twenty-two "notable" sailors from the La Teste quarter met with the commission members to discuss safety issues. According to Allègre's version of events, silence reigned when the men were encouraged by the naval commissioner of La Teste, Henri Lhotellerie, to voice their ideas, but when Allègre spoke up, his proposals, initially opposed, were eventually recognized to be worth pursuing.[16]

Allègre proposed the radical idea of introducing steam-powered, decked boats into the local fishing fleet. He argued that current fishing practices were dangerous and unproductive. He supported his argument with descriptions of the extraordinary lengths to which local men went to survive at sea when the weather turned bad. Allègre praised the solid construction and seagoing qualities of the *chaloupes,* but found that problems resulted from the use of nets for ballast.

In calm weather, out on the ocean, the nets were cast and kept afloat by buoys, which were held in place by weighted cables. The *chaloupe* anchored to the extreme west of the nets and waited eight to ten hours for the fish to accumulate; when the time was right, the crew rowed alongside the nets, hauled them in, and disentangled the fish. They would then return through the *passes.* But when a change in the conditions meant it was impossible to haul up the nets, the boats had no ballast, and thus their sails could not be hoisted, making it extremely difficult to reenter the Bassin. In these circumstances, Allègre explained, the crew would find themselves "condemned, without the protection of a deck, to remain in an horrific sea which breaks incessantly." He described how these "poor wretches," to defend themselves against the "fury of the waves," would pitch a tent by stretching a sail over a mast that rested against the bow and was held at the stern by a trestle, and secure it toward the front and along the gunwale. They would then climb underneath.

But as great waves crash constantly over the tent and threaten to sink the *chaloupe,* each man, armed with a stick with a clog at one end, works unceasingly and forcefully above his head to free the tent of the burden of water. Sometimes these precautions do not suffice, and with the water's weight threatening to capsize the vessel, an opening is cut in the tent with a knife, and the water enters the boat violently; the men then activate the pump and attempt to get out, if they can.[17]

Allègre argued that if the boats had ballast, reentering the Bassin would be feasible. For this reason, he proposed the development of steam-powered, decked vessels. He knew that it would take some arguing to convince the locals of the benefits of this change. The fishermen of La Teste had always rejected proposals for building decks on their *chaloupes.* The Conseil Général of the Gironde had offered the handsome reward of 3,000 francs to the builder of the first decked *chaloupe,* "but this encouragement was scorned, no-one came forward to claim it."[18]

After admitting his initial belief that the fishermen's resistance to decks was rooted in blind traditionalism, Allègre became convinced of the rationality of their reluctance to change. "My ideas on this subject," he declared, "have totally changed: I have come around to their view." He acknowledged that oars were "indispensable to these vessels." If the vessels were decked, the fishermen would not be able to reach the speeds necessary to haul up their nets, "for the first condition permitting a rower to place all his force onto an oar, is that he be seated solidly, comfortably, his feet strongly engaged below his seat." They also relied on their oars to extract themselves from the sandbar in difficult conditions. "In a rough sea and slack wind, how can a frail vessel, without its own motor, abandon itself to the breakers? The first wave would put it abeam; the second would throw it onto its side or the keel in the air. With oars, the pilot remains master of the direction, and the three breaks of the sandbar are soon traversed."[19] Oars, then, were the fishermen's only means of controlling their vessel in difficult conditions, so it is not surprising that they looked upon decked vessels with trepidation. But according to Allègre, steam engines would make the passage back through the heads possible in any conditions, their power replacing the rowers' efforts.

Allègre's pamphlet, *De la pêche dans le Bassin,* is the most comprehensive document relating to fishing practices on the Bassin and the La Teste coast that I have yet found. Once again, it is not the locals speaking for themselves, but an outsider who hoped to change their work patterns. However, the twenty-two fishermen and sailors who heard Allègre speak at the shipwreck inquiry commission's meeting signed a statement supporting his project, witnessed by Lhotellerie, the naval commissioner. The signatories, including Ostinde Lafon, La Teste seafarers' spokesman (*syndic des gens de mer à la Teste*), and six *patrons* (boat owners), declared that they agreed with Allègre that "a steam-powered vessel, built under special conditions, may be the instrument which has been lacking until now." They also agreed "without reservation" that this new method would offer security to local sailors and their families, "who fear for their lives. We think," they concluded, "that it is impossible to reconcile in a happier manner the advantages of work with the preservation of human life."[20] The timing favored their support for the scheme. Allègre presented his ideas to the Testerins only a month after the March 1836 catastrophe. They were still reeling, and fear had set in.

Allègre claimed that of the fifty-two men who had escaped the shipwreck (on four boats which made it back through the *passes*), only twenty-one agreed to return to sea, and only because the weather had settled. Crews were being formed with inexperienced men, including masons and unskilled laborers who had been working on the Mimizan canal.[21] The naval archives for La Teste are instructive here. Whereas the *Argus,* a ten-tonne *chaloupe* that went down in March 1836, had been crewed entirely by men from Gujan (a Bassin commune to the east of La Teste, within the same naval quarter), the four-tonne *Bonne Marie,* built in Gujan in 1836 and operating after the Grand Malheur, listed alongside five Gujanais and six Testerins a mixed crew of men from other departments including the Landes, Basses-Pyrénées, and Dordogne. These men, though technically novices, were listed as *matelots* (sailors) out of necessity. Three of the Testerin crew members were over sixty years old—a testament to the desperation of those in charge of recruitment.[22]

The loss of seventy-eight experienced fishermen in a community of several thousand people was a major blow to the local industry. Compounding this was the decision of the navy's general commissioner in Bordeaux to prohibit vessels without decks from leaving the Bassin after the 1836 disaster.[23] Only one new *chaloupe* was registered between 1837 and 1842, "a direct consequence of the shipwreck of 1836," according to Noël Gruet.[24] The community was in disarray. Allègre's offer to finance the construction and trial of a steam-powered boat could hardly be refused under these circumstances: if he took the financial risk, only he would have to pay.

Allègre, encouraged by the commission, had a steam-powered fishing boat built, which he named the *Turbot.* It was a much larger craft than the *chaloupes,* 28 meters (92 feet) long compared with their average 10 to 12 meters (33 to 39 feet), with a capacity of 86 tonnes (84.6 tons) instead of their 9 to 10 tonnes (8.9 to 9.8 tons). It could carry five hundred nets compared to fifty. Allègre tested the *Turbot* with different types of nets and seems to have been the first to use a trawl net, the paddles at the sides necessitating the casting of the nets from the rear of the vessel. The experiment with trawl nets of 11 April 1838 was too successful: the net burst open from the sheer weight of the catch. Soon after, he had a second steamer built, the *Sole.* Inspired by Allègre's example, the local entrepreneur François Legallais, who had built the first bathing establishment on the Bassin and was a member of d'Haussez's 1830 committee on *passes* improvement, financed the construction of the 64-tonne steamer, the *Testerain,* which he equipped for fishing in January 1838.[25]

By the end of 1838 both of Allègre's boats were inactive, and Legallais' *Testerain* ceased operating on the Bassin in May 1839. Allègre attempted to explain what had gone wrong in his 1841 treatise, *De la pêche dans le Bassin et sur la côte extérieure d'Arcachon* ("On fishing in the Bassin and on the exterior Arcachon coast"). He acknowledged that the steamers' engines were poorly made, lacking power and solidity, but argued that it was the novelty of their undertaking that was the key to its demise: "it must have given rise to jealousies and rivalry: we came to save the population from shipwreck and we found them united against us." He complained that "everything was against us," and that they had no choice but to liquidate. Nevertheless, he considered that "a precious experience was gained through our sacrifices, and even though it was dearly paid for, there is not one among us who does not applaud his own contribution to it, if it will result in safety for the fisherman, and usefulness for the city of Bordeaux."[26]

What had happened to the good will that Allègre had detected among the seafarers at the commission meeting in April 1836? We might take into account the visual and aural impact of the steamers: a change from the slapping of the *chaloupe*'s oars to the puffing and smoking of an enormous machine; from the sense of working within a shell, rowing in time with other bodies, to the feeling of operating on the outside (the deck) of a vessel.[27] One imagines that the fishermen experienced a loss of control: they no longer felt directly responsible for the movement of the boat across the surface of the water.

Perhaps more important, they also felt threatened by the introduction of a fishing vessel that boasted such huge catches: would this not lead to the enrichment of a few men who were already wealthy? Most fishermen could not afford to buy their own *chaloupe*: they were recruited by boat owners to join a crew, and paid either with a share of the catch or, in some cases, in wages, according to their level of experience. The few men who would be employed on the steamers would probably earn much more than those who continued to work the old way. And if they did not, then the boat owner's takings must be unacceptably high in relation to the fishermen's remuneration (i.e., if high costs did not swallow any profits). It seems that Allègre and Legallais failed to consider the probable social consequences of these innovations for the fishing community. In a manuscript dated 19 December 1836, one Bordelais commentator claimed that "Captain Allègre is seeing the inhabitants of the canton rise up against him, for they presume, with reason, that his intention is to gain a monopoly over fishing to their detriment."[28]

Even when Allègre and others changed their proposal in the early 1840s, so that the steamer's role was merely to ferry the catch back to port from smaller fishing vessels anchored outside the *passes,* local patterns of work were seen as being undermined. In what he called a "frank" assessment of the situation in March 1842, Lhotellerie, the naval commissioner in La Teste, explained to his superior M. de Prigny the discouragement, drunkenness, and passivity of the local fishermen, who were, he claimed, under the thumb of the boat owners. He considered an association between fishermen, mooted by Allègre and others, an impossibility. The small number who had survived the shipwrecks "are good and brave men, but very poor, coarse [and] so addicted to wine that they only embark on the *chaloupes* because there they can drink as much wine as they want and abandon themselves unreservedly to drunkenness." Lhotellerie believed they "could do nothing without being led and organized by the fishing boat owners, whom they call their merchants [*marchands*]" and who "are the declared enemies of anything that threatens their illicit interests." While "notable" sailors on the Bassin (i.e., ship's captains and coastal navigators [*maîtres au cabotage*]) had declared their support for Allègre's scheme, Lhotellerie claimed that "jealous" boat owners would lead the simple fishermen, "whom they keep in a dependent state until they have drowned them," to subvert the new system that, if implemented, would guarantee the fishermen's "emancipation."[29]

Even if Lhotellerie's characterization of the relationship between the fishermen and the boat owners was exaggerated—for we must not forget that he represented the navy, which took its own heavy toll on the maritime population—it appears that reformist types like Allègre would have trouble breaking through the established patterns of work and hierarchy. Allègre was—despite his stated good intentions, his "long-standing concern for our fishermen," and his "sacrifices" in their favor—an outsider, like Sauvage who had coveted the prés salés.[30] And it so happens that Allègre had bought his Arès property in 1834 from Sauvage, a connection that would not have smoothed his path in La Teste.[31]

Consider, too, the issue of safety. While a steamer might be useful for carrying fish back to La Teste from new vessels (cutters, this time) anchored outside the heads and for helping fishermen in distress, the men would still have to work on boats whose safety was not guaranteed. After 1836, decked vessels, supposed to be safer than the old *chaloupes,* sank in the *passes,* taking more men with them. The prefect noted in early 1843 that "the sailors are convinced that decked *chaloupes* hold as much danger as the [undecked] vessels known as *tilloles* [similar to *pinasses*] in this area."[32] Innovation and promises had not convinced a demoralized community, a community identified in Bordeaux by their black clothing signifying their "perpetual mourning" since the Grand Malheur.[33]

Over the same period, the efforts of a group based in Gujan made up of "inhabitants of the Arcachon coast, born among these brave men [who are] so valuable to our navy" to found a *Compagnie générale de pêche et de salaison* (General Fishing and Salting Company), appeared to gain the support of a significant number of local fishermen and boat builders. The company prospectus promised the introduction of a fleet of "unsinkable" *chaloupes* designed by the Laporte brothers in Bordeaux, as well as the construction and operation of salting, packaging, and related workshops. Their produce would be transported cheaply on the recently completed railway line. P. M. Tardis, the driving force behind the company, criticized the steamer proposal as economically unviable, being too expensive to run and having insufficient outlets for the sale and export of the catch. Tardis claimed that his own project had "lifted the low morale of the sailors of this country; and if it is welcomed, these brave and honest sailors—they have assured us, and we must believe them—will no longer hesitate to confront the sandbar in doubtful weather."[34]

While Oscar Dejean's 1858 history of Arcachon noted the General Fishing and Salting Company's "vast" headquarters in Mestras (part of Gujan, on the Bassin), he also recorded its demise after a few years.[35] He gave no reasons for its failure, but given that fifteen fishing vessels went down in the *passes* between 1841 and 1849, taking 174 men with them, it is quite possible that this included one or more of the company's "unsinkable" *chaloupes.*[36]

Despite these high rates of death and material loss, the fishing community continued to confront the *passes.* This was the life and work they knew best, whatever the risks. A degree of security was achieved through the repetition of an established set of actions, mutual trust, and the ability to predict each other's reactions in certain situations. Also, rituals had developed out of these practices, enabling fishermen to confront a difficult environment on a daily basis. So while reformers seeking to improve safety and productivity may have had the best of intentions, they threatened to upset this fragile equilibrium. After all, it was the fishermen who would have to test out the new vessels and techniques with their lives. Alain Cabantous states that for sailors, "the boat is not considered as a simple machine, a vulgar technical instrument, no matter how sophisticated it is. It [is] the object of practices, of social and cultural usages, and the basis for a symbolic expression which melds intimately the professional and the religious."[37]

Religious rituals surrounding fishing were part of a web of practices enabling the community to cope with their frequent encounters with death. These rituals included the blessing of fishing vessels, the doffing of caps to their special protector, the Virgin Mary, before approaching the *passes,* and an annual pilgrimage to the chapel on her Annunciation day, 25 March.[38] Today, it is still common for sailors to sound their horns as they pass the chapel. In 1829, Arago described "crude *pinasses*" passing, from which rose "songs of thanksgiving" addressed to the Virgin "whose temple dominates the beach and the waves." He also referred to the ex-votos (votive offerings) on the walls of the chapel devoted to her.[39]

The ex-votos, paid for by sailors to give thanks for having survived drowning, can still be seen today in Notre-Dame church in Arcachon and in the chapel dedicated to Notre-Dame des Passes at Le Moulleau. Ex-votos also operated as talismans: the souls of the drowned might guide those in distress.[40] They are a sad reminder of all those lost to the ocean and of the hope of those left behind that the souls of the departed will not wander forever in limbo. Sailors who died at sea rarely received the last sacraments, so there were serious questions for believers about the possibility of their souls being reunited with their bodies at the Resurrection.[41]

Captain Mortemart de Boisse, who visited the Bassin and landes in 1840 on behalf of the Compagnie d'Arcachon, recounted meeting an old fisherwoman on the beach one day. When he pointed out the white caps running up against the waves, she explained their significance (but not before he had offered the widow "a small pecuniary gift"):

Do you know what that is, Sir? . . . They are the souls of drowned men without tombs.—The sea, you know, rejects all that is impure. These souls' bodies also turn up on the beaches; but the poor souls remain and are obliged to tow the white wash, which is nothing but the fringe of their shroud, up to the water's edge, to wait for a prayer or a tomb, . . . eternal work, alas! until the wife or the daughter of the drowned man recognizes the wave which expires at her feet, and makes the sign of the cross over it, and says the prayer for the dead [*la prière des morts*]; then God calls the soul to him, and we see a kind of spout of water rising up to the cloud which receives it and carries it up to heaven.[42]

When we consider that wives of men presumed drowned were technically still married for as long as their husband's body stayed missing, this ritual or belief in the possibility of laying his soul to rest becomes all the more meaningful. Perhaps it allowed a lone woman to move on.

In a letter to the archbishop in 1839, the curate of Gujan raised the thorny issue of the many young widows who wished to remarry after losing their husbands in 1836. He argued that "in the interest of religion and morals," these widows should be permitted to remarry, "for several in the parish of Gujan have already passed a marriage contract, which we call '*making a beginning*' [*faire commencement*], and if they do not obtain this authorization soon, they will live as husband and wife [*en concubinage*], and what a grave calamity for this parish! Scandal is already making frightening progress and the evil can only worsen."[43]

Aside from the emotional need for such unions, remaining single was not desirable given the essential role women played in the local family economy (fishing inside the Bassin, working the vegetable patches, transporting and selling the catch, making and repairing nets). Widows had to find a practical solution, which did not necessarily accord with the Church's teaching.

This pragmatism worried Cardinal Donnet, archbishop of Bordeaux, who found the Testerins to be lax Catholics when he visited the parish in 1838 to bless the first stone of the Mimizan canal. He found that only 240 out of 3,000 Testerins took communion at Easter, the time of year when Christians were most strenuously exhorted to attend church. As a result, missionaries were sent to the area some years later; although church attendance and numbers of confirmations increased, it did not take long for the people to lapse back to their old ways.[44] Perhaps the fishing community practiced only those aspects of the faith that related directly to the perils of their work and were lax about other requirements. The lapses in their practice identified by the Church went unnoticed by travel writers who fed the stereotype of the religious fisherman and his ever-patient wife and children.

In 1849, a bourgeoise from La Teste published a pamphlet describing the annual pilgrimage to the Arcachon chapel, the proceeds of which were to be donated to the widows and orphans of "the unfortunate fishermen sailors of La Teste who have recently perished."[45] The account, offered to the wife of the prefect and "Bordelais ladies," was in the form of a journal describing a tour of the Bassin over several days in summer; it is a wonderful example of the way fishing people were represented at the time, of the way bourgeois readers *wanted* to see them. The anonymous writer noted the crews of fishermen who "raised their caps [to] the Queen of the Heavens, their devoted protector," and, when describing the "magnificent panorama" from the summit of a dune, she dwelt for a moment on the mouth of the Bassin, where waves "rose up like gigantic rocks and fell, with a frightening crash, into the bottomless abyss, where our poor sailors, passing this point known as *the Bar,* have often found their resting place."[46]

She recalled when Bassin communities made a pilgrimage to the chapel to pray to the Virgin to protect them from cholera (probably in the 1830s), describing the arrival of flotillas with members of the clergy standing at the prow, carrying silver crosses and golden banners, their bodies shining in the dawn light. Pilgrims sang litanies to the Virgin and, once disembarked, knelt at her feet. The overall effect was "thrilling: the women were crying, the men were wailing, [all] blessed by God." Later, she described the annual feast of the Annunciation on 25 March, when "heads uncovered, fishermen and helmsmen knelt humbly in their vessels, rocked by the waves, the crowd of pilgrims covering the beach." This was when crews, boats, and nets were blessed and "[e]cstasy subjugated their souls."[47]

This account reflected popular themes in the art and literature of the day. The first half of the nineteenth century, when the fashion for therapeutic bathing was spreading, was also a period of intense popular interest in the figure of the fisherman, his struggle against a merciless ocean and search for spiritual salvation. The two developments were not unrelated. Doctors declared the advantages of bathing at this time based partly on the fisherman's allegedly robust constitution, the theory being that this was due to his proximity to the sea. Along with a medicinal interest in the shore-dwelling populations came an anthropological fascination, milked by writers in illustrated magazines, who often dwelt on the tragic side of their existence. This was reflected in the guide books and travel accounts about the Bassin, all of which contained a description of the doffing of caps and singing of praises to the Virgin and a reference to the terrible toll from shipwrecks in the *passes.*

In Mareschal's 1833 "Journal du Voyage," the fishermen's veneration of the chapel cross was explained with reference to the fear inspired by the ocean: "nothing recalls us more to religious ideas than the view and frequenting of this terrible element, where the force and the prudence of man are so powerless against danger, and where he feels so greatly his dependence on the creator!"[48] This "terrible element" and the pathos of a life given over to its unpredictability every day was the subject of choice for many novelists, poets, diarists, journalists, and painters. In July 1836, Victor Hugo wrote a poem, *Océano Nox* (Night Ocean), which could well have been inspired by the details of the Grand Malheur given that this event was widely reported. His poem spoke of the many drowned sailors whose bodies were lost in the bottomless, "blind ocean." He traced the process of grieving, remembering, and forgetting of these lost souls. He pictured the "white-browed" women the fishermen left behind, sick of waiting for their husbands, as the object of others' stolen kisses, while the sailors' aged parents died waiting for them on the shore. He also played on the notion of the sea as an abyss giving up no trace of the dead, allowing no possibility of a comforting headstone. He anthropomorphized the ocean: it held "dark secrets" that it told with "desperate voices" as it surged up the beach at high tide.[49]

Tragic shipwreck stories fascinated the reading public between 1815 and 1840 and were "promoted immodestly to the rank of spectacle," as Alain Corbin puts it. In 1829 a *Journal des Naufrages* (Shipwreck Magazine) appeared, along with other periodicals of a similar nature, offering detailed accounts of shipwrecks, including names of victims. Corbin notes recorded incidents of shipwrecks being "enjoyed" by bathers watching from the safety of the shore.[50] The horror of the actual experiences of drowning and grieving thus became aestheticized; their real force, their capacity to shatter a community or at the very least a single family, could not be conveyed by the literary or artistic trope.

Even Captain Allègre, who claimed to have the interests of local fishing families at heart, offered in his *De la pêche dans le Bassin* a description of the "terrible agony" suffered by "the flowering youth of the Bassin" during the Grand Malheur of 1836, as they battled "with the conspiring elements." He concluded this passage with the comment: "Never has a catastrophe been more worthy of inspiring the brush and chisel of our artists." And in an accompanying footnote, he expanded on the imagery that might appeal to the artist: "27 to 28 cadavers have been found along the coast up to the present; only one was identified: the others, almost entirely devoured by dogs and by foxes from the landes, presented only scraps [*lambeaux*] and bones!"[51] Allègre's exclamation mark emphasizes his detachment and his shocking *aesthetic* appreciation for this gory scene. It also says something about the intended audience for his pamphlet—evidently not the local fishing families.

His audience probably included bourgeois bathers who were visiting the Bassin in increasing numbers. For during the 1840s, when the fishing community was struggling with the effects of multiple drownings and low morale, bathing was beginning to transform La Teste. A new community was developing around the notion of the sea as a therapeutic site, a place of renewal and vigor. In his 1858 history of the Bassin, Oscar Dejean noted that the General Fishing and Salting Company's headquarters in Mestras had been converted into a hotel for bathers. Agricultural developments had been the focus of reformers' and developers' energies in the first forty years of the nineteenth century, but it was the fashion for bathing that would most profoundly change the nature and organization of the Bassin's shores. The fishing community would see their world turned upside down.

PART TWO

Taming the Shore

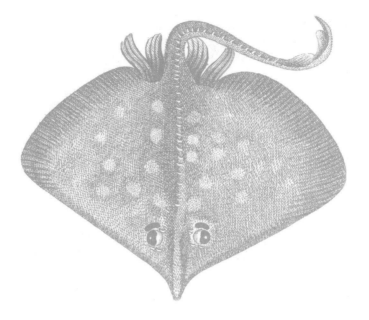

CHAPTER FIVE

An Emotional Tableau

*Arcachon is a sort of French Oceania. It is Tahiti a few kilometers from Bordeaux,
life in the wild only a gunshot away from the center of civilization.*

—Oscar Dejean, *Arcachon et ses environs*, 1858

In 1828, the writer Jacques Arago predicted during a stay on the Bassin that it
would not be long before "the comfortable citizens of Bordeaux" said to one
another: "*Let's go to the La Teste sea baths* as one would say in Paris: *Let's go to
Saint-Cloud or the waters of Enghien.*" He also suggested that, were a Landais
to open a café-restaurant along the Bordeaux–La Teste road, he would do
good business given the "large number of travelers going to La Teste" to recover their health, especially during the "bathing season."[1] An anonymous
bourgeois who spent a month at the Bassin's first bathing establishment in
1825 predicted that should the transport problem, which "distances many
people who would like to come and bathe in this magnificent Arcachon bay,"
be rectified, François Legallais' establishment would "topple the fashion for
the Royan baths, which only have one thing in their favor—the ease of the
voyage by steamboat."[2]

Arago, writing thirteen years before the railway line reached the Bassin, described the Bordeaux–La Teste road as a "prone ladder, beaten by the regular

passage of oxen."[3] Despite this deterrent, a significant number of *curistes* (cure-takers or bathers) visited La Teste and began to develop relationships with the locals and with the land and sea around them, which would furnish a model for later visitors. This was in the decade before the formation of the Compagnies d'Arcachon and des Landes, whose directors would, at least initially, show surprisingly little interest in the growing fashion for bathing, preferring their vision of an agricultural paradise. The Compagnies' projects developed (and failed) alongside the expansion of bathing practices in the 1830s, until the Compagnie directors had to acknowledge the economic potential in this new use of the shore.

In the two decades before the railway opened in 1841, a handful of guesthouses with bathing facilities appeared on the foreshore of an undeveloped beach known as Eyrac, to the west of La Teste proper: Legallais' bathing establishment in 1823; Duprat's rooms in 1829, which became Lesca's hotel in 1839; and Tindel's Nouveaux Bains d'Arcachon and Bourdain's baths, which both opened in 1836.[4] Visitors could also stay in La Teste at the more central but less beautiful Hôtel Arcachon (named for the Bassin, not for the town, which did not yet exist) or rent a fishing or *résinier's* (resin collector's) hut if they wished to stay closer to the sea. Figures from the 1850s indicate that the majority of visitors chose to rent rooms in private residences.[5]

Alain Corbin notes that the 1820s were a turning point in French attitudes toward the sea. Sea bathing, which the French aristocracy took up in the years before the Revolution of 1789 in the wake of their English counterparts, was abandoned during the revolutionary and Napoleonic wars.[6] After the peace treaties of 1815, sea bathing on the continent was resumed by the English, followed by the northern Europeans. The construction in Dieppe in 1822 of a purpose-built bathing pavilion overlooking the sea (rather than the conversion of a preexisting building or residence) indicated that at least one element of French society—the "highest aristocracy" according to Corbin—had embraced the practice of bathing. Dieppe and Boulogne were to provide models for the rest of France and indeed Europe, with their galleries and pontoons and "ambitious and orderly organization."[7]

Corbin claims that aside from these "two rival centers," France had little to offer bathers: Granville boasted a bathing "cabin" in 1827, and Royan and Biarritz were just beginning to attract visitors.[8] He makes no mention of La Teste–Eyrac. The early appearance of bathing establishments on the Bassin suggests that northern practices may have caught on more quickly than Corbin suggests. Or indeed, that local habits were being reinterpreted according to the new fashion. In 1845, Oscar Dejean, in his guide to La Teste, noted that "at each high tide the inhabitants of the region [*pays*] dive en masse into the Bassin's waters."[9] This seems to imply that Testerins of every class enjoyed bathing. We do not know whether this popular bathing pre-dated the development of the Eyrac bathing establishments, or whether visitors' practices from the 1820s onward encouraged the locals to experiment with a new approach to the water. The fishing people were not known for their skill as swimmers, and one imagines that if they spent much of their working day wading, clothed, in the Bassin, bathing would have little appeal. Other inhabitants of La Teste—laborers, for example—may have been more inclined to bathe for pleasure.

Ernest Laroche, who wrote in 1890 about his experience of the Bassin early in the century, considered that it was not until Louis-Philippe took the throne and the bourgeoisie "claimed an important role in the management of the nation's affairs" that the habit of sea bathing was taken up by other than the wealthiest sector of French society. He ignored the unregulated bathing habits of coast-dwellers: he was interested in the supervised practices of the elite. He tells us that in Bordeaux before 1830, "holidaying [*villégiature*] was little known. . . . The watering towns existed only for the great families, and even they went only on rare occasions and during the hottest part of the summer."[10]

This was a period when bathing etiquette was still being worked out, when travel accounts and diaries provided more than description: they also acted as manuals, as guides to behavior for a bourgeois reading public.[11] They articulated and promoted a way of seeing, hearing, and feeling the land- and seascape, as well as a way of perceiving the local population. In chapter 1 I touched on the outlines of an itinerary taking shape in the accounts by agricultural Compagnie representatives such as Hennequin and Mortemart de Boisse, who visited the Bassin in the 1830s. The *curiste* followed a similar path: a series of requisite outings and views, which no self-respecting visitor to the Bassin could overlook.

Although these visitors arrived with different aims from the investors—rest, convalescence, and leisurely observation rather than investigation of agricultural and commercial potential—they had much in common with the agricultural reformers. They all expressed surprise on discovering pockets of civilization in a supposed "wilderness." Like the investors, they too were *estrangeys* (outsiders or strangers), which would shape the type of relationships formed with local inhabitants. These relationships would be consolidated and formalized with the coming of the railway.

Three accounts by visitors to the Bassin before 1841 portray the place and its people in a way that was to be repeated and expanded on over the ensuing century. The writers were (1) an anonymous bourgeois from Bordeaux who kept a diary of his family's month-long stay in the summer of 1825; (2) Arago, who stayed at the same guesthouse three years later and wrote a series of letters to "Adèle," which, unlike the Bordelais' journal, was intended for publication; and (3) "J. P. P.," a local politician from Bazas in the Gironde, who wrote a brief account of his stay at Tindel's guesthouse in 1837. We see in these accounts the evolution of an image of the fishing people whose outlines we began to trace in part I and a shift for the locals from a straightforward working life to an observed, and thus at times consciously *performed,* working life.

The reason for the anonymous Bordelais' visit was the poor health of his daughter and his wife. A cure of sea baths had been prescribed in accordance with prevailing medical fashion. The Bordelais was well-read—he conscientiously demonstrated his knowledge of famous poets and philosophers at every opportunity—and it is quite possible that he had come across the recently published translation of the English doctor Alexander Buchan's guide to sea bathing.[12] The reported benefits of sea bathing must have impressed him strongly, for, as we know from previous chapters, the trip from Bordeaux to La Teste and then to Eyrac was not an easy one. His wife and child and other family members had preceded him and were already installed at Eyrac when he left Bordeaux. He and his brother-in-law had to traverse the "hideous" landes on a rickety cart in the company of an opinionated Bonapartist driver who not only "entered into our conversations with great familiarity" but overturned the cart more than once. The sensitive, royalist, self-styled poet found this most upsetting. They drove for five hours to reach the Croix d'Hins, where they bedded down fully clothed in "an awful little inn." They rose at 3 A.M. and continued on their way, arriving in La Teste seven and a half hours later, having survived a long delay due to a broken axle. They then endured one more hour with their "unfortunate" driver before reaching the top of the Pontac dune, whence they had a view of the "beautiful" Bassin and the "desired establishment."[13]

Their host, François Legallais, was a retired ship's captain who had settled in La Teste in 1810 and married a local woman—a Taffard—the following year. He built his guesthouse in 1823 on land belonging to his wife, at Eyrac. It overlooked a real, sandy beach, as opposed to the flat, muddy expanse of the prés salés closer to La Teste.[14] Legallais' establishment catered to the well off. In 1830, a twin bedroom cost 3 francs a night, breakfast and lunch at the *table d'hôte* (communal, fixed-price dining) was 3.50 francs per person (2 francs for children and domestics), and the trip from Bordeaux by *char-à-*

banc (carriage) cost 8 francs one way (5 francs for children).[15] For a family of four, then, a week's stay could cost from 177 francs (not including extras like boat trips) when the average daily wage for a laborer was 2 francs.[16]

On arriving at Legallais', the Bordelais and his companion's first action was to "run to take a first bath" in the sea, before enjoying a reunion with their wives after twelve days' separation. This spontaneous bathing experience—apparently in the absence of an approved guide or "master-bather"—suggests that the medicalization and codification of sea bathing had not yet established its hegemony, as it had in England and was to do in France over the ensuing decades.

After their swim the men rejoined the family at Legallais' guesthouse, which establishment pleased the diarist enormously. "One is most surprised," he wrote, "to find such luxury and elegance in the midst of these near-deserted dunes and on the shores of a bay inhabited almost only by poor sailors."[17] As in the Compagnie reports of the ensuing decade, we see his wonder at any signs of civilization in such an isolated spot, as well as an indication of his perception of the seafaring population. Legallais offered his guests a cocoon of civilization, of comfort and polite conversation, which only made the contrast with the surroundings more striking. A generous and delicious dinner of fish greeted the travel-weary men, who then played a game of billiards upstairs with the ladies. The Bordelais' first night's sleep was troubled "only" by his daughter Elodie's coughing.

Although Elodie had been brought to the Bassin to convalesce, the family made the most of their stay, visiting all the sites their affable host deemed worthy of their attention. The Bordelais recounted a visit by boat and foot to the sailors' chapel, beachcombing and oyster-gathering outings along the shores of the Bassin, a boat trip to Cap Ferret on the other side of the heads, an invitation into a fishermen's hut, a sardine fishing expedition and observation from the beach in front of the guesthouse of fishing *à la senne* (organized by Legallais), and a meeting with resin collectors in the forested dunes behind Legallais' establishment.[18] These activities were punctuated by regular sea baths (twice a day) and the sedentary pleasures of board games and novels.

The bourgeois' leisure activities at Eyrac followed the antique *otium* (cultivated leisure, in Latin) model described by Corbin, according to which time away from the pursuit of power was to be well spent. This was not so much a holiday as an opportunity to refresh the mind; variety was all-important. Corbin writes that *otium,* which was emulated by the "academic social elite" in France from the end of the Ancien Régime (1780s), involved "reading, the pleasures of collecting and correspondence, time set aside for contemplation,

philosophical conversation, and walking . . . Relaxation in the open air[,]
sometimes accompanied by child-like games . . . fishing or collecting stones
and shells."[19] The Bordelais did all of these.

Arago and J. P. P. experienced the Bassin through a similar cultural filter.
They too spent their time fruitfully, in the pursuit of a "cultivated leisure."[20]
It is not clear whether Arago came to the Bassin to bathe or to observe and
write, for he chose to emphasize his role as an experienced traveler with a rig-
orous, objective approach to observation and description, and he was writing
for publication. He went into more detail than the others concerning issues
such as navigational safety, the sterility of the soil, and the lifestyle (as he
imagined it) of the Landais. But like the Bordelais and J. P. P., Arago's Bassin
itinerary included visits to the chapel and the monument to Brémontier (the
Ponts et Chaussées engineer credited with the afforestation of the landes), the
dunes, and the Ile aux Oiseaux as well as observation of resin collection and
fishing for hake and sole.

While Bazas councillor J. P. P.'s trip to the Bassin was short, he managed to
squeeze in visits to the chapel, Cap Ferret, the Ile aux Oiseaux, a conversation
with fishermen, and shell gathering. All three paid homage to their hosts. J. P. P.
likened the painter Tindel's guesthouse to "a palace improvised by the inspired
breath of a powerful genie or by [legendary sorceress] Armide's magic wand,"
while the Bordelais and Arago could not praise Legallais highly enough.[21] It
seems that Tindel and Legallais both provided the perfect setting, a safe vantage
point from which their guests might explore and observe what the Bassin had to
offer.

All three writers had learned to operate according to a code of perception
that incorporated the picturesque and a Romantic sensibility. They sought out
certain views because of the emotions they were expected to inspire, and they
faithfully recorded the appropriate reactions. The Bordelais was clumsy in his
reference to these modes, whereas Arago, a published writer, had a more sophisticated grasp of these systems of contemplation and description. J. P. P.'s
descriptions of the ocean and dunes showed that he too was strongly influenced by the Romantics.

According to Corbin, the picturesque mode developed in England and
came to the continent in the late eighteenth century. By 1817 Jane Austen, in
Sanditon, was already making fun of the fashion for the utterance of stock
phrases of nature appreciation. Meanwhile, the Romantics were giving it a
new slant: the observation of nature as a form of contemplation of one's own
soul.[22] The Bordelais, Arago, and J. P. P. subscribed to both of these modes of
appreciation. The Bassin lent itself to descriptions in the picturesque mode—

it could be framed—while the ocean elicited more extreme, fearful responses from the three writers.

The Bassin offered a vision of peace and beauty. It was a haven. Compared to the mighty ocean, from which it was separated by no more than a shifting sandbank and a line of dunes, the Bassin presented, as J. P. P. put it, "the most brilliant and picturesque tableau."[23] His "enchanted gaze" rested on this "vast expanse of water," calm water that invited exploration, which was *accessible*. The anonymous Bordelais, twelve years earlier, had a similar attitude to the Bassin. This is where he and his family bathed, where one could safely experiment with "different attitudes." His brother-in-law Hippolyte showed him how to swim and "either [because] the solid floor of the Bassin inspired me with a greater security, or seawater supports the swimmer better, or finally due to these lessons which helped me a great deal, I managed almost immediately to swim on my back, and even to advance fairly rapidly." Meanwhile the Bordelais' wife and sister-in-law bathed nearby, "enveloped in large, specially-designed cotton or woolen robes," in water the color of "fine emerald."[24] They had chosen the calm Bassin water for its curative properties, and after only three days, the Bordelais recorded that the sea baths and the good air had given his daughter "color"; on the fifth day her whooping cough had almost completely gone.[25]

After the safety of the Bassin, the ocean seemed awe-inspiring, humbling. A trip to Cap Ferret to confront the ocean was an essential part of the itinerary. There, one would be reminded of the fragility of humanity and the grandeur and indifference of nature. The Bordelais declared that never had he felt "smaller, more ignorant, more insignificant" than when faced with the ocean. "I was forever exclaiming, like [Jacques-Benigne] Bossuet: Oh! I am nothing. . . . I, poor poet, know only how to receive impressions and become convinced of nature's majesty. A memory which I cannot fail to attribute to Lord Byron, whose poems have a color or dare I say an *odor* of the sea, which charms me."[26] The Bordelais expressed his rapture through other people's words—Tibullus and Virgil, Lord Byron and Madame de Staël. He thought himself a poet, so how could he fail to take up the literary conceit of the anthropomorphized ocean, the raging element that must be kept at bay?

Walking with Legallais at Cap Ferret, ahead of their companions, the Bordelais was the first of the group to see the ocean, a fact he thought worth noting. The beach formed a "barrier" against which silver waves broke "with a kind of fury, even though the weather was quite calm," while washed-up seaweed tried to "resist the fury of this terrible element."[27] He wrote of "bitter deeps" ("flots amers"), the "wrath of the elements," "the vast and treacherous

ocean" ("le vaste océan des maux")—the same language we would encounter
in Victor Hugo's writings about the sea.[28] In this way the ocean was differentiated from the calm blue waters of the Bassin.

While Arago claimed in his introduction that he intended to write an objective account of his travels, and despite his determination not to offer "a les-
son in eloquence," he too followed the prevailing literary models in his descriptions of the ocean in comparison with the Bassin. "I will only say what I
saw," he declared. "The traveler must be clear and precise in his narrations;
his imagination would harm the truth of his account; he must not listen to it.
It is the eyes which study, it is the reason which classifies."[29] Yet at Eyrac, he
told us, "limpid water, struck by the regular dip of the fisherman's large oar,
stirs a languid rhythm at your feet." Like the Bordelais and J. P. P., he felt protected from the "fatal invasions" of the ocean by the "barriers of white sand
placed there by nature to stop the fury of the deep."[30]

In 1837, J. P. P. drew from similar sources when he described the ocean as
seen from Cap Ferret:

> *Hail, bottomless abyss, magnificent Ocean*
> *Noble and sublime image of the greatness of God!*[31]

He too figured the sandy beach as a barrier against "the furious waves that
expired at my feet," but he felt safe because he knew God had said to the
ocean: "*Here are your limits; you will go no further.*" He marveled at the "im-
petuosity of the waves and the fury of the north wind [*aquilons*]," held back
only by the "moving amphitheater" of the dunes, "a place of solitude and
fear, impassable ramparts." Like the Bordelais, he wrote of "wrathful waves"
and was awestruck by "this immense gulf, which spewed forth, with a terrible
roar, its imposing masses of foam upon the shore. What a horrifying and yet
ravishing spectacle!"[32]

Although the view was predominant, all three writers made reference to
the *sound* of the ocean, for all one's senses were activated during a stay by the
sea. Corbin notes how such expressions of sensual experience echoed Byron's
Childe Harold and French author Chateaubriand's *René*.[33] The Bordelais described the Bassin's effects on his senses and sensibility on numerous occasions. Two days after he arrived, on a boat trip to the Arcachon chapel, he
noted the aroma of saltwater and pine, the reflections of sky on the surface of
the bay, and leaping porpoises—all "new sensations" that "refresh and rejuve-
nate my imagination." Bathing offered the pleasurable feeling of "a sand so
soft, so pure and so fine that one could almost be sitting on velvet" while the

"muted roar" of the sea and the pine forest—which reminded him of the verses of Tibullus and Virgil—lulled him through the night.[34]

J. P. P. also referred to the aural experience, in a poem dedicated to Tindel, the painter and guesthouse owner:

> *The whole universe is stirred by your Giant's voice*
> *Which growls in the distance during the storm.*

And in another poem he described the "raucous and wild cry" of the sea birds, who leave the "wave's breast" when the storm "rumbles." At Cap Ferret he and his companions were prompted to cross the mountainous dunes by the "wrathful waves which strike our ears"—a sign that they were excited by their fear.[35]

References to sense experiences other than sight rounded out the picture; they gave it richness and dimension. Arago counseled the reader to walk in the pine forest behind Legallais' establishment "if the sound of the Ocean's rolling waves appalls your ear"—yet another indication of the widespread fear of the open sea. In the forest, "you will hear nothing but the monotonous sound of the bell attached to the neck of the half-wild cow, and the sharp whistling of the branches moved by the breeze." He also described the physical difficulty of walking through sand, "which gives way to the slightest pressure, and opposes a rapid walking pace . . . One would think oneself on a trek [*course*] in the great Sahara desert, if only one heard from time to time the yelping of the hyena or the growl of the tiger."[36]

People also made sounds. Arago described the "raucous, monotonous, and wild cries" of the Landais, whom he considered a race of savages. Stopping in Croix d'Hins en route to La Teste, where the only food on offer was "a sacrificed chicken," he preferred to move on rather than stay in an "open room through which, during the night, noisy passengers from surrounding villages passed one after the other, without respite." Fortunately once on the shores of the Bassin, more harmonious voices might be heard, such as those of the fishermen and -women singing in praise of the Virgin as their "crude *pinasses*" passed the chapel dedicated to her.[37]

While tigers and hyenas were thin on the ground, visitors to the Bassin could assuage their thirst for otherness, for exotica, in their observations of and meetings with local people. The landes were likened to a desert punctuated by forests and populated by primitive shepherds and resin collectors, the Bassin—an oasis, of course—supported a robust seafaring population, while the ocean was the locus of adventure fantasies, turning at times to tragedy and pathos.

The Bassin was fascinating to early visitors because it was so close to a major city and yet offered all the otherness of the dominions. Arago, who had traveled to far-flung places, liked to draw out the similarities. France in 1828 was by no means culturally unified, as his first letter suggests:

> I am only ten leagues from you, my friend, and yet deserts separate us. Deserts like those in Africa, with their loneliness, their sterility, their moving sands. I am a thousand leagues from civilized France. Here live savage beings, moronic men, [and] without wishing to appear perverse, nomadic tribes . . . the inhabitants of the landes have no pleasures on earth other than the heat of the sun or the refreshing morning breeze. Beyond these peaceful joys, all is fatigue and boredom [*ennui*] for them.[38]

Arago drew a parallel between the isolated Testerins and Landais, and the inhabitants of the west coast of Australia, which he had visited some years earlier; he claimed that "the unequivocal demonstration of the tenderest care on the part of the crew of the *Uranie,* could not urge the sad indigenes of those awful lands to accept our developments [*bienfaits*]. Every innovation would undermine the liberty of these poor people, and they would prefer a painful and certain [*positif*] existence, to the incertitude of a better, but doubtful future."[39]

Arago subscribed fully to the discourse of otherness. Although on the Bassin, the other, the "horde of ghosts" inhabiting the landes who were "so close to nature" that one might almost confuse them with the animals they tended, were French subjects on French soil.[40]

Even though Legallais' guesthouse offered "order, good taste, and cleanliness transported into a wild land [*pays*]," it was no guarantee against the apparent seductions of the primitive life. The design of the building contributed to the visitor's *dépaysement,* or sense of being in another world, with its "pilastered peristyle, in the fashion of those which decorate nearly all the homes of rich colonists in India." At the end of his second letter, Arago warned Adèle that "I am becoming wild like them [the locals], and I take leave of you without airs and graces."[41]

On his boat trip to the Arcachon chapel, the Bordelais likened the local *pinasses* to the dugout canoes of Tahiti ("Otaïty"), with their "narrow flanks and curved prow." J. P. P., visiting Cap Ferret, took refuge from a storm in a fisherman's hut, which reminded him of "the tents of the nomad tribes issuing forth from the flanks of Mount Atlas."[42] The analogies they used sprang from a number of sources, but the essential ingredient was a reference to an "uncivilized" world.

One could not leave such an "exotic" place empty-handed. Beachcombing was a popular activity, for it allowed the visitors to let go a little, sink their feet into the sand, and forget their civilized selves. The Bordelais and his family rolled up their pants and skirts and walked for hours along the beach, filling their pockets and baskets with "curious objects." The Bordelais expressed delight at seeing for the first time "a crowd of little objects" in their natural environment, instead of inside display cabinets. As proof that one had returned safely from another world, it was important to take souvenirs home. Not only would they remind the traveler of times past, of adventures, but they would trigger storytelling, myth making. The returned traveler would become the expert in the salon.

Hugo expressed this desire to claim and classify the things residing in the deep (both the sea and the soul) in his 1830 poem *La Pente de la Rêverie* (The Slippery Slope of Dreams):

> I wanted to sound it, I wanted to touch
> The sand, to look at it, to scour it, to search it
> For some strange richness to bring you,
> And to say whether its bed is of rock or mire.[43]

We see this same obsession on the part of the Bordelais, who was determined to take some sea horses given him by a sardine fisherman back to Bordeaux. He kept them in seawater for six days, but on the last day they died, "too restricted no doubt in their caper jar." He pointed out defensively that "it is no little affair to pack and transport all the curiosities and shells that we have gathered."[44]

But one could take home more than shells and seaweed: anecdotes traveled especially well. A meeting with a fisherman or -woman was an essential part of the visitors' itinerary. It was not enough to observe them from a distance: one had to engage, ask questions, take a deep breath, and enter their living quarters. We can only imagine what it was like for the locals to have these city-dwellers poking around their houses. All the written sources come from the outsiders. By this stage the locals must have known there was money to be made from these curious folk. All they needed to do was act the part, tell a story, go about their business of cooking or net repairing. Perhaps they in turn were curious about the strangers? The social hierarchy did not allow them the same spontaneous incursions into the visitors' lives; the only way into the bourgeois house would be through employment as a domestic servant—not at all the same experience.

For the visitors, meetings with fishermen and -women provided entertainment and a glimpse into another world apparently full of adventure and drama. The Bordelais described several encounters with locals. Given that Gascon was the language spoken by the people of the Bassin, and that only an educated elite spoke French, we must presume that visitors like the Bordelais had someone with them to translate. On one occasion, while oyster gathering with Legallais (who may have been the translator on this day) and another guest, the men "got a fisherman's wife who was rowing with her husband to talk to them and they laughed a lot at the lass's saucy remarks."[45] Her vulgar sense of humor, enjoyed by the visitors, hardly fits the picture the Bordelais painted on another day of a population whose morals are "in general innocent and quiet"—an image in tune with the persistent fantasy of the noble savage. This last observation was made after a visit to Cap Ferret, where he and his companions entered a fishing hut, which was in fact an overturned boat—a shelter commonly used on the north shore of the Bassin for temporary accommodation during the fishing season—and questioned the fishermen while they prepared great pots of fish soup and hauled up their laden nets. He could not help comparing the scene inside the hut to the illustrations in Walter Scott's *The Antiquary*.[46] Once again the Bordelais filtered his experience through an established literary or artistic framework.

The Bordelais thought the fishermen's "simplicity" would protect them from the deep sense of melancholy and isolation that he himself claimed to experience when confronted by nature.[47] In between accounts of lovely days out with his family exploring the Bassin, the Bordelais liked to drop into Romantic mode. His Arcachon diary ended with an "elegy" in which, overcome by bitterness as he trod the shores of the Bassin, he imagined befriending the "industrious fishermen, happy people, who never/ Have known the evils my complaint reveals":

> *Beaten by the north winds which torment these seas,*
> *Exposed in turn to sun and storms,*
> *I will spread out your nets, your sails on the beaches*
> *Whereon the muttering, bitter depths come to die.*
> *At night, under your bracken rooves,*
> *Beside a weak flame*

Fed by resinous wood,
Perhaps letting my head fall on my arm,
I might find, lulled by the sound of the storm,
That rapid sleep, the only happiness of the poor:
Perhaps like you, limiting my hopes
To the web which surprises credulous fish,
In your stories, in your songs,
I will forget my long suffering.
The torment which your innocence defies
For me will end;
And by the wrath of the elements
A sail pursued from afar,
A drowned man without clothing,
A vessel ravished by the reef,
Will be the only events
To fill my entire life.

This poem reminds us of Chateaubriand's character René, who chose to live with the American Indians in a vain attempt to escape his melancholy, believing that their "innocence" protected them from emotional suffering. Perhaps the Bordelais had read Chateaubriand's preface to *René:* "The more a people advances in civilization, the more overwhelming the wave of passion."[48] In other words, for those "primitives" focused on basic survival, angst is absent. The Bordelais embraced this view; he considered the melancholy of the vacationing businessman a harder cross to bear than the loss of loved ones by drowning.

J. P. P., who also visited a fishing hut on Cap Ferret, used the meeting in a similar way: to exercise his emotions. When a storm broke, he and his companions entered one of the cabins, which he thought resembled nomads' tents. This experience "added to the brilliance and the majesty of the tableau," for the visitors had the opportunity to talk to the locals about the terrible shipwreck that had claimed seventy-eight lives a year earlier: the Grand Malheur. This is how J. P. P. described the encounter:

We interrogated these noble debris of a disaster which covered these solitary shores in mourning crepe and brought grief to the surrounding hamlets. They pointed to the immense gulf which not long ago devoured seventy-eight of their unfortunate companions, after they had fought vainly over several days against inevitable death. What an agonizing memory! And these same men did not fear to continue surrendering themselves to an element so fecund in shipwrecks? What bravery! What a denial of their existence! . . . We would have liked to stay among them to study their customs and to hear stories of their perilous adventures. It would have completed the emotional tableau of our journey.[49]

The *emotional tableau.* For a moment he had us believing that he truly empathized with the survivors of the Grand Malheur, but that last sentence revealed the extent of his detachment. We know that the survivors of the 1836 shipwreck *did* fear going back out to sea, that their community was seriously demoralized, for a long time. But for J. P. P. to acknowledge this, even merely to find it out, would have meant digging beneath a stereotype in which he and others wanted to believe. Instead, he wrote a poem in which he imagined himself visiting Notre-Dame d'Arcachon, in a pilgrim's cowl (*en capuchon*), to present his homage "after a great shipwreck." It is as though the people of the Bassin had experienced the horror of their men's death in order only to furnish the decor of a visitor's make-believe world.

J. P. P. ended his account with a promise to Tindel, his host, that he would always remember "a trip which unveiled before our eyes scenes full of emotion, pleasure, and charm."[50] The experience was a theatrical one: the visitors were spectators, and the natural and human worlds of the Bassin and ocean a series of tableaux in every genre. This phenomenon was to develop further with the coming of the railway.

CHAPTER SIX

Movement and Life

THE BORDEAUX–LA TESTE RAILWAY LINE

*All individuals are expressly forbidden to bathe in the . . . channel and near
the railway line, where respectable people walk at all times.*

—Municipal bylaw, La Teste, 8 August 1841

People trace paths of habit. Grassy verges suffer the creation of useful paths,
the stamping down of turf across one corner by impatient feet.[1] A route we
take regularly becomes embedded in our spatial awareness and practice: we can
drive in automatic mode and realize on arriving home that we have not consciously registered any red or green lights. When an element of this habitual
path is changed, when a wall is erected, a tree cut down, a footpath narrowed,
we are forced to register the change and adapt our bodily response to the space.

On the Bassin d'Arcachon, networks of spatial practice, patterns of movement traced by bodies, were consolidated through repetition over the centuries. The attempts by "improvers" of the early 1800s to transform the natural environment—successful or not—challenged the Bassin inhabitants'
established practices, their ways of negotiating and living in this space. One
project that brought profound changes to the lived space of the communities
on the Bassin was the construction of the Bordeaux–La Teste railway line,
which opened in July 1841. This passenger line—one of France's earliest—

facilitated rapid travel between Bordeaux and La Teste. The new railway allowed the fifty-two-kilometer (thirty-two-mile) trip to be completed in less than two hours, in relative comfort.[2] With it, conceptions of La Teste's place within the department—and the nation—changed dramatically. No longer was it a backwater ignored by city-dwellers. It was now a place where one might actually *choose* to go.

A notary from Bordeaux, Louis Godinet, had sought the government's authorization to construct a railway line between his hometown and La Teste in 1835, in the same year that Isaac Pereire gained the concession for the Paris–Saint Germain line.[3] The prefect of the Gironde, Lacoste, supported Godinet, and accompanying his letter of 26 October 1836 to the general director of the Ponts et Chaussées, was a proposal for a bill of law recognizing the "public utility" of the railway, which would create "an easy, rapid, and economic communication route" between Bordeaux and the "commercial port" of La Teste. It would greatly improve on the speed of passage of produce from the landes and the Bassin via the departmental road, which Lacoste likened to a "trough." Tourism did not appear to be a consideration at this stage. The railway line was planned primarily for the transport of timber, resin products, and fresh fish to Bordeaux—in tune with the aims of the agricultural Compagnies, although competitive with their canal plans. The draft bill concluded by authorizing Godinet and his partner Roché to "establish a railway line . . . and to collect the profit from the fixed rights [*droits*] by means of the tariff attached to the project."[4]

Godinet and Roché spent 15,000 francs on the preliminary inquiry, only to be told in October 1836 that the Ponts et Chaussées administration had decided to open up the railroad concession to competition. The winner of the tendering process was M. Fortuné de Vergez, a Paris-based engineer who outbid his competitors by proposing a reduction of the concession period by sixty years. At this stage, the Paris–Saint Germain was the only other passenger line in all of France, and it was only 21 kilometers (13 miles) long, compared to the 52 kilometers (32 miles) proposed for the Bordeaux–La Teste line. This indicates the risk involved as well as the great promise that the government and investors saw in the landes and the hoped-for commercial port of La Teste.

A limited company (Société Anonyme) was created, and on 1 March 1838 Vergez and the brothers Bayard de la Vingtrie signed a contract to build the railroad.[5] Ten thousand 500-franc shares were released, and their value rose immediately to 650 francs. The prospectus offered a vision of Girondins discovering a whole new region. "The population of Bordeaux, currently deprived of public countryside [*campagnes publiques*] and above all of sea baths, will be

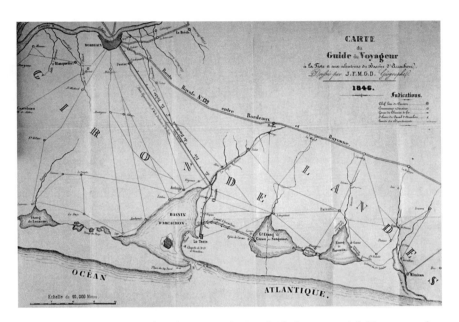

FIG. 6. Bordeaux–La Teste railway line. From O. D., *Guide du voyageur à la Teste et aux alentours du Bassin d'Arcachon* (Bordeaux: P. Chaumas-Gayet, 1845), n.p. Bibliothèque Municipale de Bordeaux.

carried as one to the edge of the Ocean, from which it will be separated by no more than an hour and a half."[6] Three years earlier, the prefect's letter of support for the initial railway proposal did not even mention bathing. The *concessionnaires* were now actively promoting the railway's contribution to this practice—an indication of the extent to which bathing had entrenched itself in public awareness during the 1830s.

Before construction could begin, the company faced a barrage of obstacles, including arguments over the position of the Bordeaux station and wrangles over whose property the line would pass through. Delays and corrections to initial plans blew out the budget. The company had to request reimbursement of the bond, of which the government agreed to return four-fifths. They also obtained an extension of the concession to seventy years. By early 1841 the line was finally ready, but not long before the scheduled opening, the La Hume railway bridge collapsed, delaying the launch once again. We might ask whether this was due to faulty engineering or to the unstable terrain on which the bridge was built—the prés salés.

Once the bridge was rebuilt, the official opening was rescheduled for 6 July 1841. Bordelais newspapers painted grand visions of the region's future. "Opulent and enlightened men" would bring the Bassin communes to life, one journalist claimed:

> In their hands vast forests will rise, improved flocks will multiply, salt meadows will be created, fish reservoirs, rich pastures and harvests. When the rising sun hits the white dunes reflected in the water and the somber green of the pines contrasts with the foreground of the picture; when the retreating tide calls forth the intrepid fishermen of La Teste . . . ; when, in their elongated canoes, the women, as hardy as their husbands, fill their boats with oysters gathered on the bare shores or with fish speared in the transparent water, there is no more ravishing sight than that of the Bassin d'Arcachon, animated by the flotilla making its way out to sea, by these thousand *tillots* [sic] which ply its coves and bays, these clouds of aquatic birds playing on the beaches and islands.[7]

Notice the same imagery used by the anonymous Bordelais in 1825—the vision of an earthly paradise populated by exotic seafarers—alongside the improving discourse of the Compagnies (what this place might become), and all this now within easy reach, available to the residents of Bordeaux in less than two hours.

The La Teste council's provisions on 4 July 1841 for the opening two days hence betrayed a mix of trepidation and excitement. A welcome party was organized, and the national guard and the gendarmes were to maintain order. A ball was scheduled in the afternoon, and five cannon shots were to be fired upon the arrival of the archbishop and the authorities from Bordeaux.[8] While the presence of the gendarmerie and national guard was required for appearance's sake, the councillors may also have feared scenes of overexcitement, even hysteria. This was, after all, the first railway line to open in the Southwest, preceding by eleven years the connection between Bordeaux and Paris. Anything might happen!

A huge crowd assembled in Bordeaux to watch the train's departure. Speeches were made, and Bishop Donnet bestowed his blessing. A journalist compared the engine to an impatient racehorse, pawing at the ground and releasing "clouds of foam, blood and smoke" from its "enflamed nostrils."[9] The ticket-bearing guests climbed aboard as the regimental band played, and the train moved off. It reached La Teste an hour and three quarters later. The prefect, Baron Sers, made a speech in which he envisaged La Teste providing a vital link with the Spanish coast via steamship. A banquet was held after which the company visited the shores of the Bassin "to admire the beauty of the spectacle which unfolded before their eyes."[10] The train then returned to Bordeaux, crowds of onlookers lining the track.

The next day the railway was opened to the general public. Georges Bouchon describes scenes of fear and panic: "they dared not climb aboard the wagons; laughter and cries of terror were provoked by the locomotive's whistle or a puff of steam. Many good souls dared not affront the 'monster.'"[11] It seems that the notables who had boarded the train the day before had managed to hide their panic! The first three days saw large numbers of first-time travelers, but a lull ensued. There were complaints about the price of tickets and about the carriages: a journalist in the legitimist newspaper *La Guienne* compared the third-class wagons to cattle cars.[12] The company made improvements and introduced cheap return fares for Sundays in summer.

The railway line, at least initially, was not the great success its first investors had hoped for. Despite a sharp rise in tourist numbers in the summer months, the takings were not sufficient to keep the company afloat. The problem lay partly in the failure of the government to support the improvement of the La Teste port and in the disappointing outcome of the Compagnies' agricultural development projects in the hinterland, including the canal. In October 1848, the government took over management of the railway line; this impoundment lasted five years, although the trains continued to run during this time. In September 1853, the line was absorbed by the Pereire brothers' newly formed Compagnie des Chemins de fer du Midi et du Canal latéral à la Garonne (Midi Railway and Garonne Lateral Canal Company, or

Compagnie du Midi for short). From then on, its fortunes were to improve dramatically.

The railway line may not have lived up to its creators' expectations in its first decade, but it still transformed the Bassin.[13] As in every other village where a railway station was built, there was a reorientation of the Testerins' daily activities: they had to adapt to new focal points, spatial and temporal. The path between the station and the water's edge became significant. The locals' conception of time was also deeply affected by the incursion of these parallel tracks. Times of arrival and departure, now unaffected by climatic conditions, dictated bursts of activity. The coastal village rhythms so closely tied to tides and winds were overlaid by a new timetable: a timetable printed on paper, known and recognized by all.[14]

Properties were cut in two, and land close to the station had new value. The question of property values became a thorny one. Roads and canals, the railway's complements, were made defunct or more useful than ever according to their position. New patterns of behavior, which revolved around servicing the visitors, developed in response to arrival and departure times.

Testerin councillors considered that the railway had given an essential boost to the town's economy and defended its continuation in the face of the railway company's severe financial problems. When, in 1846, the municipal council heard that the Bordeaux–Bayonne railway line might be constructed from scratch, instead of incorporating the La Teste line as far as Lamothe, they painted a picture of the changes experienced by the commune since 1841. They considered the "hardy and generous creation" of the railway line to have been "much less a speculation than a work of social regeneration." They compared La Teste six years ago—a place suffering from "inertia, from languor, from the stagnation of business, from the dearth of transactions resulting from the lack of communication and population which is now so close to us," to a place characterized by "movement and life, in the form of clearing, planting, building, and industrial and commercial relations which are becoming more and more active and profitable; in a word, a complete transformation." The council feared that should La Teste be bypassed by the new Bayonne line, "the well-being of a population of 15,000 souls would be condemned to total ruin."[15] Here, we see the councillors playing their role as culture-brokers, walking the fine line between encouraging development and protecting the interests of local inhabitants.

While tourism had not been an important consideration during planning, from 1841 on the number of visitors arriving by rail increased dramatically. The year 1841 has been identified as a turning point in the development of modern travel and its social organization: highlights include the appearance of the first national railway timetable (in Britain), the first Atlantic steamship service, the creation of the Wells Fargo (later American Express) company, and the first Thomas Cook tour.[16] On the Bassin, new guesthouses sprang up and expanded. Those situated at Eyrac beach and Mouëng (pronounced "Mougne" and situated between La Teste and Eyrac) were not easily reached by foot or cart from La Teste: boats were the most efficient means of transport around the Bassin. This meant that from the outset, local fishermen and -women were instrumental in the development of a functional tourist industry.

Contemporary accounts describe boatwomen carrying train passengers *on their backs* across the marshy foreshore and through the shallows to their boats and rowing them to their lodgings farther west along the Bassin's edge. These were people known for their wariness of strangers and for their reluctance to embrace "progress" as envisaged by engineers and investors, but they adapted readily to new opportunities. They had always worked as transporters (*caboteurs*) in the summer months, so this work could be seen as an extension of familiar work patterns. They also had some bargaining power, as they provided the only reliable means of transport in the area.

In 1849, an anonymous Testerin woman who wrote a pamphlet on the festival of the Arcachon chapel described her experience with local boatwomen. She and her companions "climbed aboard a light dinghy [*nacelle*] piloted by able boatwomen, who handled the oars of their little boat adroitly and vigorously, rowing with assurance, neither filling nor submerging it, despite the impact of the waves."[17] These assurances to her readers that they would be in safe hands should they make the same journey, suggest that it was seen as unusual for women, even fisherwomen, to be in charge of a vessel. Popular images of the time tended to show the archetypal fisherwoman standing on the shore, waiting for her man. While the Testerine praised the trip across the water, she thought the passage between the boat and the shore—with the boatwomen carrying her and her friend on their backs—less successful. "Not being distrustful enough of their mobility, our feet and slippers were soaked when they put us down."[18] The comfort of the boatwomen, who must have been wet from at least the waist down as they waded through the shore break, was not mentioned.

These women also carried men on their shoulders. "It is upon their robust shoulders that we hoist ourselves," Oscar Dejean explained in his *Guide du voyageur à La Teste,* "when the tide is too low to embark or to land in muddy places."[19] It appears that women did similar work in Boulogne, on France's Channel coast. William Hickey described a party of men arriving at

Fig. 7. "On the boatwomen's shoulders." Drawing by Gustave Labat. From G. Bouchon, *Historique du chemin de fer de Bordeaux à La Teste et à Arcachon* (Bordeaux: G. Gounouilhou/L'Esprit du Temps, 1891 [1991]), 55. Bibliothèque Municipale de Bordeaux.

Boulogne in their cutter at low tide. They climbed into a small sailing boat, which grounded thirty yards from the harbor. They were then approached by "a parcel of Amazonian fish women, with their petticoats rolled close up, their whole thighs being bare." The men were lifted up by "these masculine creatures" and carried to shore. One man, "struck by the appearance of a fine, plump, naked thigh, wanted to ascertain whether the feel would correspond with the looks of the flesh, and put down his hand for that purpose; but the very instant that he did so the two women that had hold of him let go, and plumped him flat upon his back in the water, to the great entertainment of us all, who thought he deserved the ducking for his folly."[20] As the women of La Teste also tucked their skirts up, exposing their thighs, one can imagine similar scenes taking place between these women and the visitors arriving by train. The pious Testerine of course made no reference to anything like this in her pamphlet.

The entertainment value of the women's role as pilots was not lost on La Teste's administrators. Back in August 1839, they had enlisted six boatwomen to take the Duc d'Orléans in a *pinasse* to the Arcachon chapel during his one-day visit to the Bassin.[21] Six years later, however, attitudes had changed. In April 1845, the La Teste council raised fares for the passage from La Teste to Eyrac to cover the costs of a new bylaw requiring boatwomen to be accompanied by a male sailor "for the satisfaction and security of travelers."[22] While the reasons for this new regulation were not given, it indicates the spreading influence of a bourgeois morality that enforced a particular vision of femininity and masculinity unable to accommodate such an inversion of the gender order as a woman carrying a man on her shoulders.

The fishing people found they were called on to provide more than transport-related services. As we have seen, they became objects of curiosity to the newcomers and were expected to perform for them. Visitors liked to watch them fish and often requested—and paid—to be taken out on fishing trips. The theater of the fishing expedition was described in some detail by writer Anthelme Roux, in a humorous novella published in 1853 about a Romantically minded young woman's teasing of her suitor during summer holidays on the Bassin d'Arcachon. The story was padded with descriptions of the resort, with advice on bathing and other activities: it was in essence a guide in the form of a novella. It was published as a companion piece to a similar "resort" novella set in Nice.[23] Fanelly, the willful heroine, who disdained the "vulgar" crab-catching so popular among bourgeois women, preferred the more dramatic *pêche à la fouine* (harpoon fishing). Roux described the pleasure derived from watching a fisherman at work:

He is perched on one side of his vessel, which drifts without wrinkling the surface
of the Bassin; he is upright, immobile, and he spies out his prey with a concentration that nothing can disturb. He has spotted it. At this moment, the spectator
identifies with the fisherman: each holds his breath, for fear of making the slightest
sound. . . . For an object of such little value, the emotion is raised to the highest
power.[24]

We might compare this moment of identification, enjoyed by the visitor as a
source of emotional excitement, to the experience offered by another popular
resort activity of the time: gambling. The suspense before the catch was similar
to the moment before the roulette wheel stopped or the next card was dealt.

The boatmen and -women were also asked to race each other within sight
of the guesthouses on the foreshore. Only a fortnight after the opening of the
railway, the council announced that a "new fête" had been proposed by some
"commendable" visitors to the Bassin. Sailors of the La Teste quarter were
therefore alerted that, to celebrate the festival of Saint Anne, "a nautical tour-
nament or race will take place on the Coast in view of the Bathing Establishments" on Monday, 26 July.

The conditions stipulated that the competitors must row and that only
small *tilloles* (a kind of rowboat or *pinasse*) would be admitted. Each *tillole*
would have two men or two women on board. The race was to take place
after the celebration of mass. The prizes were handsome: fifty francs for the
winning men (equivalent to three to four weeks' wages), thirty francs for
the women (equivalent to one month's wages). The mayor requested the
participation of both local and visiting communities in this "new spectacle . . . which cannot fail to excite their curiosity." The race would lend a
fillip to this annual, well-attended festival.[25] In August 1848, the first official
regatta was held, after which the Bassin became known for its yachting.[26]

While guesthouse operators and administrators strove to provide suitable entertainment for well-heeled visitors, the leisure pursuits of poorer
bathers—mainly locals or Bordelais taking advantage of cheap Sunday
fares—were thought to pose a threat to decorum. The council thus created
bylaws regulating the behavior of both the newcomers and those locals
who took advantage of the visitors' presence. The text of these bylaws reveals a great deal about the way people utilized the spaces around the new
railway station.

Only one month after the opening of the railway line, the mayor of La
Teste, basing his decisions on national laws passed between 1789 and the
Code Pénal, decreed that "considering that daily during high tide, young

people and children bathe in the channel which was recently created in the salt pasture (pré salé) at the end of the street leading from the railway, which is injurious to morals and is a public outrage to modesty, in committing the most inconvenient indecencies," ruled that "all individuals are expressly forbidden to bathe in the said channel and near the railway line, where respectable people walk at all times."[27] It is likely that poorer bathers swam with no clothes on, or in their undergarments.

The channel dug between the railway station and the port was not meant for swimming: it was intended to facilitate the transfer of passengers and goods from the Bassin's boats. Compared to the muddy and shallow prés salés though, the new channel must have seemed an ideal swimming spot, saving poorer bathers from traveling to Eyrac, where the wealthier visitors bathed. The "respectable people" were those who made the trip from La Teste to Eyrac by hired *pinasse* and were thus obliged to look at these outrageous young people bathing around them in inappropriate (or no) garb, as they left the port for their lodgings.

This kind of regulation was a feature common to bathing centers elsewhere in Europe. John Walton discusses a "regulatory crisis" in Victorian England during the 1840s and '50s. In Blackpool, for example, day-trippers bathed naked in front of the "best houses," provoking legislative action.[28] Corbin considers that "the norms of modesty and the fear of social or sexual contact became accentuated between 1811 and 1850," but notes regional differences, comparing the regulatory impulse evident in northern continental resorts with a more laissez-faire approach in Biarritz (to the south of Arcachon). My research suggests that Testerin councillors were more sensitive than their Basque neighbors.[29]

In July 1847 the council passed a bylaw governing the bathers' movements, costume, and comportment. "Good morals," the bylaw declared, "demand that bathers conduct themselves with decency on the shore and in the water." Men bathing in the prés salés or on the Bassin shore within a kilometer (⅝ of a mile) to the east of the Arcachon avenue were obliged to wear "wide trousers" (presumably so as not to show the shape of their anatomy) and to "remain, as far as possible, removed from the places where Ladies bathe." They must undress and dress in bathing cabins, or, "if for any reason it is necessary that they undress in their apartments, they must cover their bodies with a woolen shirt." Women's dress regulations were much more restrictive: they were required to wear "a large gown reaching their heels for the approach to the baths and while bathing." Relations between bathers were even subject to municipal control, with article 7 stipulating that "bathers and people of both sexes are prohibited from speaking to each other or making indecent gestures while bathing and on the beach."[30]

It seems likely that this law was targeting working-class Testerins or poorer bathers from surrounding areas. It is also possible that beneficiaries of the reduced Sunday return fares available by this time—mostly Bordelais who were discovering the pleasures of bathing for the first time—had not embraced the bathing etiquette of their wealthier, better-read fellow visitors. The stipulation that women bathers wear ankle-length robes served to differentiate them from the fisherwomen, who tucked their skirts up above their thighs while working. It is clear that La Teste's notables were sending a strong message to their constituents about the way an elite of *estrangeys* expected them to behave. They could no longer act as if they were living in an isolated backwater: They were under public scrutiny. They were *being watched.*

As early as 1825, the anonymous Bordelais diarist had noted with concern while visiting Duprat's bathing establishment at Mouëng, to the east of Legallais' guesthouse, that fishing vessels, nets, and huts were close to the bathing area, "such that the modesty of female bathers must often suffer from the proximity of these good sailors."[31] So the Bordelais was fully aware that just as he and his companions watched the locals with curiosity, those same people, or objects of observation, were in turn observers—observers who did not necessarily obey the same set of rules as the bourgeois visitors. To bathe was to be exposed—even if covered from head to foot—and one did not want to make a *spectacle* of oneself.

Victor Hugo, visiting Biarritz in 1843, described how young local women swam in serge chemises, "often full of holes, without worrying what they showed." He dreaded the day when Biarritz would become fashionable for more than the elite and the locals who already frequented it in the summer months, for he envisaged prudery replacing "the free and innocent familiarity of these young women who play with the sea." Setting aside Hugo's evident voyeurism, which gave him a particular reason to regret the eventual suppression of these liberties, we can see that his vision of a "modest and rapacious" future for Biarritz applied equally well to La Teste.[32] In order to attract the economic benefits of visitors, one must learn to *act like them,* and on occasion, to act *for* them.

Uncouth bathers were not the only people who needed to be kept in line. The local fisherwomen and -men who greeted the visitors at the station were also considered a threat to good order, essential though their services might be. We have already noted the bylaw enforcing the presence of a man alongside boatwomen transporting visitors in their *pinasses.* An 1847 municipal bylaw concerning bathing practices dealt with another aspect of transport from the railway station to the guesthouses: traffic. Traffic around the station had become chaotic, so the council placed restrictions on parking and standing zones for passenger vehicles, luggage carts, and horses in an attempt to free up circulation on the avenue leading to Eyrac.

The random placement of vehicles was not the only concern. Article 3 stipulated that "boatmen or boatwomen wishing to offer their water transport services to travelers" must remain "outside the roundabout in the avenue opposite the railway hotel" at arrival times. All service providers were warned against "bothering the travelers . . . being expected to remain within the limits of sensible restraint and allowing travelers their liberty of action."[33] These documents paint a vivid picture of a town brought to life at certain moments of the day, and of local authorities struggling to maintain control over a burgeoning tourist-oriented community. Spatial and behavioral boundaries were considered necessary to the smooth operation of the resort.

In a descriptive guide to the La Teste railway line, J.-B. Couve wrote a verse for each station. This is how he pictured the traveler disembarking at La Teste:

> *What a commotion*
> *I hear in the Station!*
> *Each cries out: out of my way!*
> *To find his belongings:*
> *One seeks his mother,*
> *Another her father;*
> *The single man,*
> *Alas! seeks nothing.*
> *One, treating the lighthouse*
> *As a very rare thing,*
> *Wants us to prepare*
> *To take a boat trip.*
> *Another boasts*
> *Of a poor skinny horse*
> *Which tempts me little*
> *To climb the hillside.*[34]

This picture was reinforced by Roux, who, in *Fanelly aux bains d'Arcachon,* warned visitors to the Bassin not to be tempted to leave the train at Gujan (two stops before La Teste) "despite the insistence of boatmen, who hail you with their least raucous voice."[35] No longer was La Teste an isolated backwater. Wolfgang Schivelbusch notes in *Railway Journey* the way in which train travel in its early days was perceived to have annihilated space and time: the speed of displacement seemed to shrink distances.[36] In the case of La Teste, the metropolis—Bordeaux—was suddenly closer. The scenes around the station at arrival times were reminiscent of a crowded city, not of a "miserable *bourgade*" (village or townlet) on the edge of the desert.[37]

This new proximity to the city had its disadvantages: in summer the trains brought not only bathers but also "individuals of doubtful morality," drawn by recent "major works" (like the canal). The presence of these potentially dangerous types led the council to request its own brigade of gendarmes for La Teste in 1847.[38] In previous years the council had considered employing a police commissioner but lacked the funds to do so.[39] In November 1847 the matter was raised again, this time with a greater sense of urgency. The council called on the relevant minister to support its request for a police station, pointing out that the town's population of four thousand regularly jumped to five thousand and more—the minimum required for the creation of a local police station. The minister was urged to act if he agreed that La Teste, "where each year a numerous, brilliant and elite society assembles . . . is as a result exposed to malevolent and greedy attempts, the target of criminal enterprises by that class of men which the Law ceaselessly seeks out and which the railways by their promptitude of locomotion favor in the execution of their misdemeanors." Workers drawn to the landes by the ongoing "improvement" projects were included in this criminal element: these "masses of workers of every condition and from every country, most of them stripped of resources, in continual revolt against law and society" were hardly desirable guests. According to the council, the forests and dunes around La Teste provided convenient refuges for these outlaws—quite a different representation of the landscape from that offered in guidebooks.[40]

The matter of the regulation of behavior would come to preoccupy doctors as well as administrators. Dunes and forests, represented as havens for criminals at times, were also being figured by doctors as sites of recovery, along with the "salutary waters" of the Bassin: reviving, pure, tranquil places for invalids to heal their bodies and minds. This medical discourse, centered on therapeutic bathing practices and the benefits of breathing resinous air (which we will investigate in chapter 7), fed into the growing *aesthetic* appreciation of the sea and shore and drove the rapid appropriation of the foreshore of what would become Arcachon.

The hitherto fairly random, unregulated development of the foreshore on either side of Eyrac was coming under increasing municipal scrutiny and control, especially since the completion of the road from La Teste to Eyrac in 1845. The extension of this road toward the western end of the beach (as far as the chapel) in 1849 and the prefectorial decision to permit enclosure of properties, despite this area being subject to communal usage rights (*droits d'usage*), led to an acceleration in the construction of houses. Between 1822 and 1844, 18 houses were built along this strip of beach; between 1845 and 1848, 47 houses appeared; and, in an impressive jump, another 272 sprang up over the next six years. Most were being built in a long line facing the water.[41] Social distinctions were already apparent in the organization of the settlement. The farther west one traveled (and the farther away from La Teste), the grander the houses. In 1859, Henry Ribadieu described Arcachon, by then a commune in its own right, as a four-kilometer- (two-and-a-half-mile-) long "*ville-rue*" (one-street town) with footpaths, boutiques, and street lamps.[42] It would not be long before this thin strip would expand into the forested dunes.

The La Teste council, which in 1847 requested an extension of the road westward from Eyrac to the Arcachon chapel, declared that the sea baths and the recently built jetty had brought "movement and life to the shores of the Bassin d'Arcachon and as a result a complete change in the state of the area, a change born of progress and one resulting in greatly increased well-being in our region."[43] This well-being, though, did not necessarily extend to the fishing community. While the growing "floating population" of summertime bathers created demands for new services from the locals, the shore that had been their work space was being swallowed up.

On 23 March 1846, the La Teste council expressed concern that the foreshore of the Bassin between l'Aiguillon (to the east) and the Arcachon chapel (to the west) had been "invaded by new houses and walls which have been built in such a manner that along nearly the entire length it is impossible to land on the coast." This was creating problems "so grave that should we neglect them, the most pressing needs and most legitimate interests of the country [*pays*] and of commerce in general will be greatly harmed."[44] Here was the essential paradox of the development of tourism. The locals' work and the spatial practices essential to their livelihood, while increasingly the object of the bathers' fascinated gaze, were being threatened by the bathers' very presence.

CHAPTER SEVEN

The Pacific Conquests of Hygiene

For the medical corps in our region, it is an established custom,
consistent in its results, to recommend the profession of fisherman to any individual
threatened by pulmonary tuberculosis, whether directly or by heredity.

—Dr. Fernand Lalesque, *La cure marine de la tuberculose*, 1900

In 1744, fish-sellers from La Teste appealed to the intendant of Guienne to authorize repairs to the sandy track between La Teste and Bordeaux.[1] They argued that they were not the only ones using the track: Bordelais cure-seekers also needed it to be practicable. It seems that doctors of medicine in Bordeaux were sending their patients to the Bassin d'Arcachon for sea baths as a cure for rabies—some eighty years before François Legallais built what is considered to have been the first bathing establishment in La Teste–Eyrac.[2] While this evidence of early bathing activity is surprising, we should not confuse its sporadic nature with the turning point of the 1820s, when permanent bathing establishments appeared on the Bassin's shores. Legallais opened his guesthouse in 1823, on the advice of local doctor Jean Hameau, who had presumably recognized a demand for accommodation suitable to his patients' class.[3]

In 1835, Dr. Hameau, regarded by some medical historians as a precursor of Louis Pasteur due to his early (and at the time unappreciated) claims concerning viruses, published a book called *Quelques avis sur les bains de mer*

(Some advice on sea bathing).[4] He claimed that, in his twenty-eight years of service in the area, he had seen the annual arrival of "a large number of invalids" who came to bathe in the "crystalline waters of this superb bay" with great success: proof of this lay in the "crutches and other painful things [*objets de douleur*] hanging in the pretty chapel which graces this shore."[5]

In the same year, Hameau's Testerin colleague Dr. Auguste Lalesque, who had been employed by one of the agricultural Compagnies operating in the area, published a medical topography of La Teste that may well have been inspired by Hameau's doctoral thesis of 1807, "Essai sur la topographie physico-médicale de La Teste." Both of these works described the influence of the local environment on the various "classes" (Hameau) or "tribes" (Lalesque) of La Teste. Lalesque claimed in his foreword that "localities imprint on their inhabitants a physiognomy of constitutions as much as a physiognomy of illnesses and an almost invariable type of treatment."[6] True to the tradition established in medical topographies in the previous century, which, Corbin argues, tended to "exaggerate the strength, fertility, and longevity of shore-dwellers," representations of the Bassin fisherman as a paragon of health featured in Lalesque's work, and continued to appear throughout the century in medical texts and guides to Arcachon.[7] These representations informed the development of therapeutic strategies that increasingly emphasized the benefits of sea bathing.

Arago had claimed in 1828 not to be surprised by the "air of health and strength which shows in the burnt faces of the inhabitants of La Teste and the towns surrounding the Bassin d'Arcachon," for he believed that fishing encouraged good health.[8] Lalesque's medical topography took this much further: his observations of the different "tribes" inhabiting the area (which included the sedentary professionals in the town of La Teste, agricultural laborers, and the fishing and resin-collecting populations) and their particular physiological characteristics, temperament, diet, clothing, and fertility rates, led him to declare that the local mariners were exceptionally healthy despite their rough living conditions.[9] In comparison to their non-seagoing Testerin neighbors, they personified "vigor." They suffered "neither the obesity of persons of independent means [*rentiers*], nor the pallor of other sedentary inhabitants, nor the puny appearance of the resin collectors." They were of average height, "their faces ruddy, their beards thick and black, their chests broad, their muscles voluminous and well-defined under a rare cellular tissue: they are gay, lively, agile, and present a sanguine and sanguine-bilious temperament."[10]

Lalesque used the language of temperaments, based on the reworking by

Greek physician Galen (c. 130–200) of Hippocrates' humors, according to which the predominance of four body fluids (including blood and bile) determined a person's physical and mental qualities. Not until the development of cell pathology in the nineteenth century would this system be discredited. The *Oxford Dictionary* defines *sanguine* as "(Hist.) of the temperament in which the blood predominates over the other humours, with ruddy complexion and courageous hopeful amorous disposition" and "bilious" as "(fig.) Choleric, peevish, ill-tempered."[11]

Lalesque ruled out diet, clothing, housing, and work as factors influencing their difference from the other "tribes" of the area, arguing instead that their respiration of air "ceaselessly renewed by the winds and beaten by the sea" was responsible for their "rich blood." On the basis that "sea water has the double advantage of cleaning the body and strengthening health in an unequivocal manner," he recommended sea baths to his readers as a regular hygienic practice in summer, particularly for workers, noting that "this practice, which has only entered common usage in recent times, is spreading, but not fast enough."[12] The benefits of living by the sea were proved by the salutary effects of a seaside sojourn on sickly children who had grown up in other regions among unhealthy "vegetable emanations." The doctor noted the case of a young herdsman suffering from "tubercules at the summit of the two lungs" who, coming out of a long illness, "became a fisherman." Three months later "he was unrecognizable, so strong was his constitution."[13]

Dr. Hameau concurred. He recorded his amazement at the prompt return to "flourishing health" of patients undertaking a cure of baths. "I have seen young men so weak that they seemed unlikely to live for much longer, take up fishing, and become men of athletic build."[14] Dr. Lalesque's nephew Fernand, who published widely on tuberculosis in the second half of the century, noted in 1900 the long-established local practice of recommending the "profession of fisherman" to patients threatened by tuberculosis, based on the "climatic and innate immunity of our fishermen."[15] Of course, the fishing "profession" would be recommended only to those of similar socio-economic status to the fishermen—peasants and working class. For the bourgeois client, this recommendation referred to the patient's proximity to the sea, eating of fresh fish, breathing sea air, and supervised sea bathing.

Emulation of the local population's behavior was not to be self-prescribed, however. One should not simply do as the hardy mariners did. Dr. Hameau warned readers of his *Quelques avis sur les bains de mer* that "sea baths can do much good or much harm. . . . Taking them without rule or measure, they can be harmful; this is why it is prudent, when one is sick, to consult a doctor."[16] In his 1845 guide to La Teste, "O. D." echoed Hameau, informing bathers that it was "a grave error to believe that sea water can in no way harm people who enjoy perfect health."[17] He advised that they consult either Dr. Lalesque or Dr. Hameau upon arriving in La Teste and listed basic bathing precautions. Both "O. D." and Dr. Hameau warned bathers against emulating the locals "who dive with impunity into the sea at any moment." They were "used to it," benefiting from a "second nature."[18] So, while the example of the fishing population's excellent health was given as an inspiration to invalids, newcomers to the shore must follow strict instructions when bathing, as much from a medical as a social or moral perspective. The doctors' authority must be recognized. In this, the La Teste medical establishment followed the example set in spa towns over the first half of the century.[19]

The basic principles that bathers needed to respect, according to "O. D.," were that they should not enter the water when in a sweat nor before completing their digestion, but only when they felt their "head and stomach to be free" (presumably of alcohol and food). Dr. Hameau listed other "essential things that must be observed before bathing": women should not bathe during their "critical time" (presumably when menstruating); "hemorrhoidal flow" and diarrhea were other contraindications. For those in generally good health, any discomfort, headaches, dizziness, "lassitudes in the limbs with no apparent cause," were all signs that one should not bathe without first consulting a doctor.[20]

Other factors to consider, according to the medical establishment, were the time of day—the locals favored dusk, but the bather's level of experience should determine the appropriate hour—and the condition of the beach. Dr. Hameau offered his readers a vision of the ideal setting. The bathing spot should be "disposed in such a manner that there be only sea water, that it be very clear, that the beach be beautiful, easily approached, and the winds, by leveling the swell, form gentle and light waves." This of course, did not apply to the open ocean.

Finding or creating these perfect conditions for bathers would prove a difficult task, as we will discover, for the local fishing community had a different vision of the beach, one that revolved around their needs as workers. But medical texts and guidebooks tended not to acknowledge this problem. Indeed, after describing the best conditions for bathing, Dr. Hameau declared that Legallais' establishment provided all of these advantages "to a high degree" and that no other establishment was as "happily situated."[21] Here we see a fine example of the interlocking interests of doctors and investors, a precursor to the close collaboration between the medical profession and the developers of Arcachon's new quarter, the Ville d'hiver (Winter City) in the years to come.

Clearly it was in the interests of both doctors and investors to promote the Bassin d'Arcachon as a place for cures. Doctors were instrumental in the creation of this aspect of the new bathing place's identity: its close association with the ailments it was supposed to cure or relieve. Under his chapter entitled "Illnesses for which Cold baths are useful or harmful," Dr. Hameau claimed in 1835 that medical books were "almost silent" on this question and that by "opening his career" (in this field) he hoped to alleviate humanity's suffering with his contribution.[22] He claimed that cold baths were always useful in the following cases: "a general or partial weakness of the muscular action (resulting from a sedentary life, intellectual work, or venereal excesses), lymphatic engorgement, chronic [*ancien*] rheumatism, nervous ailments, specifically madness, as well as the majority of other mental distortions [*altérations*]." He went into some detail about hysteria, which he characterized as a women's disease (no surprises there), and hypochondria, considered more common among men. Baths could help hysterics "when the illness is not too chronic, and has not had too great an influence on the uterus or the brain," but as these women tended to feel the cold, their immersions "should be brief and governed according to the delay or promptitude of the reaction." The specificity of Hameau's advice reinforced his argument that bathing should be carefully monitored and not left to the discretion of the bather.[23] In his 1845 guide, "O. D." extended Hameau's list of ailments for which sea baths were helpful to include "St. Vitus's dance, epilepsy, trembling, neuralgia, sciatic gout, paralysis, children's convulsions" and asthma.[24]

This medical contribution to the promotion of the Bassin would be echoed in guidebooks touting sea baths as a cure throughout the century. One striking example was the *Album Illustré des Villes d'Eaux et de Bains de Mer* (Illustrated Album of Spa Towns and Bathing Resorts) of 1896, which classified resorts by illnesses: the reader could look up a disease and find a list of the places one might seek a cure for it. Arcachon was listed under the following headings: amenorrhea (especially for "excitable anemic lymphatics"), anemia, chronic catarrhal bronchitis (Arcachon's pine forest rated a mention here), neurosis, phthisis (e.g., pulmonary tuberculosis on which, the guide claimed, "water cures are without effect . . . but [are] favorable for fighting symptoms and improving the general state"), rheumatic gout, and scrofula. After discussing Arcachon's climate and the qualities of its seawater—which were "sedative" compared to the beaches of northern France—the guide listed the resort's doctors.[25] In this way, the resort was represented in and through the imagined, ailing bodies of its potential visitors.

Although medical texts and guidebooks implied that doctors were the ultimate authority in the matter of bathing as a therapeutic practice, we should not assume that their warnings and restrictions were always heeded by bathers. The Abbé Véchambre, in his *Bains maritimes d'Arcachon* (Arcachon Sea Baths) of 1853, believed that "without being initiated into Hippocratic doctrine, one could still . . . recommend [sea baths] to the most robust temperaments," even going so far as to encourage "intrepid" swimmers to head for the Ile aux Oiseaux. He wrote a little poem defying the reader "To prove that our Bassin / Has ever engulfed a swimmer in its embrace."[26]

The passage of the municipal bylaws of the 1840s indicates that unsupervised or "free" bathing was common (and disturbing) enough, to elicit the authorities' concern. The doctors' grasp on practices could never be complete, particularly when thousands of bathers were arriving at the Bassin every summer. As bathers came to appreciate their immersion as a pleasurable activity, and learned to swim or at least to wade in deep and drop under the water unaided, they were more likely to pull away from the supervision of bathing guides and doctors. Bathing would gradually become as much a source of fun as a means of regaining one's health.

The medical profession would have more success wielding their power in the Ville d'hiver. Doctors were involved from the beginning in the creation of this purpose-built, exclusive open sanatorium, a space that would allow them to penetrate every aspect of the lives of wealthy invalids, who willingly (for the most part) subjected themselves to their medical advisor's gaze. A short history of the creation of Arcachon and in particular of the Ville d'hiver appears in most guidebooks and literary descriptions of the resort. Dominique Rouillard, in his impressive study of the Norman resorts of Houlgate-Beuzeval and Trouville, identifies what he calls the "foundation myth" essential to the construction of an image of a new bathing resort. This myth describes the magical metamorphosis of a once deserted or unappreciated coastal site into a thriving town, realized by a farsighted individual, a hero-founder. Central to the moment of transformation is the coming of the railway, which activates construction and brings people and modernity to the "desert."[27]

In 1853, Jules Mareschal wrote of the extraordinary change that had occurred on the Bassin's shores over twenty years. It was as though a "magic wand" had transformed a "desolate" and "wild" coastline into a place of "luxury and pleasure," with elegant houses materializing "as if by enchantment."[28] Arcachon's motto, *Heri solitudo, hodie vicus, cras civitas*—yesterday solitude, today town, tomorrow city—devised in 1860 by the new commune's first mayor, Lamarque de Plaisance, is a concentrated version of this foundation myth. On the occasion of the first, brief visit to Arcachon in October 1859 by Napoleon III, the Empress, and the Imperial Prince, this creation story was drawn upon by the mayor, the parish priest, the cardinal-archbishop (in Bordeaux), and journalists who wrote about the day. The cardinal spoke of "the gracious city which has sprung up as if by magic on a once solitary beach"; Father Mouls suggested that Arcachon might be "the only town in France created, as if by magic, under Your Majesty's ever glorious Empire;" and a journalist from *L'Indicateur* praised the town's progress, noting that it boasted the "conveniences of the city, here where not long ago one saw nothing but sand and pine trees." Mayor Lamarque de Plaisance explained the town's motto and looked forward to the "brilliant future" awaiting what was once a "vast solitude." The proposed Ville d'hiver, soon to be built in "our salutary forest," represented that future. "Science," he declared, "recommended the project; the goodwill of the honorable President of the Compagnie du Midi [Emile Pereire, who had bought the La Teste railway line] is ready to execute it."[29]

Here we have the trio of hero-founders: two individuals—Lamarque de Plaisance, the first mayor, and Emile Pereire, the bringer of the railway to Arcachon and promoter of the Ville d'hiver—and a discipline—"science," or "medicine"—which was represented in turns by the local medical profession and individuals such as Dr. Emile Pereyra, who, the story goes, suggested in the early 1850s to his cousins the Pereire brothers (one of whom was an asthmatic) that the Bassin's climate would benefit tuberculosis sufferers and other invalids.[30] Lamarque de Plaisance was the local visionary, Pereyra and his medical colleagues the voice(s) of reason or knowledge, and Emile Pereire the executor of the dream, the indispensable financier. The story was somewhat flexible, allowing for the acknowledgment of figures such as Thomas Illyricus (a fifteenth-century monk who, on a retreat in Eyrac, prayed to the Virgin Mary to save some ships in distress, found a statue of Mary washed up on the beach, and built a chapel there in her honor), Adalbert Deganne, railway engineer and prominent local property developer, and Paul Regnauld, the engineer in charge of the Ville d'hiver.

The Pereire brothers, Emile and Isaac—fervent Saint-Simonians, railway pioneers, and founders of the Crédit Mobilier, one of France's first modern banks—bought the failing Bordeaux–La Teste railway line in 1852, incorporating it into their Compagnie des chemins de fer du Midi (Compagnie du

Midi). They had in view the extension of the line to Bayonne (from Lamothe, one of the existing stations on the La Teste line), and the drainage and plantation of large expanses of landes. They could not fail to notice the growing popularity of the summer bathing season on the Bassin and, inspired by the claims of medical practitioners, saw the potential for a winter season that would make the railway line viable outside of the summer months. The Compagnie du Midi envisaged the extension of the railway from La Teste to Arcachon from the moment of its acquisition of the line in 1852, which it achieved in concert with the engineer Adalbert Deganne. The railway arrived in Arcachon on 26 July 1857, just after the town was made a commune separate from La Teste—thanks to Lamarque de Plaisance, former mayor of La Teste, who had worked tirelessly to this end between 1852 and 1857, and who was rewarded by being named first mayor of Arcachon. The arrival of the railway and Arcachon's coming of age would thus always be linked in narratives about the town's beginnings.[31]

After several years of legal maneuvering, Emile Pereire managed to achieve the alienation (conversion from state to private property) of part of Arcachon's state forest, over which the inhabitants of La Teste had usage rights going back centuries. Pereire's purchase of 53 hectares 90 centares (133 acres) for himself and 43 hectares (106 acres) for the Compagnie du Midi was confirmed in October 1861. Four years earlier, in May 1857, he had written to the minister of finances explaining his vision for Arcachon and requesting the concession of 400 hectares (988 acres), on one half of which the company would build "a casino and its dependencies, promenades for pedestrians and riders, [and] villas [*pavillons*] in various locations," promising to follow this up with an investment of 300,000 francs in the two years following the concession. The company would have the right to use the other half of the concession in accordance with its own interests. Pereire spelt out his vision for a winter season in the forest, which would appeal to people from surrounding areas seeking "a milder temperature and air more favorable to the cure of many illnesses." The new municipal council eagerly supported Pereire's appeal to the minister, claiming that "the shelter formed by the dunes and forests creates favorable conditions for a winter stay and the cure of certain illnesses, in particular pulmonary phthisis."[32] Claims for Arcachon's hygienic climate and therapeutic possibilities were thus central to the promotion and development of the new quarter, the Ville d'hiver.

In the 1840s and 1850s, Drs. Emile Pereyra and Isidore Sarraméa had published arguments for the Arcachon forest as a winter resort for consumptives. Dr. Sarraméa, who was chief surgeon of Bordeaux hospices, had even envisaged the creation of an agricultural school in the forest for young offenders who were susceptible to lymphatism, scrofula, and tuberculosis.[33] His project never saw the light, but his 1860 pamphlet, *Un regard sur Arcachon,* reinforced the representation of Arcachon's forests and shore as sites of renewal and as fertile ground for medical intervention. He called on the "weak, tired, sick," seeking "strength, rest, health," to go the new resort. "There, one can breathe into one's lungs the great air of the immensity; there, saline emanations, enlivening fragrances of iodized seaweed, ribbons of bronzed moiré studded overnight with phosphorescent spangles, penetrate every pore."[34] Jacques Léonard, in his history of the French medical profession in the nineteenth century, notes the extraordinary speculative boom in "curism" propelled by doctors from 1850 on; Sarraméa's representation of Arcachon is a classic example of this.[35]

Writing in the period when Emile Pereire was negotiating with the government to purchase vast tracts of Arcachon forest, Sarraméa envisioned a mighty role for medicine in this "virgin" territory:

> Ardent investigator of all that might be good and useful to humanity, medicine has not failed in its task. Leaping forth along the rail network directed by engineers toward unknown regions, it has cut paths through the desert, interrogated its forests, atmosphere, sands, plants and waters. Before these treasures and the marvelous arrangement [*agencement*] of the best hygienic conditions for physical, intellectual, and moral medication, enlightened by the lessons of experience and by careful examination, medicine said to itself:—And I too, like literature and poetry, I will take hold of this beautiful nature, which unites salubrity, grace, and magnificence.[36]

We cannot fail to note the similarities between this passage and the vision of the investors who wrote about the Bassin in the 1830s, hoping to discover untold riches in the "hideous virginity" of the landes. Sarraméa, however, was already beginning to see the fruits of the exploratory impulse.

Sarraméa argued for the central role that medicine must play in the organization of the proposed Ville d'hiver. He declared that "science will be happy to provide all the hygienic requirements which must prevail in the buildings and the organization of this beneficent institution" and finished with a warning to the "intelligent administrators and happy owners of this fortunate soil" not to depart from the initial impulse to create a space devoted to the improvement of public health, not to forget that "science conquered the desert," indeed that "science created you"—"you" referring to the town that had arisen "as if by magic" (once again). He feared that, should speculation get out of hand, a hygienic, restful, family-oriented resort would be transformed into a noisy city bursting with sources of "entertainment." If Arcachon could only retain its "purity of atmosphere," its people would find that "hygiene will smile upon you and be your patron."[37]

These medical "patrons" of the Ville d'hiver were ridiculed in a short-lived local newspaper, *Le Détroqueur*, which appeared in 1880, some twenty years after Sarraméa's pamphlet. *Le Détroqueur* claimed to "defend the interests of the working class of our maritime population and principally the sailors, small-scale oyster farmers, and all the laborers employed in any capacity whatsoever in oyster farming on our Bassin." The verb *détroquer* refers to the process of levering oyster shells from the lime- and sand-covered tiles on which they grow. Its publication in both Gascon and French suggests that the editor, Eugène Faure, hoped to appeal to the local population's strong regional identity, while giving non-Gascon speakers—mainly outsiders and Frenchified bourgeois—the opportunity to understand his taunts. At ten centimes a copy, it was within reach of workers.[38]

In the cast of characters in *Le Détroqueur*'s second issue (14 May 1880), councillor (Albert) Fonbené's area of expertise was described in pharmaceutical terms, as "purgatives, vomitives, laxatives" and (Clément) Sémiac's as "laxatives, vomitives, purgatives": a humorous reference to French playwright Jean-Baptiste Molière's *The Imaginary Invalid*. In the twelfth issue, the appointment of the mayor Dr. Hameau as "medical inspector of sea baths" was criticized. The paper asked: "[W]hat work, what reports has he made? . . . He has never done anything!" and quipped that "any other individual chosen in the animal, vegetable, or mineral worlds, M. George a hippopotamus, a turnip, or a freestone . . . would have done just as much as M. Hameau."[39] The paper's jibes belie the real power exercised by the medical profession in the new town. Dr. Hameau and his deputies successfully sued the editor for libel. Faure was fined four thousand francs and imprisoned for thirty-eight days, and the paper closed down after twenty-five issues.[40] The "pure atmosphere" envisaged by Dr. Sarraméa—and promoted by his colleagues—had no room for *Le Détroqueur*'s parody of serious medicine.

Doctors did indeed play an important role in the design of Ville d'hiver. One local historian claims that Hameau and Lalesque collaborated with Regnauld on the choice of a sinuous layout of pine-treed lanes, which would protect invalid residents from wind tunnels.[41] Bernard Marrey notes that the fashion for curvilinear "parcs à l'anglaise" (like the Parc Monceau in Paris, another creation of the Pereires, which was *not* designed with medical aims) happened to coincide with this medically endorsed plan, although Jacques

Gubler proposes as a more useful reference the U.S. and British "urban park" models, underpinned by a reformist ideology and hygienic concerns.[42] In any case, the mutual reinforcement of these aesthetic and medical aspects meant that the Ville d'hiver could be promoted to its wealthy clientele as both hygienic and à la mode.

The spatial configuration of the Ville d'hiver can be understood on a number of levels, for the medical influence interlocked with or reinforced a strong social message about the new quarter. Maps of Arcachon reveal the markedly different layout of the Winter quarter, as well as its physical separation from the rest of the town. The Ville d'hiver's curvilinear design distinguished it aesthetically from the rectilinear commercial center of Arcachon, known as the Ville d'été (Summer City)—it had all the "beautiful disorder" that writer Anthelme Roux felt was lacking in La Teste in 1853.[43] The new quarter sat above and behind a dune, overlooking the original settlement, its elevation symbolic of the social status of the families who could afford to stay there. The Ville d'hiver was also more closely associated with the pine forest than with the sea; it was protected, enclosed, tranquil. And apart from the park given over to the grand, new Casino Mauresque (see chapter 9), the new quarter was, unlike the Ville d'été with its mix of businesses and dwellings, purely residential.

This spatial distinction reinforced the quarter's exclusivity, its uniqueness; the Ville d'hiver represented a civilized, and yet "natural" seeming (because sinuous and forested) haven away from the bustle down below. Guides tended to emphasize that Arcachon was made up of "two cities," even though other "cities" had been created, namely the Ville d'automne (Autumn City, between the Ville d'été and poorer eastern quarters of Aiguillon and Saint Ferdinand that housed fishing and building industry workers) and the Ville de printemps (Spring City), at the western end of the beach, radiating around Notre Dame church. As these other quarters adjoined the Ville d'éte, they were associated more with the active commercial seafront than with the Ville d'hiver, which was always singled out. P. A. de Lannoy's guide of 1900 spoke of Arcachon's "double character" that "ensures its vitality. It is cut into two cities: the summer one, with its beach of fine crunchy sand . . . ; the other, soaring above the Peymaou plateau, a true winter conservatory, in the peace and warmth of the pine trees."[44]

In a conversation reported (or fabricated) by Louis Branlat in 1886, two women on the train to Arcachon spelt out the distinction between these "cities":

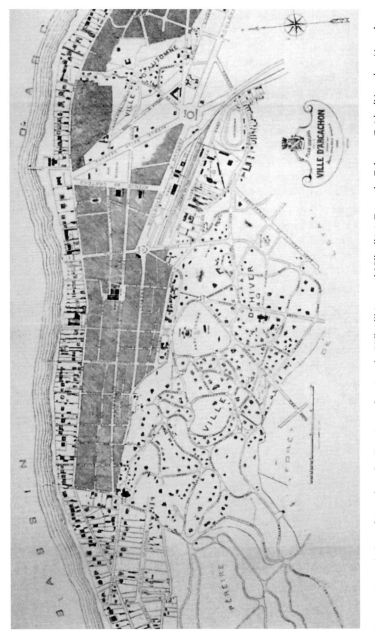

FIG. 8. General plan of Arcachon, by Ormières, showing the Ville d'hiver and Ville d'été. From de Gabory, *Guide d'Arcachon* (Arcachon: Mme Delamare, 1896), foldout. Bibliothèque Municipale de Bordeaux.

—Will you be staying long in Arcachon, Madame?

—Eh! my goodness, for a month, Madame.

—Ah! really, me too.

—Perhaps we could see each other?

—Of course, Madame.

—Your children are lovely, I would very much like them as companions for mine. For you see, on the beach, one doesn't know with whom they might associate.

—Oh! you're right there, Madame. The people today mix in everywhere, at the baths any old milliner [*la première modiste venue*] comes across as a great lady and amazes one with her sumptuousness.

—Are you staying near the beach?

—No; in the forest, where we have rented a very beautiful villa. In any case I am a little weak in the lungs, the air from the pines will do me good, I believe. And socially, it is less mixed, much less.

—What a shame! I have rented on the beach; so we will see each other less often. But you see, my children are a little pale, so I judged that exercise, races on the sand, the air of the Bassin would give them more strength. Otherwise I would have been in the forest.[45]

Branlat's little joke is that either one of these women might well be *la première modiste venue*—a milliner playing the role of a lady. The conversation elicits some of the social meanings attached to the beach and the forest in this divided resort.

Arcachon council minutes from the 1890s offer us a glimpse of another perspective on the Ville d'hiver's privileged position. Certain councillors were frustrated at the lack of services provided to the eastern, working-class end of town: the town crier was rarely heard there, the church was too small and its budget insufficient to service its congregation, and a tram line proposed in the late nineteenth century was to skirt this more populous area and serve the wealthier western end of the commune.[46] So the division between the Ville d'hiver and the rest of Arcachon was not simply aesthetic; it had a *concrete* meaning for local residents.

There was also the matter of protecting the enclave from unwanted visitors. Exploration went both ways. Visitors to Arcachon—who of course included Ville d'hiver families—were encouraged by guidebooks to visit the industrial quarters and to look at the fisheries and the local population at work. This kind of exploration also operated in the other direction, with visitors from down below walking up the hill to inspect the forested lanes and ornate villas of the quarter and, perhaps, to peer at sofa-ridden invalids in their closed verandahs or to spot a minor royal. A more disturbing kind of invasion was reported by councillor Roger Expert, who proposed that children under the age of fourteen be stopped from "marauding" in the Ville d'hiver and running amok in the forest, "doing obscene things"; he demanded that they be kept in school, be made to report their activities, or be imprisoned until their parents came to retrieve them![47] These were surely local children from the poorer quarters, as wealthy families staying in the Ville d'hiver would have hired tutors for their children or at least servants to keep an eye on them. Expert's proposal is reminiscent of the municipal bylaws of the 1840s that sought to control the behavior of locals on the beaches; spaces newly defined as health-giving were to be regulated to ensure that the newcomers' vision and expectations were satisfied. Locals must act accordingly.

The concerns about invasion by minors would have been particularly troubling for those who sought to maintain the Ville d'hiver's role as a curative space. The desire for control over the quarter as a whole extended to the villas and the bodies of their inhabitants, a tendency that intensified in the late nineteenth century, when bacillophobia—a pervasive fear of germs, as traced by David Barnes in his *The Making of a Social Disease*—took hold of the national psyche.[48]

The villas built in many and various styles in the Ville d'hiver—which became increasingly fanciful as the century wore on—were microcosms of the philosophy that informed the quarter as a whole. They claimed a kind of individualism or otherness (though subsumed within the designed "whole" of the quarter) tempered by a concern with the latest developments in hygienic and therapeutic practice. The use of closed-in verandahs and the choice of orientation (to maximize exposure to sun while protecting patients from winds) were two of the medically determined features of the villas. But, as Eliane Keller points out, villa owners' tendency to show off with ornate façades—towers, sculpted gables, and the like—worried doctors like Hameau, who in 1887 considered that hygiene was being sacrificed to taste and fashion.[49] This was when the fear of contagion was shaping up as a social force, in the wake of Robert Koch's 1882 identification of the tubercle bacillus and the growing medical acknowledgment of the consequences of this finding—namely that microbes and their carriers were the enemies to be targeted.

In the 1860s, when the Ville d'hiver was being designed, tuberculosis was not considered to be contagious, despite Jean-Antoine Villemin's finding in 1865 that it could be inoculated into rabbits. His experiments were discredited, the Academy of Medicine considering the contagion theory to be out of date (because harking back to much earlier notions) and dangerous because it

FIG. 9 Arcachon. La Rue du Casino (Casino Mauresque overlooking the Ville d'été). Collection of the author.

might ignite widespread panic. So inherited disposition, alcoholism, and sexual excess continued to be blamed for the consumption scourge. It was not until the late 1880s that the contagion model came to be accepted by the medical profession. Recognizing the *cause* of tuberculosis did not improve the chances of curing patients, however. It only refocused hygienists' concerns, leading them to campaign against spitting and dry sweeping (which raised bacillus-containing dust) and for the regular airing and disinfection of consumptives' rooms.[50]

The growing paranoia about microbe-carrying invalids led doctors to reassess the design of their wealthy patients' homes. While the villas in the Ville d'hiver had been carefully oriented to protect their residents from strong winds and give them access to full sun, doctors came to see the need for interiors that could be easily and thoroughly disinfected and would harbor no germs. The end of the 1890s saw the construction of "hygienic villas" in the Ville d'hiver, first devised in 1896 by Dr. Fernand Lalesque and architect Marcel Ormières. Fancy moldings, cornices, ceiling roses, drapes, and wall hangings were rejected in favor of washable walls with rounded corners, facilitating thorough disinfection, a service organized by Arcachon doctors until it was made a municipal responsibility in the early 1900s. Disinfection involved the "formalinization [*formolisation*] of the patient's room, the sterilization of contaminated objects, the antiseptic washing of parquet floors, skirting boards and paneling," and the special treatment of laundry, kept in a separate bag.[51] These developments coincided with the peak of what Barnes calls the "war against tuberculosis."[52] At this time, doctors and hygienists considered that everything about the consumptive must be monitored to prevent the spread of France's greatest killer—seen as a threat to the nation's economic, military, and moral strength.

In these pre-antibiotics days, tuberculosis therapy was based on three main principles: fresh air, rest, and overfeeding (*suralimentation*)—a program feasible only for the rich. The poor, who were the worst hit by the disease, lacked the means to follow such a treatment.[53] Arcachon's doctors, who ministered mainly to the wealthy, published studies on their treatment regimes, thereby promoting the therapeutic possibilities of the Arcachon climate. Dr. Fernand Lalesque, writing prolifically at the turn of the century, reinforced the association between Arcachon and cures for illness.

In his 1890 *Le climat d'Arcachon étudié à l'aide des appareils enregistreurs* (Arcachon's climate studied with the aid of recording devices), Lalesque claimed that Arcachon's thermal and hygrometric stability supported his argument that the resort was "singularly privileged and that it should have first place among those [resorts] whose oscillations have the narrowest range."[54] His graphs, with their precise rendition of peaks, troughs, and plateaus, presented an image of Arcachon that we can compare to other representations of the Bassin's land and seascape, whether functional (maps), artistic (e.g., sketches or watercolors) or promotional (postcards). While they have different meanings and different purposes, they all attempt to create a permanent record, a readable trace, of some aspect of the environment. The contours of the place are thus registered in different forms, each seeking to pin Arcachon down in some way, to transcend its changeable, ungraspable qualities, and to enable projections into the future.

The representation of Arcachon in climatic graphs formed part of the justificatory material for the medical profession's intimate control of patients' lives. Complementing this kind of representation were Lalesque's fever charts, which appeared in his *Climathérapie française: La cure libre de la tuberculose pulmonaire* (Open cure of pulmonary tuberculosis), published in the *Journal de Médecine de Bordeaux* in 1899 and then as a separate pamphlet. These charts showed the response of anonymous patients to various fresh air therapies in Arcachon. In the caption beneath each chart, Lalesque briefly described the patient's manifestation of tuberculosis (e.g., "right sub-clavicular moist cracks; dry pleurisy at bottom left") followed by an explanation of the groups of zigzag lines that showed the patient's temperature ranges both before and after Lalesque's treatment. The presentation of both climatic and patient charts for Arcachon reinforced the link between control over place and over bodies, through measurement.

Lalesque presented his *Cure libre* in a public lecture organized by the Syndicat Médical des Stations Pyrénéennes (Medical Association of Pyrenean Resorts) as a contribution to the debate concerning the benefits of sanatoria for the treatment of tuberculosis. While the discussions to which he referred centered mostly around the possibility of establishing sanatoria for the poor, Lalesque wished to publicize the observations he had made in his treatment of wealthy tuberculosis sufferers in the "open" sanatorium of the Ville d'hiver. His claims were controversial on two levels. First, they challenged the medical orthodoxy that favored the *cure d'altitude,* or mountain retreat, for tuberculosis sufferers: as he noted in a later brochure on the *cure marine,* many doctors in this period recommended that consumptives stay away from the sea, while he argued that "chronic pulmonary tuberculosis, the most common, is healed just as well on the plains as in the mountains, by the sea as in the desert." Dr. Henri Lamarque, for one, would have disagreed with Lalesque's approach here: he counseled thermal curists against following their mountain retreat with a stay beside the sea. He considered that thermal treatments brought "a certain excitation," which should be followed with calm and rest. "This calm, this rest cannot exist beside the sea: the air, the wind, the sound of the waves, the intense life of busy resorts are all the more perturbing, given that mineral waters put the nervous system and organic functions into a very impressionable state."[55]

Second, Lamarque's claims challenged the established preference for "closed" sanatoria. Lalesque spoke of the benefits of the so-called open cure (*cure libre*), also known as the "home-sanatorium" cure, seeking to reassure doctors who feared that this approach did not guarantee invalids' strict observance of hygienic practices.[56] What Lalesque communicated was the extent to which doctors ruled the lives of their tubercular patients in the open sanatorium. He claimed there were two types of "open cure invalids": those who were ignorant of the latest medical discoveries concerning airing (*aération*) and who insisted on closing themselves in stuffy rooms for fear of catching a chill (i.e., the ones "for whom everything becomes a pretext for argument and resistance") and those who were already versed in "good hygienic notions" and happily followed their doctor's advice. The first kind, the recalcitrants, called for the doctor's tenacity. He must never "disarm." He must be prepared to "return incessantly to the attack, he must know how to make unimportant concessions one day, and withdraw them the following day, for their benefit [*avec bénéfice*]; in a word, he must know how to win the invalids' confidence."[57]

The invalids' trust was essential given the intimate knowledge doctors sought concerning every aspect of their lives. Lalesque expressed this succinctly in his definition of the doctor's "solicitude" for his patient.

> To show this solicitude is to regulate down to the smallest details the installation of the patient. It means guiding his choice of *quartier* [quarter], villa, the room he will inhabit. It means showing him, for daytime airing, in the lounge room, on the verandah or in the garden, according to the weather, according to the direction of the sun and the wind, the position of his chaise longue. It means . . . indicating the position of the bed, choosing the door or the window to be opened, giving the size of this opening, finally marking the direction of the screen [*paravent*] designed to protect the patient from the too-direct arrival of air. All of this, regulated minutely, accompanied by a program governing [*ponctuant*] the hygiene of the skin, clothing and diet, encourages patients, gains their trust and wins them over.[58]

Lalesque also required that his patients keep a detailed journal of their daily activities (or passivities!). These diaries included the following: temperature night and day; severity and nature of cough at different times; number and color of expectorations; and patterns of perspiration, diet (an exact account of everything consumed), appetite, bladder, and bowel function. Following these observations were general comments on how the day was spent (airing, or location of rest) and the patient's subjective sense of well-being.

Lalesque demanded that his patients spend hours each day resting on chaise longues or hammocks, shielded by movable screens, and limit their exercise to the bare minimum. Armed with a thermometer and scales, he judged their recuperation according to their level of "organic combustion" and their weight gain. He argued that a patient's own impressions were not trustworthy and that these measuring instruments ensured accurate observations.[59] We see, then, the extent of the doctor's claim to control over his patients' lives. And we understand better the guidebook writer de Lannoy's description of the Ville d'hiver's "becalmed atmosphere," where one might "rediscover oneself."[60] Lying in a hammock all day under the pines, noting down the minutiae of his existence, the patient was focused on himself, on his changing states of body and mind. This "obsessional self-centered arithmetic," as Corbin calls it, was an essential part of the doctor-invalid relationship developing over this period.[61]

And yet there was the occasional opportunity to come out of one's shell: while Lalesque recommended in 1897—against prevailing opinion—that his patients alternate rest days in the forest with days sitting on a protected, sunny Bassin beach, by 1900 he proposed that "for certain invalids, I advise staying on the beach, in any season, and outings on the water, even in a strong breeze."[62] He claimed that the "special topographic circumstances" of the Bassin permitted such an approach. Above all, the Bassin must not be confused with the ocean.

> On the beach, neither undulations, nor waves, nor dazzling light. On a fine and golden sand, packed down beneath the treading foot [tassé au pied qui le foule], the clear, silver, calm, and polished sea spreads out in languid folds, without a murmur, without a sound, grandly silent, in striking contrast to its state several leagues out from land. From the sky, a soft velvety blue, falls an even softer light, giving infinite transparency and lightness to the atmosphere. In sum, the Bassin d'Arcachon is the sea with all possible inconveniences subdued.[63]

The most important benefit of the Bassin's topography, according to Lalesque, was the quality of the air. Despite its being protected from the harshness of the ocean, the Bassin received pure winds from the Atlantic, for no

Une cure d'air et de repos avec un autre dispo-
sitif du Paravent-Abri. par temps calme, la
valve supérieure abritant du soleil.

FIG. 10. "Fresh air and rest therapy with another arrangement of the Screen-Shelter, in calm weather, the superior flap providing protection from the sun." One of Dr. Fernand Lalesque's chaise longue–ridden tuberculosis patients. From Dr. Fernand Lalesque, *Clima-thérapie française: La cure libre de la tuberculose pulmonaire (Conférence publique faite le 4 juin 1899)* (Bordeaux: Gounouilhou, 1899), fig. 5. Bibliothèque Municipale de Bordeaux.

settlement lay in their path to "dirty" them. He gave as evidence measurements of the number of microorganisms per meter cubed, comparing Arcachon's 150 to the Rue de Rivoli's (in Paris) 5,480.[64]

In light of these findings, Lalesque recommended sea outings for certain patients; he cited the case of a very ill young woman who "never feels better, who never breathes more fully than during a *cure en bateau* [boat cure]. She experiences such well-being that even on very windy days, with a strong swell, she does not interrupt this treatment."[65] He noted that the shape of the local *pinasses* was perfectly suited for a chaise longue (see fig. 11). The boat could be either anchored just offshore, leaving the invalid alone to be "gently rocked by the waves," or in motion, "either rowed or under sail, carrying the patient lying on his chaise longue, sheltered from the sun by a large parasol, made merry by the coming and going of fishermen and the thousand incidents of sea life."[66] Lalesque's description of the boat's motion failed to acknowledge the presence of someone at the helm, for when the second option was favored, a boatman or -woman would be the patient's pilot.

Lalesque's reference to the entertainment value of the "coming and going" of fishermen and vessels on the Bassin suggests that the patient's feeling part of the active world (though warmly wrapped and recumbent) was part of the therapeutic experience. However, the invalid needed to be protected from too close a contact with the fishing population. In one of Lalesque's accompanying photographs (see fig. 12), we see a patient, whose gender is difficult to determine, under a parasol, with a female companion in a large hat seated in the middle of the boat, between the recumbent patient and the working boatman. This implies that it was not acceptable to leave the invalid alone with the pilot—at least not in the case of young women, for whom the close, unmediated company of a rough-mannered local would have been considered undesirable given that bourgeois families were paranoid about mixing even with others of their own class. This close proximity of invalids who would usually be confined to the Ville d'hiver and other, *healthy* members of the Arcachon population would be a source for another kind of anxiety.

As the bacillophobia ignited by Koch's findings spread to the general population, contact between well and unwell communities began to concern some Arcachon residents, although it was not so much the fishing community for whom the fear-mongers spoke up but for the precious summertime tourists, who might be discouraged from coming to Arcachon because of its long-established association with tuberculosis. We have noted the local doctors' early disinfection policy, but by the turn of the century, we see a more

FIG. 11. The open marine cure. "Anchored vessel, on a breezy day. The patient, lying on a chaise longue, carefully wrapped in a blanket and cape, protected from the wind by a parasol, waits, after several hours of fresh air and rest therapy, for the descending tide to leave the boat dry on the sand." From Dr. Fernand Lalesque, *Climathérapie française: La cure libre de la tuberculose pulmonaire (Conférence publique faite le 4 juin 1899)* (Bordeaux: Gounouilhou, 1899), fig. 10. Bibliothèque Municipale de Bordeaux.

Barque en marche, par temps calme. Le malade étendu ou assis sur sa chaise-longue est protégé du soleil par un large parasol mobile.

FIG. 12. "Boat on the move, in calm weather. The patient, lying or sitting on a chaise longue, is protected from the sun by a large mobile parasol." From Dr. Fernand Lalesque, *Climathérapie française: La cure libre de la tuberculose pulmonaire (Conférence publique faite le 4 juin 1899)* (Bordeaux: Gounouilhou, 1899), fig. 11. Bibliothèque Municipale de Bordeaux.

explicit, public recognition of the fear of what the invalids might leave behind. For example, in L. de P.'s 1901 guide to Arcachon, under the heading "Ville d'hiver," the reader is reassured that "Before the opening of each winter season, meticulous preparations are made for the disinfection of premises, and the use of pocket spittoons, which is becoming more common among invalids, protects the public from any risk of contagion."[67] During the bacillophobic era, droplets of saliva were identified as one of the main sources of infection. Arcachon doctors prided themselves on their town's record of having sold 750 pocket spittoons between 1897 and 1899. In 1908 another guidebook declared in its section on the Ville d'hiver that "the disinfection of premises is carried out with the greatest care"; it also carried an advertisement for the Villa Peyronnet in Arcachon that used the *cure d'air* as a drawcard but warned in italics that "*we refuse all contagious invalids.*"[68]

The fear of contagion would eventually become such an important issue that municipal election campaigns would be fought over the future identity of the resort—as a curative or pleasure space. The close identification of Arcachon with illness, although essential to the resort's creation and development, would need to be shaken off to appeal to a wider range of vacationers.

CHAPTER EIGHT

Whistles and Pickets, or "Dejecta of All Sorts"

In this place, tennis has planted its pickets,
stretched out its nets, and the ladies come running,
trying to outdo each other.

—De Lannoy, *Guide aux plages girondines*, 1900

At half past four on the afternoon of 27 July 1872, Jean Mauriac, the mayor of Arcachon, inspected the stretch of sand between the rues François Legallais and Nelly in the company of an officer of the Ponts et Chaussées, the police superintendent, and the commune's forestry guard. Their mission was to determine "whether the pontoon boats transformed into dwellings" by Testerin fishing families remained on the beach, in contravention of certain prefectorial and municipal decisions. The pontoons were unwieldy, flat-bottomed boats often used, and inhabited, by guards who protected oyster farms from marauders.[1] The mayor and his companions reported six pontoon owners whose vessels, dragged high above the watermark, "prevented the free circulation of bathers."

The pontoon owners present that day declared that they had been given permission to keep their boats there by Huas, the naval registration officer, an employee of the ministry for the navy. Arnaud Cazaux had beached his pontoon in front of the 150-room Grand Hotel (built in 1863–64 for the railway

Fig. 13. Pontoon boat on beach below the Deganne Château, Arcachon. Collection of Richard Lahaye.

company and situated at the Bassin end of the street that led to the impressive
Casino Mauresque, or Moorish Casino, also of 1863). Cazaux told Mauriac,
"in a quite provocative, if not threatening, tone," that this was indeed his pontoon and that it was the harbormaster who had instructed him to place it
there. In fact, he claimed that the captain of the La Teste port, or harbormaster, "had recommended that he clutter up the beach as much as possible; that
moreover he had the right to stay there given that his pontoon was equipped
for fishing and that he had his own enrolled crew [*rôle d'équipage*]."[2] Not long
after Mauriac made his reports, a note in the margins of a letter that Autran,
the navy's commissioner general, wrote to the prefect, warned that "the sailors
are very upset with M. Mauriac and I would not like to see them revolt against
municipal authority, whatever wrongs the council may have committed."[3]

Why this battle over the pontoons? We can understand this episode as part
of what Jean-Didier Urbain calls the "era of the clean slate: the time of the
holiday pacification of the shore—an inaugural operation 'attuning space
with desire.'"[4] The "desire" was for a safe version of the nature described by
Romantic poets. "Pacification" involved constructing the beach to meet that
desire by removing all that did not fit. The beach, for centuries a work space
for locals, was being reinvented as a safe, clean, unencumbered, "natural"
space where a physical and moral renewal was possible for stressed urban-
dwelling bourgeois. This spiritual reinvigoration, this escape from the pres-
sures and dirt of the city, called for a communion with purifying nature, in
this case the sea and shore. For the beach to be made "natural," for it to become a threshold for the cleansing sea, it must be emptied of any reminders
of labor, of poverty, of everyday living: pontoons, nets, and rubbish. It had to
be differentiated from the bourgeois' places of work.[5]

We have seen in chapter 6 that as early as the 1840s, before Arcachon became a commune in its own right, the naval authorities representing the
Bassin's fishermen were concerned about the limitations that new foreshore
developments placed on the sailors' access to the shore.[6] Twenty years later,
Arcachon was a flourishing resort whose fortunes rested on the continued development of therapeutic bathing and related activities. In the eyes of the municipal authorities, the fishing community's interests now came second to
those of the newcomers.

In the summer of 1866, mayor Charles Héricart de Thury declared in a letter to the prefect that, "above all, to ensure the future of Arcachon, it is necessary to clear the Beach of all the obstacles which might deter bathers from
coming." These included seaweed hiding dead fish "which emit a vile
stench," broken plates and bottles that cut bathers' feet, and, finally, the ob-

structive "old pontoons" whose inhabitants "dirty [the beach] with dejecta of all sorts."[7] The beach as it was would not do: it had to be *purified*. Even nature—in this case seaweed—was not necessarily welcome. Thus began the campaign that Mauriac took up with such gusto in the early 1870s.

The pontoons' presence was, ironically, a direct result of the development of bathing on the Arcachon coast. Their owners, all from La Teste, set up their temporary homes for the summer season where they could make the most of the beachgoers' presence. In 1866, a report on the state of fishing on the Bassin explained that the small colony of sailors living in Arcachon came from villages right around the Bassin, and that they and Testerin sailors "found the complement of their existence in the guardianship of Arcachon villas, yachts and oyster farms, and also in the promenading on the Bassin of visitors who come for the sea baths," as well as of Bordelais day-trippers who came on the cheap *trains de plaisir* on Sundays and public holidays.[8]

According to Mauriac's report of July 1872, a sign on one of the pontoons proclaimed its owner to be "Hippolyte Dupart, boatman; bathing and swimming; flame fisherman," while Jeune Gabriel's sign declared him to be a "boatman-fisherman of all kinds, [who] gives swimming lessons."[9] However, while many councillors and developers profited from the bathing season, the Testerin pontoon owners' contribution to the new town's commercial activity was seen as a threat to the process of reconstructing the beach.

Much to the council's dismay, pontoon owners offered more than swimming lessons and boat trips: they sold oysters, drinks, and other products from their shelters. According to Mauriac, they had an unfair advantage over the shopkeepers in the village: they avoided the municipal trading fee (*droit de plaçage*) paid by all merchants because the council had no right to collect dues on the beach, which lay within the maritime domain. This problem of "rent-free" trading space, whether pontoons or stalls on the sand, was one that confronted other seaside resorts (e.g., Blackpool) at this time.[10]

In a letter to the prefect in October 1872, Autran responded to Mauriac's July reports by quoting his man on the ground, Huas. Huas, the naval registration officer in La Teste, was the staunch defender of the fishing community's right to operate freely within the maritime domain. His support showed that it was in the navy's interests to protect fishing communities, because they provided men for the navy. Indeed, as registered sailors, they could be called up to serve on navy ships for as long as one in every three to four years.[11] How ironic that the naval authorities, who must have been hated at times for their heavy demands on sailors, proved to be their strongest supporters when it came to protecting their access to the maritime domain.

Huas's support for the Testerin fishermen infuriated Mauriac. The previous summer, the mayor had claimed that Huas "only sees and only wants to see what he believes to be in the interest of his sailors, [and] pays no attention to any of our claims"; Mauriac had then requested permission to "force the naval registration officer to effect the removal of the boats from the shore"— in vain.[12]

In his October 1872 letter, Autran noted Huas' claim that Mauriac had misapplied a municipal bylaw of 1871 based on a prefectorial decree of 1866, which prohibited the parking of "old boats transformed into dwellings" on the section of beach frequented by bathers. Huas claimed that this could not apply to the sailors reported in July because their vessels were "nearly all brand new, solidly built and regularly equipped for fishing." Autran hoped to see the end of "the incessant harassment to which the mayor of Arcachon subjects the sailors of the La Teste quarter" and finished his letter by drawing the prefect's attention to another, damaging claim by Huas—namely "that other pontoon boats, in particular that belonging to Mr. Dehillotte, coastal navigator [*maître au cabotage*], were in a similar situation to that of the accused, and that despite this he [Mauriac] did not report Mr. Dehillotte."[13] Huas had also told Autran that Dehillotte paid a trading fee (*indemnité de plaçage*) to the municipality. If this were true, it meant that the council was prepared to overlook "obstruction" of the beach if it could benefit financially (if illegally) from the pontoon owners' presence.

Auguste Lalesque, mayor of La Teste, the hometown of the pontoon owners, wrote to the prefect on the same day as Autran to report his constituents' version of events, which supported Huas's trading fee claim. The Testerins had told Lalesque that two years earlier (1870), the Arcachon council had tried to remove them from the beach between the Grand Hotel and Nelly Street, but that they had "resisted these efforts with the force of inertia." They had then been told they could leave their pontoons where they were if they paid a yearly communal tax. "Some refused," they claimed, "and others consented quickly, for the sake of peace, if they would receive receipt for their payment." The Arcachon council then passed bylaws requiring that the pontoon owners in question "move to any other part of the same coast," leading the sailors of La Teste to wonder "why that which was permitted on some other section of the shore was prohibited here, given that no part of the shore could be singled out with prerogatives or legal exceptions."[14]

Mauriac was on the back foot. He wrote to the prefect in November defending his actions and accusing Autran and Huas of displaying "bad will" toward him. He claimed that if the pontoons were new, they were nevertheless designed not for fishing but for living in, and that their inhabitants "indulged in all kinds of crimes and bad behavior."[15] He did not explain what he meant by this. But he complained that Huas had protected his sailors with "the alibi [*sauf conduit*] of a crew list, granted uniquely for the occasion, and in order to play what might be called a trick on the administration." Mauriac denied collecting any dues from Dehillotte and called on Autran to produce evidence for Huas's claims.

Three days later Mauriac wrote to the prefect again, pointing out that Dehillotte had "set himself up permanently on the Arcachon beach, not to fish but to sell oysters which he sells retail, in competition with the local merchants." He sold oysters "10 centimes cheaper per dozen" and paid none of the charges required of other merchants. Dehillote's justification was "the privilege attached to his crew list." Mauriac calculated that out of 28,398 oysters brought into Arcachon for the consumption of its inhabitants between 1 September and 8 October, "Dehillotte alone sold 14,100, roughly half."

Mauriac argued that unless the municipality were given the power to collect revenue across "the entire Territory of the Commune" (i.e., including the maritime domain), a beach market would compete directly and unfairly with the town market.[16] Given these protestations, why then was Dehillotte not reported along with other oyster farmers during Mauriac's July inspection, as the other Testerins claimed was the case? If Mauriac had indeed overlooked Dehillotte's presence on the beach in return for a regular payment, the council was probably benefiting handsomely given his impressive turnover.

Mauriac failed to sway the prefect: in January 1873 the prefectorial council declared that the mayor had no authority over the seashore and annulled his reports of the previous summer, claiming they were "a serious attack on the liberty of navigation and the sailors' industry." This infuriated Mauriac. He vented his spleen at a council meeting in May, claiming that the pontoons were "places of debauchery and even of prostitution" (so that is what he meant in November by "crimes and bad behavior"!) and that if the prefectorial decision was not challenged, "we should consider the Bassin's beach lost and Arcachon deprived of the advantages . . . of the exceptional location it offers for the safety of bathers."[17]

We should be wary of accepting Mauriac's accusation of prostitution at face value. This was, after all, a last, desperate plea in the face of defeat. Mauriac needed to find something strong enough to sway the prefect, who had been unmoved by the pontoon owners' alleged obstruction of the beach and the threat of unfair commercial competition. Given the nineteenth-century discourse around prostitution, fed by the pervasive fear of physical (venereal) and moral corruption from the 'dangerous classes'—Corbin calls it "the point of convergence of collective deliria and the meeting point of all anxieties"—Mauriac's accusation of prostitution raised the specter of a dirty, "unnatural" beach, polluted by the same evils as the cities from which the tourists were fleeing.[18] This was the antithesis of a clean, secure beach, a space that ought to be free of unpleasant associations, where the bourgeois stroller might contemplate nature unimpeded. Renewed twice a day with the incoming tide, this sandy strip was the ideal site for a moral and physical regeneration—if only it could be rid of those dirty, ugly "places of debauchery."[19]

If we reread the 1872 reports in light of this latest accusation by Mauriac, a seventh report made in August, a fortnight after the six we have already discussed, is illuminating. Mauriac and Peseux (the forestry guard) returned to the beach with Pérès (gendarme brigadier), to determine the validity of "numerous complaints made to us daily by visitors concerning the parking of old pontoon boats whose chains and anchors . . . often provoke accidents among bathers and strollers." They arrived as the tide was withdrawing and found "an old pontoon boat," beached and dry, below a property belonging to a M. Coussillan and close to Ramond's hot baths. The boat had been shored up with a "protective wall of sand preventing it from leaning to the left or the right," a ladder operated as a staircase, and a canvas awning had been erected at the rear, "taking up an area of about ten square meters held up at one end by the said boat and at the other by two stakes planted in the ground."[20]

The municipal officers approached a group of women who were sitting in the shade of the pontoon, who told them that the owner was at the lighthouse. When Mauriac threatened to impound the boat if they did not reveal his identity, Pierre Lallegrand emerged from inside the pontoon to admit to ownership. Like the others, he was from La Teste, but he had set up only eight days earlier; that is, shortly after the other Testerins had been reported. He too claimed the support of the naval registration officer Huas.

A gathering of women: was this enough for Mauriac to declare the existence of prostitution? When working, the fisherwomen of the Bassin wore pantaloons, sometimes baring their calves, and this at a time when bourgeois women bathed in outfits designed to "encrypt silhouette and complexion, bodily form and substance, thereby removing them from the gaze of the other."[21] Working-class and peasant women, on the other hand, were considered likely candidates for prostitution, and the increasing numbers of visitors passing through Arcachon may well have created a demand for their services. If we take into account John Merriman's study of the nineteenth-century fear

of the edges of towns, the shore—as the periphery or margin *par excellence*—
was a potential site for threatening activities like unregulated prostitution.[22]
In the 1866 *Notice sur la pêche dans le quartier de la Teste* (Notice on fishing in
the La Teste quarter), as part of an analysis of the "material and moral situation" of the fishing community, it was reported that "the taste for dressing up
is winning over the sailors' daughters and with it will come the accompanying
vices and miseries."[23]

In an 1879 report to the prefect, however, La Teste's police superintendent
claimed that neither independent prostitutes nor brothels operated in his
commune.[24] Clearly, Mauriac could not rely on the police to substantiate his
claims. And as the maritime prefect (a vice-admiral) pointed out in his letter
to the prefect of the Gironde in 1874, if "illicit industries" were a problem, it
was the responsibility of the local police to curb them: it was of no concern to
the navy and outside its jurisdiction.[25]

Mauriac did not have even the full support of all the bathers whose interests he claimed to represent. Some time after piecing together the pontoon
issue, I came across a public inquiry into a council proposal to build an "embankment with road" between Arcachon's main beach and its foreshore villas.
This was referred to as the inquiry into the Boulevard de la Plage (for it would
affect the owners of properties situated on the Boulevard, which backed onto
the beach).[26] The timing of this proposal sheds light on Mauriac's increased
pressure on the fishing community from 1872 on.

In December 1872, Harry Scott Johnston, a member of the board of the
Société Immobilière d'Arcachon (which developed the Ville d'hiver), wrote to
the prefect to complain that the Arcachon council had misrepresented the
board's views on the proposed promenade. The council had claimed in its
February 1872 minutes (several months before Mauriac's beach inspections)
that the Société Immobilière approved of the project and undertook to finance and build the section in front of the Grand Hotel. According to Johnston, the Société's board had voted *against* the proposal and called for the
"preservation of the beach as it is."[27]

In his report on the Boulevard proposal, the chief investigator (*enquêteur*)
M. Gaussens listed some of the benefits of building a promenade along the
foreshore. Mayor Mauriac's stamp on the project is unmistakable. It would
be laid with gravel, "always clean and well maintained, instead of moving
sand, into which pedestrians' feet sink, seaweed and stinking remains of fish
of all sorts. The current obstacles to circulation by fishermen's nets and the
beaching of pontoons, whose surrounds harbor infection during the bathing
season, will of necessity disappear if the promenades are established." The

promenade, then, would be instrumental in the creation of Mauriac's ideal beach.

Gaussens' report on the inquiry was surprisingly upbeat considering that, of the thirty-seven men who presented to respond to the project, only three were in favor. All of the opponents claimed that Arcachon's beach was unique and sought-after precisely because it was *not* separated by a thoroughfare from the foreshore villas. This meant that the children of villa owners could run down to the sand without fear, and be watched from afar by their parents. Several complainants referred to the beach as the "land of children" (*patrie des enfants*). M. Moureau's objection contained a touching description of the beach as a children's paradise, to which Arcachon owed its "reputation" and "fashionability." "Arcachon *is* the beach," he declared. "It is the soft sand which breaks their falls, it is the fine sand which does not hurt their delicate feet; it is the liberty to roll in this white sand which does not dirty their clothes. Arcachon is for them, and rightly so, precisely a place with neither stone walls [*perré*] nor embankments."[28] This situation pleased the children's parents, too, for the villas' direct contact with the sand, the safety of the gently sloping beach, and the shallow water contributed significantly to high property values along the foreshore, values that would, they argued, be diminished by the construction of the promenade.

Not only would the promenade threaten access and property values, but it would ruin the beach itself. Protesters claimed to have observed the dramatic erosion of the beach in other parts of Arcachon, in one case due to the construction on the shore of a bathing establishment. The building of an embankment would, they argued, inevitably cause the sand to disappear, and the currents would dig a deeper channel near the shore, creating danger for bathers. Arcachon would lose its claim to fame, its "beautiful," "unified," and "tranquil" beach; it would be deserted by summer tourists and the commune ruined.[29]

Some protesters also claimed that the erosion of the beach would adversely affect the local sailors: their frail boats, at present easily drawn up onto the sand in rough weather, would crash against the new embankment. M. Moureau noted that the navy had not been consulted on the project, a serious breach of procedure that must be rectified given that the beach was part of the maritime domain. He was not the only one to note that the commune had no jurisdiction over this domain.

Finally, all expressed concern that the parlous state of the commune's finances ruled out any such expensive undertaking. M. Lafon asked how a commune with a debt of 600,000 francs could possibly be in a position to borrow 800,000 francs for the promenade project (although the investigator claimed the project would cost between 20,000 and 26,000 francs, so Lafon's calculations appear to be exaggerated). M. Moureau, placing the matter into the national context, wondered whether "they had chosen the best moment to introduce local taxes for fantasy creations when France needs to devote all her resources to one unique goal, to rid ourselves of the foreigner who crushes our nation?" (He was referring to the heavy indemnity France was required to pay under the terms of the Frankfurt Treaty of May 1871). M. Guérard pointed out that other, more essential public works such as the construction of a schoolhouse and of footpaths on the Avenue de la Gare, as well as the insulation of the St. Ferdinand church, were all waiting on council funds.[30]

Many of the complainants were *forts imposés* (highest communal tax payers) as well as proprietors of villas, so their interests were directly affected: *They* would be hit by local taxes to pay for the project. *Their* property values would drop, and *their* children would have to cross the road. While these opponents to the project may have been close to Mauriac in a social sense, there were clearly political differences. This inquiry is yet another illustration of the delicate position of municipal councillors who were constantly juggling the opposing interests within their community, and often within their own ranks. In his attempt to "pacify" the shore, Mauriac had to deal with bathers and villa owners who had their own interests and preferences to defend, just as, when trying to clear the pontoons, he had confronted fishermen and -women who invoked Colbert's edict, and naval authorities who supported the rights of their sailors. Each group made its own claim to the beach, even while declaring that it belonged to the maritime domain.

On the issue of beach maintenance, however, the mayor had the support of those who opposed the promenade. For example, de Cabanne, agent for the Société Immobilière, called for the "most complete clearing of the beach," and John Durand, a villa owner, called on the council to carry out "a more severe policing of the beach's maintenance."[31] So, while the promenade would not be built for another forty years (one assumes the objectors carried the day in 1872), the issue of control over the beach continued to vex the authorities.

The greatest hurdle to municipal attempts to free up the beach for bathers was the fishing community's use of the sand for the drying out and repair of their nets and boats. In September 1873, the board of directors of the Société Immobilière d'Arcachon wrote to the prefect to complain that the bathing and hydrotherapy establishment attached to the Grand Hotel suffered as a result of the "hindrances created by sailors to [bathers'] access to the sea." Long nets hung between wooden pickets planted in the sand, and boats anchored

just offshore, prevented bathers' access to the water and caused them injury
when they tripped over mooring ropes. The board requested that a strip forty
meters (forty-four yards) wide below the hotel be kept free of nets and other
fishing paraphernalia, claiming that "the beach being six kilometers [3.72
miles] long, there can be no harm to the seagoing population of the Bassin
d'Arcachon."[32]

While only a handful of Testerin families beached their pontoons on the
Arcachon beach in the summer months, nearly all the Bassin's fishing communities used the same stretch of sand for the essential activities of net drying and
boat repairs. As early as 1869, Mauriac had proposed "that the drying of nets
on the beach be prohibited outright."[33] Confusion over the division of powers
where the maritime domain was concerned led the prefect to establish, in December 1873, a committee whose brief was to study "the measures necessary to
assure the policing of the beach," its maintenance, zones for the drying of nets
and careening of boats, and the manner of mooring and beaching vessels.[34]
The committee's meetings must have been heated given that Mauriac and
Huas were both members. Other members included Dmokowski, the Ponts et
Chaussées officer who had accompanied Mauriac to the beach in July 1872;
Désiré Legallais, hotelier and retired ship's captain; and Johnston, Bordelais
merchant and director of one of the first steam-trawler fishing companies on
the Bassin.[35]

Johnston, as a board member of the Société Immobilière, was one of the
complainants in the letter to the prefect concerning the nets below the Grand
Hotel, not long before the formation of the beach policing committee. Johnston figured prominently in the life of Arcachon. His family was one of the
first to build a villa at Eyrac; before Arcachon became a separate commune,
he was involved in the industrialization of fishing on the Bassin; and in December 1872 he bought the eastern end of the contested prés salés.[36] His foreshore villa was next door to the Deganne Château—a copy of the Château de
Boursault—built by railway engineer and two-time mayor Adalbert Deganne.[37] Johnston's regular letters to the prefect reveal his preoccupations,
one of which was the zoning and policing of the beach.

With their claim that the fishing community had enough beach for its
purposes and would therefore not be affected by the removal of nets from the
area below the Grand Hotel, Johnston and his supporters overrode the fishermen's local knowledge and preferences with their own hierarchy of worth for
each section of the beach. The villa owners valued a particular stretch of
beach according to the view it offered, its proximity to bathing establishments and amenities, its width, slope, and the quality of its sand. They were

(1618) ARCACHON. — Le Château Deganne et Promenade sur la Plage.

FIG. 14. The Deganne Chateau and a walk on the beach. Collection of Richard Lahaye.

not prepared to acknowledge that the fishing community might have its own scale of values. The Société Immobilière's proposal assumed that for the sea workers, any part of the beach would do, whereas the bathers and strollers required exclusive access to a choice patch.

Of course, the Bassin's various fishing communities had their own, quite different representation of this most useful stretch of shore. They had divided it up according to commune and specialization: people from Arès and Andernos, for example, had agreements with Testerins and Arcachonnais (Arcachon residents) as to where they could work.[38] The 1873 beach committee took some account of the fishing communities' agreed divisions of the beach in its first proposed zoning, but this early concession would be whittled away over the years.

The committee's maps represented sections devoted to different activities: net drying, careening, and passages for bathers. Their clean black lines are reminiscent of the hydrographic maps of the *passes*-improvers: a fantasized orderliness, a tool for planning, for projecting into the future—very different from the chaotic, peopled, changing space that we know the beach to have been. Controlling the strips allocated to net drying and boat repairs, which were indispensable to the survival of the artisanal industry, would prove a difficult task. Many families continued to work for themselves, even after fleets of steam trawlers were introduced to Arcachon in the 1860s. Unlike Johnston's trawler business, which was concentrated around a privately financed jetty and sheds at the eastern end of the beach, away from vacationers' villas, the artisanal fishing people spread themselves around the bay's beaches, invoking Colbert's 1681 edict that declared the maritime domain available to all—just as they had done when the prés salés were threatened.

The local fishermen's tendency to prefer independence over employment with the new trawler fleets might help explain Johnston's antipathy toward the artisanal fishing community who persisted in using the sand as a work space. While Urbain argues that the industrialization of fishing was an important factor in the disappearance of fishing communities from the beach-es, in this region there was no sudden rush for the fisheries.[39] Bassin families preferred mostly to work independently; many took up oyster farming and appropriated of sections of mud flats for this purpose, which contributed to the spreading of productive activities around the bay rather than their concentration.

Back in 1866 the writer of the *Notice sur la pêche* had noted that the organization of artisanal fishing in La Teste was favorable to the majority, "for more than half of the fishermen have the quality and the benefits of owners

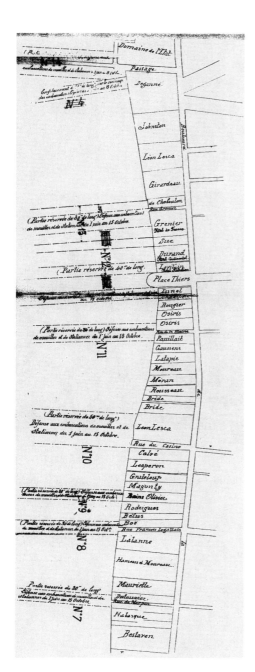

FIG. 15. A fantasised orderliness: one of many attempts to divide the Arcachon shore into zones for fishing work and bathing. Johnston's foreshore property is situated just south of a careening zone. Detail from Ponts et Chaussées division of the Arcachon beach, 31 August, 1893. © Archives Départementales de la Gironde, AD 33, SP 2865 (formerly at 3 S/Cô 17).

320 — ARCACHON-SAINT-FERDINAND - *Pêcheries de l'Océan*   M. D.

FIG. 16. Industrial fishing on the Bassin: the Pêcheries de l'Océan. Collection of Richard Lahaye.

[*patrons*] . . . out of 1180 registered, 629 live in their own home, and 362 own small parcels of grapevines, wheat fields, meadows or pine plantations."[40] This independence survived the expansion (and decline) of industrialized fishing over the ensuing decade.

René Pérotin, who wrote a book about Arcachon steam trawling in 1911, noted that only half of the 320 sailors working on the trawlers were locals.[41] The other half were Bretons and northerners who had settled in the area for this work. Pérotin likened steam trawlers to factories, while René Rougerie, a local writer, thought that "the world of trawlers has always been seen as an antagonist on the Bassin, even a threat to small scale artisanal fishing on the bay."[42] According to Pérotin, the local fisherman who chose to work on the trawlers did so to survive: "not because he likes it, for nearly all prefer the liberty and the independence they enjoy on their *pinasses,* even though they are not the owners, but sardines do not turn up every day and one has to make a living."[43]

A very different picture of artisanal fishing was painted nearly fifty years later by a professor at the Maritime Institute, one that Johnston would probably have endorsed. For Marcel Hérubel, writing in 1911, the deprived "small-time fishermen" were "attached by routine and misery to the scrap of ocean where their fathers struggled, to the same antiquated techniques." They were weighed down by "the tyranny of the past," condemned to work the same patch, "unceasingly scouring and re-scouring, for a slice of bread, the same fishing grounds with *finer and finer nets*—like the *chevrette* net—creating each year a deeper desert."[44] Hérubel argued that the answer to this disastrous situation lay in intensive fishing by large steam-powered trawlers. Arcachon was to become the second most important fishing port in France by 1911, but the industrialization process was slower than Urbain has suggested, for it required the conversion into employees of fiercely independent fishermen and women. By continuing to work independently, they had the freedom to pick up extra work servicing bathers, looking after yachts, and guarding oyster farms.[45] Johnston would have to put up with the careening zone on the beach below his villa for some time.

In the decade following the Société Immobilière's complaint about fishing paraphernalia below the Grand Hotel, the council continued to pressure the fishing community to make way for bathers. Johnston and the board of the Société Immobilière had argued in 1873 that the fishermen working below the Grand Hotel would not be disadvantaged by their removal to another site, but a petition from those targeted by the campaign suggests otherwise. In 1883, thirty fishermen appealed to the minister for the navy and colonies, reporting that their pickets had been removed to another part of the beach, only to be rejected a second time, by a different group of proprietors. The petitioners explained that nets must be dried immediately upon the fishing boats' return, for if they were left to sit, damp and warm, they would decay. Some had fishing material worth several thousand francs—"their only possession"—and fishing was "their only means of existence," providing "daily bread to nearly all the households of this coast." Should they be prevented from maintaining their material, they would "lose what they have painfully acquired and be deprived of work (the only kind they know) and in consequence be exposed to the most pressing need."[46]

For the petitioners, the measures against net drying showed that the councillors cared more about potential revenue from visitors than about the well-being of the local fishing community. This perception had been expressed humorously back in 1880 in the satirical paper *Le Détroqueur*. In a scathing attack on the priorities of Arcachon's administrators, *Le Détroqueur* had published a "fanciful record" of the newly elected council's first meeting, containing a hilarious scenario in which Dr. Hameau, the mayor and so-called "General of the Jesuits"—a hypocrite, according to the discourse of the time—proposed that the council chop down the pine forest, drain the Bassin, and build a huge casino in its place.[47] According to the playful script, Hameau invited his colleagues to consider the disasters suffered by "our seafaring families . . . The tempest, the horrible tempest, causes great damage here. It is unfortunately impossible to fight it; but, thanks be to God, there is one element we can fight, that is, water. Thus I propose that we buy a pump to drain all the water from the Bassin."

Marcel Dubos, a councillor described as an "oyster banker," replied: "That would necessitate a pump . . . a pump . . . a steam pump!" while Dignac, "stand-in" (*bouche-trou* or, literally, "hole filler"), cried: "But you are encroaching on the prerogatives of the navy, and I, old alligator as they call me, cannot allow the Bassin to be dried out." Councillor Millien added: "And my whaling boat [*baleinière*]?"[48] Hameau appeased them by declaring that all these "small inconveniences" would be outweighed by the money to be earned from all the fish that would be left flapping on the floor of the emptied Bassin, as well as the revenue from the "immense casino" that they would build once they had filled the enormous hole with sand from the surrounding dunes.[49] Even though the imagined meeting was a farce, the underlying message was clear: the councillors would rise above their personal differences and sacrifice the future of the Bassin and its people for short-term financial gain.

And yet, there is evidence that the fishing community and some bathing entrepreneurs found ways to accommodate each other's needs—at least when they came from a similar socioeconomic background. For it was not only oyster farmers and net dryers who were seen by administrators to be ruining the beach but also managers of baths for a lower-class clientele. In April 1885, a maritime services engineer, with the support of the mayor, Jean Méran, refused the application of Marie Lacaze, retired haberdasher, for the renewal of her family's concession for the hot and cold baths on the Arcachon beach. The concession had been granted to her father, Gérard Lacaze, in 1850, before Arcachon's separation from La Teste, and had been managed after M. Lacaze's death by Marie's brother-in-law M. Ramond, until he too died in 1884. The engineer noted that a new concession, rather than a simple renewal, would be required since the bathing establishment had been swept away by a storm the month before Mme. Lacaze's application. The mayor did not favor any new concessions on the Arcachon beach, and both the engineer and his superior agreed with him, arguing that the baths in question had been situated on the section of beach "most popular with bathers"—between the Grand Hotel and the new Place Thiers—and had thus "created a certain obstacle to circulation." Moreover, "their primitive mode of construction contrasted disagreeably with the neighboring villas."

The storm's fortuitous destruction of the baths meant that this eyesore would no longer confront visitors. Indeed, the engineer noted, "They [the baths] had only been retained out of consideration for the unhappy situation of the Ramond family."[50] The family, beset by financial problems, was also burdened by their ailing mother, who was suffering from dementia and monomania. A doctor's certificate from April 1883 reported: "her current monomania is suicide, she seeks constantly to leave the house and throw herself in the Bassin or in a well near the house; she cannot be left for an instant."[51]

The Lacaze baths may have been of "unsightly appearance," and their owners an unfortunate burden on the commune, but the fishing community appreciated them. In a letter to the prefect on 29 March 1885, Mme. Sentout (née Ramond), requesting permission to rebuild the destroyed baths, attached a petition signed by "numerous local inhabitants and sailors." According to Mme. Sentout, they were grateful to her for allowing them to store their nets free of charge and acknowledged the "great service" her establishment offered "to those imprudent people straying too far from the shore," to whom she supplied, "for no cost at all, all the special, essential and indispensable medicines for restoring them to life."[52] The petition, signed by more than fifty individuals, asked that the baths, which acted to stabilize the beach and provided shelter for the fishermen, be rebuilt.

We see here that cooperation was possible between the operators of a bathing establishment and the local fishing community. But the incorporation of the Lacaze Ramond baths into the fishing work space meant that they did not fit easily with the vision for the resort held dear by Arcachon's more influential promoters. Back in 1865, Ramond had also managed floating hot baths on the La Teste prés salés, and in a letter to the prefect he acknowledged that they served a working-class clientele; it is possible that his Arcachon establishment attracted the same class of bather, which may have contributed to its poor reputation with the new resort's administrators.[53] Remember that Pierre Lallegrand's pontoon boat—the one in whose shade sat a group of women whom Mauriac implied were prostitutes—had been beached just near the Ramond baths.

Despite the prefectorial committee's regular pronouncements concerning the zoning of the Arcachon shore, the problem of coexistence was still unresolved in the 1890s. The situation had worsened since the 1870s, as the beach had diminished in size, the sand slowly disappearing. This led to an intensification of the spatial conflict. In June 1892 a petition was signed by fifty-four inhabitants of the Eyrac quarter (evidently not members of the fishing community) who requested the removal from the maritime domain of huts and surrounding debris from oyster farms, which made it difficult for property owners to rent out their villas "because of the stench in this location and the huts' ugly appearance."[54] And earlier that month, café owner Repetto's request to the council for permission to place a tent and tables on the footpath near the beach was refused because it was already "invaded by all sorts of displays of merchandise, giving the town, which ought to be clean and elegant, the appearance of an outer suburb [banlieue]. This is very unpleasant for visitors."[55]

An Arcachon councillor in 1891 complained that oyster sellers were "invading" the beach, and in the same meeting it was suggested that the pontoons from which oyster farmers sold their products be obliged to remain afloat and at least ten meters (eleven yards) from the "dry sand" between 15 June and 15 October.[56] In 1894, a councillor asked "to whom the policing of the beach fell? For he considers that it is carried out by no-one."[57] Johnston shared this concern. In September 1895 he wrote a letter to the prefect in which he queried the effectiveness of the policing of the beaches. By this stage the beach had diminished to such an extent that the only strip of sand remaining lay between the Eyrac jetty and the Hôtel de France, roughly two hundred meters (220 yards) long. The western half of this zone was reserved for bathers, the area in front of Johnston's property for careening, and the stretch outside the château next door for the hanging of nets. "Movement," he complained, "is in consequence rendered completely impossible in that portion, and is greatly restricted in front of my chalet." It seems that a two-meter strip of the château's retaining wall was being used for the disposal of rubbish, whose "miasmas" were infecting the quarter. No doubt the late summer heat enriched the stench.

Johnston argued that the position of the careening zone reduced the value of his property. In 1891 he had made a similar complaint: the constant whistle-blowing of passing passenger steamers was driving him crazy. "This noise," he grumbled, "makes living alongside the Beach intolerable, and is detrimental to the properties close to the jetty."[58] Four months earlier, in a proposal for the regulation of the port, the maritime services engineers had included an article forbidding "steamboats servicing the public or other [groups], from whistling, unless to announce their departure or arrival . . . To this effect a single whistle blow of 4 to 5 seconds at the most is authorized. All other whistle blowing is prohibited, except in case of danger or absolute necessity during the trip." They also forbade "cannon shots or lighting firecrackers on leisure boats . . . outside of festive days (regattas, races, etc.) or public celebrations."[59] Tourism was a noisy business. But beach work was worse.

In his 1895 letter against the careening zone, Johnston declared that it had become "unbearable" to stay in his chalet, "due to the noise of hammers and so on which begin at dawn and continue unceasingly until sunset." Adding insult to injury, his access to the beach was "blocked" by boats being repaired on the sand. Could it be that some of the fishermen repairing their boats below his villa whacked their hammers especially hard when they saw Johnston, the father of industrialized fishing, emerge onto his terrace on a fine morning? His letters certainly offer us an aural seascape different from the one described in the guide books. Johnston wished for a separation between his work space—the fisheries some half a kilometer to the east of his property—and his holiday home. But he had built his villa on the edge of someone else's work space.

Johnston's concerns were exacerbated by the reduction in the surface area available to bathers. In his 1895 letter he took up the case of bathers living "within the town," who came to the beach "in great numbers, only to leave very quickly due to the inconveniences." He thought they deserved "some satisfaction." The noise and the obstacles to promenading were not all that

bothered him: water from the sewers was running straight onto the beach because pipes had broken. Johnston expressed concern for the future of the resort should these problems not be rectified, as the number of visitors appeared to be dropping already.[60]

In September 1892, an Arcachon councillor observed that the beach,
which had "contributed so much" to the town's development, was "on the
verge of completely disappearing." He found it "painful" to declare that despite expensive defensive work to rebuild the beach, "that goal has not been
achieved."[61] The diminution of the sand brought beach workers and bathers
into even closer proximity. So the conflict over the net-drying zone continued into the next century. In 1902, the deputy mayor of Arcachon wrote to
the prefect complaining that "due to the degradation of the beach, the only
part still accessible to the public in the center of town, at high tide, is in
front of the château and the Aquarium, that is, within the port. Now, below
the château there is a forest of pickets upon which fishing nets are always
hanging." He made a series of proposals for the removal of the nets to other
sections of the beach, but none of them was satisfactory. Not only would the
net dryers get in the way of bathers, but fishermen and -women from one
commune would be pushed into zones recognized as the domain of sea
workers from other Bassin communes.[62]

The deputy mayor seeking to resolve the net question admitted that some
fishermen might be inconvenienced by the greater distance from their usual
place of disembarkation, but, he argued with impressive *sangfroid:* "you will
consider as I do, Monsieur le Préfet, that the interests of *a few individuals*
must bow to the *general interest.*"[63] In other words, the fishing community
was now considered to be a minority group: its members had become the in-
vaders of their own territory. They might be locals with ancient claims to the
beach based on recognition of the maritime domain and the rights of sailors
registered with the navy, but the visitors outnumbered them.

In 1905, the Chamber of Commerce in Bordeaux heard a report on the division of the Arcachon port: the increase in numbers of people visiting the
beach in front of the Deganne Château—now the municipal casino—had led
the council to request that between 1 July and 1 October, this zone be "abandoned completely to the public"—that is, kept free of nets. The Chamber
supported the proposal.[64] So, on paper, Arcachon belonged to the newcomers, for the summer months at least.

We must be wary, though, of reading the anti-beachwork campaign as expressive of a desire to rid the commune of the fishermen and -women's presence. Guidebooks always included fishermen and -women in their list of in-

teresting features of the Bassin; offered descriptions of the fishing methods practiced on the Bassin; and outlined the history of oyster farming, citing the impressive numbers of oysters grown and exported. They often suggested that visitors observe fishermen at work—night "flame" fishing was a popular spectacle—but while the presence of the local sea workers was woven into the tapestry of the colorful bathing scene, they were by no means the central figures on the sand: the beach was figured primarily as a space given over to bathers and watchers.[65]

CHAPTER NINE

A Magnificent Panorama

*No doubt [visitors] find [Arcachon's] position very beautiful, but they cannot
find a place to stop and contemplate it[;] they are obliged to undertake an unbearable
march in the overpowering heat, over moving sands or across wet sea grasses.*

—Baron Michel, "Projet d'un établissement de Bains-promenade," 24 October 1882

In a postcard of Arcachon entitled *La jetée devant le Casino* (the jetty in front
of the casino), we see a scene worthy of the panoramas that were so popular in
Paris at the end of the nineteenth century (see fig. 17). Men in straw boaters
and women in swishing white skirts lean over the jetty railings to watch the
activity on the water below them. In the foreground, on the water, three
pinasses prepare for an outing. In one boat, manned by two sailors in soft
caps, a tiny dinghy full of empty baskets fits snugly into one end; a small
party of vacationers, protected by hats and a parasol, perches at the far end,
the women's backs turned to the viewer (and to the boatmen). While the
people on the jetty peer down at the boats below, some of the boatmen look
back up at them. And rearing up behind the crowded jetty is the spectacular,
turreted beachfront casino converted from the Chateau Deganne in 1903—
Archacon's second casino. The photographer has composed the picture so
that the jetty creates a strong line from the lower right corner to the center of
the frame, drawing the eye deep into the picture.[1]

FIG. 17. The Eyrac jetty, near the Deganne casino. Collection of Richard Lahaye.

Performances, carefully framed, were essential to the culture of the seaside resort and involved actors from all walks of life: not only official entertainers at the casino and the fishing community but also vacationers and invalids themselves. While visitors to the beach spoke of "views" and "scenes," they too were part of the scene: They behaved according to certain social expectations, wore appropriate clothes, walked or bathed at appropriate hours; they *showed* themselves to other visitors. And what better platform for this display than the jetty-promenade, that indispensable feature of seaside resorts?

The pleasures of looking and being looked at were perfected on and around this structure, for it acted as both auditorium and stage. From this vantage–point on the jetty, one could look out at the natural grandeur of the Bassin, at fishing activities, or at organized regattas and also *back toward the shore*. That is, the structure that jutted out over the water enabled the viewer to observe the beach and the foreshore as though they too were stages. And the jetty itself provided an ideal platform on which the promenader could show him- or herself to advantage, to be observed by those sitting on hired chairs on the beach. In this way, multiple gazes intersected with each other. This was a true panorama: one could look in any direction and be entertained by an ever-changing spectacle. As Dominique Rouillard notes, the roles of spectator and actor became one: each person was an "observed spectator," or watched watcher.[2]

Arcachon has three jetties: (1) the Eyrac, built between 1843 and 1845, destroyed by a storm in 1882 and rebuilt in 1898, (2) the grander and more solid Thiers jetty-promenade, opened in 1903, and (3) the modest Chapelle jetty, below the then-much-visited Notre Dame church. At one time there was a fourth, the Legallais, which failed to survive rough weather. The Eyrac jetty— built before Arcachon's separation from La Teste and on the heels of the railway line—was an important development for the nascent bathing resort. It was built close to the first "center" of what would later become Arcachon; that is, where the earliest bathing houses had sprung up. In 1847, the La Teste council credited the jetty and the bathing establishments with "having brought movement and life to this point of the Bassin's shores, and consequently a complete change to the state of the area, a change born of progress and which tends more and more to improve the well-being of our region."[3] The jetty, used for both embarking and disembarking passengers and goods from boats *and* as a promenade, seemed to act as a magnet. Even after the opening of the Thiers jetty-promenade, the Eyrac, situated alongside the Deganne Château-turned-casino, continued to draw a crowd.

While the Eyrac jetty remained a popular destination for promenaders, the new Thiers jetty, opened in 1903, was more impressive. It was built to extend outward from the existing Place Thiers, a public square on the beachfront; a postcard of the Place shows its use as a viewing platform (see fig. 18). Like the Eyrac, this jetty serviced passenger boats, but above all it provided a promenading destination. *La Place Thiers* is a study of backs: backs of well-dressed visitors, skirts topped by striped and plain parasols, their owners peering over the parapet at the world of the beach, which is obscured by the viewers whom we (the postcard readers) are viewing. A triangular movement is established with the bulking of figures in the left-hand corner and the line of foreshore hotels and villas leading toward the center of the frame.[4]

Postcards show that the built-up foreshore was a key element of the view from the jetty. It was both auditorium and backdrop, for the villa owners and hotel residents looked out from their windows and balconies at the theater below them, while promenaders looked back. The history of the jetties reveals the processes of set design and casting that lay behind the seaside spectacle as it appeared in promotional imagery. Although the Thiers jetty—known as the "jetty-promenade" to distinguish it from the more prosaic Eyrac "landing stage" (*débarcadère*)—was not built until 1901–03, similar structures had been proposed for Arcachon by private entrepreneurs as early as the 1880s. An examination of some of these proposals lends insight into what the jetty—and the beach it overlooked—represented at this time.

The earliest proposal documented in the departmental archives was by the Paris-based Baron Michel (Raymond-Laurent-Victor), whose self-reported credentials included chevalier of the Legion of Honour, retired navy lieutenant, and treasurer-paymaster.[5] In 1881, he requested the concession of an area of the Bassin for the creation of a bathing establishment and of a strip (100 by 15 meters [109 by 16 yards]) for a jetty-promenade, which would link the baths to the beach.[6] In October 1882 he submitted a description of the project and an extraordinary drawing of the proposed structure (see fig. 19). It is, in effect, a postcard of an *imaginary* Arcachon.

To understand the scale of and vision behind the Baron's project, which might otherwise seem excessive, we need to take into account architectural precedents in Arcachon, as well as parallels with British developments. In Britain, supervised medicinal bathing and the development of an "architecture of pleasure" predated continental efforts by decades.[7] A boom in pier building began there in the 1860s and continued until the turn of the century. In his social history of the English seaside resort, John Walton considers that Brighton's Palace Pier with its "golden oriental domes and delicate filigree ironwork arches" marked "the apotheosis of the pleasure pier."[8] Arcachon's architecture echoed the playful styles emerging across the Channel.

FIG. 18. La Place Thiers. Collection of Richard Lahaye.

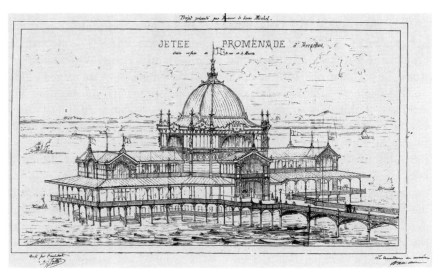

FIG. 19. Baron Michel's jetty-promenade proposal, 1882. © Archives Départementales de la Gironde, AD 33, SP 957 (previously at S non coté Domaine Maritime 14).

The architects of Arcachon's Ville d'hiver and associated buildings, financed by the Pereire brothers' Société Immobilière, preferred the exotic and
the ornate, in line with prevailing fashions. A prime example is the extraordinary Casino Mauresque (Moorish casino), which opened in 1863. De Gabory,
in his 1896 *Guide d'Arcachon*, described this "monument" in its four-hectare
(ten-acre) park as "a mixture of the Alhambra of Granada and the Cordoba
mosque . . . bathed in the perfume of exotic flowers, hanging like the [Baby-
lonian] gardens of Sémiramis and with the alluring beauty of those of the
Armide." The extravagantly ornamented, richly colored casino evoked "the
dreamy fantasy of the Orient."[9]

De Gabory enumerated the casino's many features, including "Arabic and
Sarrasin decor" and "Islamic enamel and earthenware tiles."[10] These features
evoked the baths so often depicted in nineteenth-century Orientalist art-
works, a national obsession since 1830 when France invaded Algeria. The
casino's decor also reinforced the sense of being elsewhere, on vacation. The
architect of this wonder was Paul Regnauld, also responsible for the solid
Grand Hotel on the beachfront and the impressive, though less financially
successful, four-story Chinese buffet restaurant, opened in the summer of
1864 close to the railway station and (unfortunately for us) demolished in
1882. *Le Journal d'Arcachon* hailed Regnauld as a "great magician, who has
managed to transport the Alhambra into our desert [*landes*]."[11] The villas in
the Ville d'hiver, of which the first twenty-two, financed by the Société Immobilière, were built under Regnauld's direction between 1862 and 1864, also
made playful reference to architectural styles from other lands and periods; in
this way they were personalized for their wealthy winter tenants. They were
nevertheless built using the most up-to-date processes and materials; many of
them were partially prefabricated and transported to Arcachon on the recently extended railway line.[12]

Buildings like these offered a vision of an exotic paradise while providing
modern comforts and entertainment as well as the familiarity of one's own
customs, domestic and social. According to Jean-Didier Urbain, architectural
fantasies like those in the Ville d'hiver signified a "rupture with the rest of the
world . . . the demarcation of a separate universe."[13] This mixture of the "exotic"—an eternally popular theme among writers describing Arcachon, from
Jacques Arago in 1828 to Paul Joanne in 1908—and the modern, was integral
to the success of the resort.[14] Visitors wanted to feel distant from the familiar
and mundane and yet have their preoccupation with health and convenience
catered to. In this time of startling technological developments in transport,
energy sources, and communications, advertisements for Arcachon hotels

172 ARCACHON. — Le Casino Mauresque.

FIG. 20. Casino Mauresque (Moorish Casino). Collection of Richard Lahaye.

in Joanne's 1908 guide combined descriptions of each establishment's position and view with lists of modern conveniences such as "Heated bathrooms, Electric lighting, Lift."[15]

Baron Michel's project, which might otherwise seem preposterous in its size and opulence, makes sense in this context. The 1882 drawing of the complex is a stunning image of a magical palace hovering over the water (see fig. 19). An enormous dome tops three floors of glass and iron galleries. A two-storey-high archway with iron filigree work greets the promenader, and flags fly at every corner of the building, proclaiming its importance to sailing vessels—a nautical attraction the draftsman has taken care to depict, along with a sky studded with clouds and the distant outline of the north coast of the Bassin. The Baron's 1881 blueprint included a café-bar, games room, ladies' room, ballroom (*Salle des Fêtes*) with a stage at one end, and reading and conversation rooms. These various entertainment settings followed the example set by spa towns and casinos, with the added attraction of the structure being placed over the sea.[16]

The Baron's project description makes it very clear that although all visitors to the Bassin might enjoy *looking* at this establishment from the vantage point of the jetty-promenade or the beach, it would not be open to everyone. This project was aimed at well-to-do bathers who could not bring themselves to use the bathing cabins on the beach but did not have the means or the time to rent a private foreshore villa. As long as a suitable bathing establishment was lacking, he wrote, "in order to put on their bathing costume, they are obliged to venture into alleys which are often unclean and poorly kept, and to enclose themselves in cramped, difficult-to-close cabins, whose flimsy adjoining walls [*mitoyenneté*] are particularly embarrassing for the ladies"—cabins he likened to "a slab in the morgue." Although such visitors might find Arcachon beautiful, he said, they were frustrated by the lack of a place where they could stop and contemplate its admirable position and attractions; instead "they must undertake a wearying march across moving sands or wet seaweed." The overall effect, he argued, was "deplorable," and better-class visitors were staying away from Arcachon: the proof lay in the absence of grand hotels (perhaps Arcachon's Grand Hotel did not measure up to his high standards?) and of "the rich outfits [*toilettes*] and pretty society, which are the ornament and animation of other bathing resorts." Rich families vacationing on the Bassin tended to stay in their "magnificent villas," rarely showing themselves in public.[17]

François Mauriac wrote of these villa owners in his 1921 novel *Préséances*. He described the "ladies" from Bordeaux's great families, who "live in their square meter of garden, exchanging measured greetings across common walls." Their villas overlook the Bassin, whose waves "attack" the beach and terraces. Mauriac also described Sundays when "*trains de plaisir* unleash a public, beaming at first, but soon in despair due to the absence of beach and because the villas lined up as if for battle confiscate the sea in favor of 'the best circles' [*ce monde-là*]. People have spent a whole day in Gravette [Arcachon], without so much as seeing the crest of a wave."[18]

The end result? What remained of the beach was given over to people whom the Baron Michel called a "second-rate public, which spends little, makes a lot of noise, and whose free manners hasten the departure of misled tourists."[19] This is a very different picture from that offered in postcards, which, of course, could never represent the aural dimension of the beach experience. The Baron also claimed that the sand was littered with broken tiles (from the oyster farms) and shards of plates and bottles (probably from all those self-catering day-trippers).

Whereas Mayor de Thury's complaints of the early 1860s had focused on the oyster farmers as the source of trouble, the Baron targeted lower-class bathers. The Baron's mission was to provide the hitherto ignored, "better-class" visitors with an *elegant* meeting place, where they could bathe in clean and secure surroundings, and from which they might "contemplate the magnificent panorama of the Bassin and the town." Entry to the pier after 11 A.M. would cost fifty centimes, and another fifty centimes would be charged for the use of bathing cabins, thereby keeping out the rabble at prime bathing and promenading hours. The beach adjoining the jetty would be clean and well-lit, so that "honest families" could enjoy the Bassin after sunset.[20]

The Baron emphasized repeatedly the importance of creating a refuge away from the "crush"—the "crowd" and the "filth" on the beach. His project was, in essence, to create an *alternative* space, a replacement for the beach, which would provide the same—and more—benefits (sea water, a view, a meeting place) but without the inconveniences of mixing with people of other classes, the element of the unexpected, or the confrontation with unkempt nature (sand, seaweed) that so bothered him. This was his imaginary Arcachon: his idealized representation of a space whose "lived" characteristics horrified him.

In addition to catering to a "better-class" bathing clientele, the Baron claimed to address other, local needs in his project description. First, he argued that the jetty-promenade would help stabilize the beach, a matter of great concern to town promoters who were witnessing the gradual disappearance of the sand over this period. The jetty, he said, would break the current responsible for removing the sand, and the beach would be restored to its "original limits." This, he claimed, was the most significant justification for the utility of the project.

His second claim to public utility was the availability of the jetty to Bassin excursionists, sailors, and oyster farmers for a landing stage and (temporary) mooring—for a fee. He noted that the provision of "unsinkable" water safety-craft belonging to the Société de Secours des Naufragés would prevent drownings, and that two electric lights would also be attached to the jetty, to guide sailors "on dark and misty nights," an offer guaranteed to enthuse "the numerous and courageous seafaring population which spends its laborious existence on the difficult work of oyster farming and fishing." So, the Baron was aware that he would need to accommodate the wishes of the local population; his imaginary Arcachon was not entirely divorced from reality.[21]

However, the Baron's demand that the municipality accord him a number of "privileges," including the provision of twenty promenading boats and a double steamer service, the prohibition of chair- and cabin-hiring tents on the beach, and the undertaking not to grant any bathing cabin concessions within a zone of 600 meters (656 yards), might be seen as a threat to some local businesses.[22] The council must have found his demands excessive, for his project never saw the light. He also had competition.

At about the same time as the Baron, an engineer named John Lawson proposed an iron jetty 140 meters (153 yards) long, ending with a platform measuring 32 by 16 (eventually 32) meters (35 by 17.5 yards), which would hold a café-restaurant, a reading room, and a tobacconist's "&a &a."—this last unspecified possibility causing consternation among local traders. The plans accompanying his concession request in July 1882 were more modest than the Baron's and more convincing from a technical point of view. No bathing establishment was proposed, and the buildings on the jetty and platform were much smaller and simpler. In the early 1890s, proposals for a jetty-promenade with casino attached would also be made by a M. G. de St. Clair, and then by Brisson and Delamare and Company.[23]

In June 1883, a public inquiry into Lawson's proposal was overseen by Léon Lesca, regional councillor (*conseiller général*) and cofounder with Harry Scott Johnston of the first steam-trawler company in 1866. In fact, Johnston was the first resident to support Lawson's jetty proposal, declaring himself in favor of this "necessary complement of a bathing resort as significant as ours." He noted its appeal for those visitors not lucky enough to own a villa on the foreshore: it would provide much-desired relief from the "great heat" of the summer season. Johnston's approval was echoed in a statement signed by 291 supporters of the pier project.

But 261 signatures appeared on a petition *against* the Lawson project, which argued that the commercial center of Arcachon would be displaced, established businesses in town deprived of income, and some boat operators ruined by Lawson's monopoly. The jetty-promenade would benefit only "several new identities" (i.e., outsiders) to the detriment of locals who had "acquired ancient rights."[24] Once again, we see that various groups within the community understood Arcachon in different ways. The disagreement over what constituted the town's center—a common refrain that also emerged during discussions about a proposed tramway over the same period—arose out of a particular spatial conception of Arcachon, a sense of where activity was concentrated and how that determined the distribution of economic power within the town. The prejudice against outsiders proposing to transform the lived space was nothing new. And the jetty would effectively create a *new* space, by extending out over the water; its developer would have an unfair advantage over those confined to the existing, limited thoroughfares on dry land.

Although Lesca defended Lawson's proposal, claiming that it would stimulate business, offer fresh air and an "attractive spectacle with the Bassin on one side and the magnificent façade of the Casino Mauresque on the other," and provide a safer embarkation than the current system of locals' carrying visitors on their backs through the shallows (a practice described in the earliest guidebooks to La Teste and still the norm fifty years later), Lawson's jetty never eventuated.[25] In the summer of 1892 he withdrew his application, claiming that similar projects in other parts of France, including Nice (where a grandiose jetty-promenade had been built), had not generated the anticipated profits.[26] None of the other privately sponsored projects saw the light either. By December 1899, though, the municipality considered a second jetty indispensable to prevent further beach erosion. The mayor pointed out that for people living within the town and for day-trippers, "at high tide, they can only go to see the Bassin from Place Thiers or the Eyrac jetty; this last is thus so encumbered that the embarkation and disembarkation of tourists on the Cap-Ferret steamers is becoming difficult, if not impossible."[27]

In the end, the Thiers jetty was built with municipal and government funds, with neither casino nor bathing establishment attached. It was a simple jetty, used for promenades and the embarkation and disembarkation of (mainly) pleasure boats. But the failed proposals reveal something about the way Arcachon was imagined in the 1880s and 1890s. The beach—now overpopulated, poorly maintained, and diminishing in size through erosion—no longer satisfied visitors who wished to breathe fresh air and show themselves to advantage. Overcrowding ruined sight lines: performances

154.- ARCACHON.- Côte d'Argent. - Grosse Mer - BR - 2644-

FIG. 21. Arcachon, Côte d'Argent, Heavy Sea. Collection Jacques Clémens. Editions Alan Sutton, 1997. Reproduced with permission.

FIG. 22. Effect of waves on the jetty-promenade. Collection of the author.

could not be read from within a crush of bodies. And bodies were not the
only eyesore—their coverings were also offensive: in December 1898, the
council prohibited cabin hirers from hanging their bathing costumes and
towels out to dry along the road.[28] One could no longer be sure that the
beach was a healthful site; it was difficult to control and distressingly popular.
The air one breathed there was mingled with the smells of other bodies and of
rotting seaweed and fishy nets. So the jetty was promoted as an alternative
space to the beach. By standing *over* the sea, and away from the beach, one
obtained direct, unpolluted access to the briny air. Resort doctors, who put
into practice the climatological (and more specifically climatotherapeutic)
discourses that flourished under the Third Republic, encouraged this search
for atmospheric purity.[29]

The jetty, then, was an essential element in the theater of the seaside resort—a kind of proscenium, transcending the ugliness of everyday life and offering the tantalizing possibility of another world. The councillors and investors were this theater's front-of-house managers and production designers,
but the ad hoc nature of development and the uncontrollable impulses of real
people prevented them from creating a completely satisfying tableau.

Of course, the jetty was much more than a stage. The jetty-building impulse expressed a desire to extend the land beyond its natural boundaries, to
cheat nature: it was an act of defiance against strong seas, currents, and winds.
This challenge was represented in the many postcards that show jetties with-
standing storms: waves crashing against their pylons, threatening to engulf
these ambitious man-made structures. This time it was nature's turn to perform. In a postcard captioned "Grosse Mer" (Heavy Sea, fig. 21), foreshore villas and the Thiers jetty are under watery siege, and no one is about. But the
villa windows are like eyes that look out over the threatening waves, and the
walls that frame them are unperturbed. Another postcard labeled "Effet de
vagues sur la jetée-promenade" (Effect of waves on the jetty-promenade, fig.
22), taken from the seaweed-strewn beach, reveals the deserted jetty against a
hand-tinted pink horizon, a great jet of white water hitting its flanks. The gas
lamps stand tall, and in the background, we can just make out a sail. Although
humans are absent from the scene, their creations survive this assault by the elements. If the sea cannot be "suspended," it can at least be challenged.

CHAPTER TEN

Posing for Posterity

*These days, cities and villages are changing unceasingly. Old picturesque houses
are being replaced by barracks. . . . We believe, then, that the view cards in collectors' albums
will fix in our memory these things which will no longer exist in twenty years.*

—Interview with Humblot, postcard publisher, in *Le Figaro Illustré,* 1904

Arcachon was a new town situated on old territory, and its identity, never quite stable, needed to be shaped and re-shaped to ensure its continued appeal to the visitors who had become the mainstay of the local economy. Promoters needed to tap into existing and emerging discourses of health, leisure, nature, and (familiar) otherness. One way to create an identity for Arcachon, as we saw in chapter 9, was to represent it pictorially, in postcards, guidebook illustrations, and posters. Illustrators and photographers working for postcard manufacturers relied on the compositional approaches of established art schools—that is, on a readily identifiable pictorial vocabulary. In this way, the particularity of a place could be framed by recognizable aesthetic conventions: the potential visitor would know what to expect.[1]

Postcards capture the performances that were so central to the life of a beach resort. When aware of the photographer, the people who appear on these small, captioned squares of cardboard are presenting themselves to the viewer, performing themselves or their "part." We can see the acting out of "tradition" by locals, the performing of rituals of sociability by visitors, and the conscious design, or at least framing, of backdrops by promoters and administrators. Postcard manufacturers were offering recommended views, signs of "*here*ness," or exotica for the tourist gaze. If we examine some of these moments, most of them consciously posed, we might reach behind the surface to find the movements and meetings, and occasionally conflicts, played out both on- and off-stage.

At the turn of the century, postcards were a novel and popular means of representation and communication. They first appeared in France during the 1870 war with Prussia, as a means of sending open letters to Paris from besieged Strasbourg by balloon, and were legally recognized in 1872, with the administration of the Third Republic reserving for itself the monopoly on production. But it was not until the Universal Exposition of 1889, with the launch of the first illustrated postcard depicting the Eiffel Tower, that the postcard came into its own. Three hundred thousand of these were printed, and they were sold on the first floor of the Tower during the Exposition. New developments over this period in photographic and printing techniques—in particular phototype—meant that images could be mass-produced and offered cheaply to an enthusiastic public. The increasing geographical mobility of the population, for tourism and work, and the improved organization of the postal system also contributed to the rise of the postcard, which was quick to write, cheap to send, and collectible. It has been estimated that, by 1907, between three hundred million and six hundred million postcards were being produced in France every year—an extraordinary number for a country of just under forty million people.[2]

Postcards presented an encyclopedic vision of the changing nation. Photographers, both publishers' employees sent into the field and freelancers seeking commissions, sought to capture the contemporary world in all its manifestations, as well as aspects of what was seen as "traditional" life—fragile and thus requiring documentation. They were also, quite literally, souvenirs for the French public, in an era before the advent of amateur photography. We have access, then, to a wide range of images of Arcachon, a close analysis of which can reveal the way people looked at this place and its people—the nature of the "tourist gaze," to use John Urry's expression. Postcard imagery fed the visitor's anticipation of what to expect from Arcachon and expressed an idea of what was worth communicating to others about this place.[3] The visitors' expectations necessarily affected their likely relationship to the Arcachon—the *lived* Arcachon—that this book has tried to reconstruct through other sources.

Local fishermen and -women, and especially oyster farmers, appeared with great regularity on postcards of Arcachon. Given that this book seeks to reveal the experience of local people and how they saw themselves represented by outsiders, this chapter begins with an analysis of some postcards depicting them and their work. Although we are looking through the lens of an outsider/photographer, a critical and contextualized interpretation is still possible: a turning backward of the gaze, toward the maker of the image and toward imagined or possible readers (including ourselves).

Postcards were made and bought for many different markets—not solely for tourists. In many cases, people bought postcards because they or their friends and family featured in them. While this chapter focuses on postcards targeting a vacationing public, the images that so attracted visitors to Arcachon might well have adorned the walls of the very people pictured in them. We should not immediately assume that the people featured were victims of an objectifying gaze. While we can identify hidden contradictions or visual lies in some of these images, we must simultaneously recognize the agency of the people who played out their work before the camera. Their reaction to the urgings of a photographer were surely many and various, from fascination with a new technology, to embarrassment, to ridicule of a man standing under a black cloth looking at them through a hole in a box, to a willingness to pose in work mode in the hope of pecuniary reward or, at least, an image of themselves to show their families.

The postcard *Parqueurs et parqueuses au travail* (oyster-farming men and women at work) shows oyster farmers gathering the shellfish at low tide, on glistening, foot-printed sand banks (*crassats*).[4] Filled bags have been placed at uneven intervals around the "park," or oyster farm. Crooked sticks protrude from the mud in the middle ground, and behind the workers we see the bow of a beached boat, sitting on what appear to be rails leading across and out of the picture. In the background, a mass of the same low protruding sticks creates an effect of vegetation, and behind them, longer, more slender stakes rise up at the edge of the water. The women are in the foreground. They wear baggy pants, long-sleeved, dark shirts, and *benaizes* (hats worn by oyster-farming women and supposedly localized to the Buch and Médoc regions), which obscure their faces. The *benaize* comprised a section of fabric reinforced by wicker or reed that shaded the face and a long piece of floating fabric protecting the nape of the neck from the sun.

The *benaize* featured in many postcards and in the proto-Fauve painter Louis Valtat's 1895 sketches and paintings of oyster farmers on the Bassin, as well as in an article on oyster farming that appeared in *L'Illustration, Journal*

73. - ARCACHON. - Côte d'Argent. - Parqueurs et Parqueuses au travail - BR - 576

FIG. 23. Oyster-farming men and women at work. Collection of Richard Lahaye.

Universel in 1892.[5] It seems to have symbolized a regional tradition; it marked out the working women of the Bassin as different from those of other places. And yet, according to local historian and geographer Charles Daney, there is no record of the *benaize* in early travelers' accounts, nor does it appear in engravings.[6] Could it have been created—or at least rediscovered—in the 1860s and '70s, when oyster cultivation (as opposed to gathering from natural deposits) was established on the Bassin? While it is unlikely that oyster-farming women donned them purely to please the tourists—they were practical, after all—what the prevalence of the *benaize* in postcards does indicate is a search by the makers of representations, by promoters of the region's attractions, for a highly recognizable symbol of the local culture—a culture that they tended to see as fragile.[7] But what they presented as a recording of "tradition," a preserving of custom or costume, may have been an act of invention.

Given that postcards claimed to present an "authentic" picture of local life and people, images of women in *benaizes* suggested that this was the age-old costume of a community still operating according to "ancient ways," when in fact oyster-farming techniques were relatively new. Aline Valette, in an 1898 article in the Parisian, feminist newspaper *La Fronde,* acknowledged the unusual status of the industry on the Bassin. Oyster farming had developed only over the previous forty years, coinciding with industrialization in other sectors, but all the same, she argued, it was a trade of the "old type, in which the worker and the boss are one, although helped by co-workers when the need arises." Women's role was essential, but, as in other industries, they were paid only half the man's wage.[8] A more classic evocation of "progress" appeared in postcards showing the new steam-trawler companies' headquarters, their fleets, large numbers of employees, vast canning halls, and ice factories.

But back to the postcard in question, in which these *benaize*-wearing women are bent over, digging in the mud. This is a space entirely separate from that inhabited by the tourists. The postmark dates it at 1913, but there is nothing in the picture to convey any sense of time. Indeed, the photograph may well have been taken long before, as the same postcards were often reproduced for years on end; the postmark does not always indicate the production date. This apparently timeless image is also carefully composed. It is picturesque in James Buzard's definition of the term; that is, it is a balanced and complete scene, appearing to occur without intervention, spontaneously.[9] Even if the photographer did not actually pose his subjects, he chose a viewpoint that accentuated their oneness with the landscape; they appear, in their facelessness and their positions of subjugation, like *features* of this curious maritime scene rather than as individuals with whom one could identify or communicate.

The women in the foreground are strange figures, their shapes distorted (by turn-of-the-century standards) by their outfits and their postures. One woman, who stands tall, looking down at the rack that supports her basket of oysters, seems manlike, her body misshapen by thick, creased clothes and her feet in large wooden clogs. Where elite women's clothing of the time emphasized small waists and feet, generous busts and hips, proclaiming their wearers' femininity and unsuitability for work with delicate trimmings and flowery hats, but hiding the dangerous (because seductive) legs, the outfits of these oyster-farming women had the opposite effect: waists blew out, the shape of their legs was revealed, and their faces—the site of tell-tale eyes—were hidden from view by their *benaizes*. The 1892 *Illustration* article confirms that contemporary viewers saw these women as oddly unfeminine. Its author, P. Kauffmann described them as wearing "original and half-masculine clothing, blouse and trousers in red cloth; they have bare legs and their feet ensconced in large wooden pattens [*patins*]."[10]

Their bare legs, a source of great interest to commentators and photographers, often were emphasized by depicting the women bending over. This is the case in the postcard we have been describing, as well as in one of the etchings accompanying Kauffmann's article. In the lower-right foreground of the postcard *Parqueurs et parqueuses au travail,* a woman bends down, her backside to camera, an ankle visible as she leans to one side. In Kauffmann's illustration, a row of women (with one man) appears like a series of trestles: legs apart, rumps in the air, faces hidden as they dig at the mud. In contrast, a *bourgeoise* might be shown pulling up her dress to reveal her legs when wading in the water (as in *Le "Quart de Bain," Débarcadère* (On "Bathing Watch," Jetty), postmarked 1909), but such images had a humorous, even slightly scandalous tone to them.[11] They served to highlight the femininity of the women who dared reveal their shapely calves. Laughing or curious men looked on, responding to their actions. Back in 1853, novelist Anthelme Roux described the crowds of shell-collecting *bourgeoises,* "their clothes hitched up to the knees, with no intention of showing them, and showing nevertheless a self-effacing ankle, an elegant leg, and the finishing touch: an unshod foot, as dainty as the foot of a Chinese woman."[12]

In the oyster-farming postcard, there is no shared moment of humor or flirtatious complicity between viewer (holding the postcard) and subject (or object). These hard-working women inhabit a different world: they look away or down. There is no inviting glance, no encouragement to the viewer. The same is true of the postcard *Parqueuses se rendant au travail* (oyster women going to work)—another powerful image that is picturesque in its

FIG. 24. On "bathing watch" at the jetty. Collection of Richard Lahaye.

apparently spontaneous, marvelous composition—in which three trousered women, their backsides to camera (that familiar pose), their heads down, push a cart laden with oystering materials (baskets, tools, and the like) across the sand toward the water's edge, while a fourth figure—it is unclear whether a man or woman—brings up the rear, carrying an enormous basket that obscures his or her top half, giving the appearance of a pack horse: only the legs are visible below the load. We do not immediately notice a man pulling the cart, in the horse's position. The pushing women's backsides and calves are at the center of the image. And yet they seem unaware that their photograph is being taken. Their energies are focused on the task at hand. They are like beasts of burden. (Let us not forget that this pose would have been held for some time for the photographer; though it *represents* movement forward, across the sand, the image was made through enforced stillness. One imagines the photographer calling out to the bent-over workers: "Please, just hold it for another few seconds . . . nearly there . . ."). In another (perhaps earlier?) printing of this same postcard, the masculine noun was used to describe the workers pictured: *parqueurs* rather than *parqueuses*. The masculine noun may have been used because, in French, the presence of a sole man among women makes a plural noun masculine. It is also possible that the printer thought the workers *were* all men, until corrected by the photographer for subsequent reprints.[13]

Could an erotic charge be gained from such images of woman as packhorse? Griselda Pollock argues in her article on Arthur Munby's collection of photographs of women miners (1850–1910) that such a figure, both woman and not-woman, could be both exciting and disturbing because she embodied the pre-Oedipal "grand, powerful, and mercifully as yet undifferentiated maternal body." Pollock stresses the significance of the revealed leg in the nineteenth century, for the impact has worn off in our bare-it-all times. She argues that the vision of women in trousers, while confusing ingrained gender divisions, simultaneously invited the viewer to "imagine the specificity of what happens between their legs."[14]

Kauffmann's article confirms this contemporary fascination with bare legs, as does another postcard showing a theatrical troupe dressed as Arcachonnais oyster farmers: six women in short aprons over knee-length pantaloons, holding rakes and baskets, their espadrilled feet strapped onto *patins,* stand on either side of a man in a sailor's cap holding a large net with a sign on it saying "Arcachon." The women are *not* wearing *benaizes.* And espadrilles were not part of Arcachonnais attire, but they signified the seaside for urban theatergoers. In any case, it was probably the unveiled (though black-stockinged)

26. — ARCACHON. Parqueuses se rendant au travail.

J. H. B. Ed., Bx.

FIG. 25. Oyster-farming women going to work. Collection of Richard Lahaye.

legs that were of greatest interest for this troupe's public, not the accuracy of
their depiction of a regional costume.[15]

There are postcards of Arcachon oyster-farming women that acknowledge
more explicitly this fascination with their otherness, close-up images that remove them from the context of their work. These are posed shots of women
in their *benaizes* and pantaloons, staring straight at the camera, as in *Parqueuses,* postmarked 1908 (see fig. 26). In this image, two women stand side
by side, their feet in water, one holding a basket (empty, suggesting they are
about to start work, or perhaps giving away the posed nature of the shot), the
other holding a tool for levering oysters from their supports. They look
straight into the lens, and one woman has her arm placed on the shoulder of
what appears to be her sister, possibly even her twin. Other than the fact that
they are surrounded by water, the background is of little importance. What is
significant is their appearance: the strangeness of their outfits (with calves revealed), their calm self-assurance, and the fact that they are not embarrassed
by their state of undress.

An image like this one fits the genre of *types* that forms such a large part of
the postcard repertoire. There are many examples of such images in the Arcachon archive—posed shots of individuals or groups looking straight at the
camera, usually in such a way as to display their clothing (often worn, patched,
or in some way distinctive) and a tool, basket, or some other sign of their
work. Examples include *Types du Bassin d'Arcachon[:] Marchandes attendant
l'arrivée des pêcheurs* (Bassin d'Arcachon types[:] Women fish-sellers awaiting
the fishermen's return), *Vieux Marin* (Old Sailor) and *Type de Pêcheur* (Typical
Fisherman, see fig. 27). Each of these would have belonged to a series of images, churned out by postcard publishing houses with collectors in mind. A series might depict different trades or agricultural activities in one region or one
trade across a number of regions. This way, the collector could claim to own a
"full set," a classified range of *types*.

The representation of *types* was an established practice in France before the
invention of the postcard. From the eighteenth century on, series of litho-
graphs of figures in regional costume were an important commercial enterprise for French printers. This industry burgeoned from the 1830s, when it
was expanded to include colonial territories.[16] Gustave de Galard's litho-
graphs show that the figure of the La Teste fisherwoman was already part of
the stable of images on offer by 1814.[17] From the mid-1800s, with the invention of cheaper techniques for the reproduction of images, these stock figures
reached a mass audience. Emotionally resonant versions of such *types* were
also the subject of many a Salon painter's works later in the century, as in

Pierre-Marie Beyle's *Fleur des Grèves,* in which a young fisherwoman looks wistfully off to the side as she carries her baskets of fish across the wet sand.[18]

While in the early 1800s these series of images might have provided an overall impression of aesthetic, purely formal differences subsumable within the idea of the nation, by the turn of the century their significance had changed somewhat. A nostalgic view was possible because these people had come to represent the past or "tradition" (even if practices such as fishing and oystering were ongoing and evolving), as opposed to the growing industrial working class that was seen as a threat to order. Unlike the expanding working class, these supposedly unchanging, "traditional folk" represented an idea of the "true" Frenchman or -woman, the peasant (in this case attached to the sea rather than the soil) from whom the urban bourgeois vacationer or cure-taker felt increasingly alienated. The ongoing rural exodus and consequent urban growth across France meant that the connection with the land was weakening for many.[19] The frequency of images of and references to vacationers playing at being fishermen—rolling up their pants and skirts and dipping a long-handled prawn net into the Bassin's water, for example, or offering to help the locals at their work—suggests that these *types* held a fascination as representatives of a way of life with which city-dwellers had lost touch and which they liked to play at reliving, if only for a moment.

A scene from Guy de Maupassant's 1888 novel *Pierre and Jean,* set on the Normandy coast, illustrates this form of play. The protagonists go on a prawn-fishing outing, so they borrow appropriate clothing from a local hostel owner, La Belle Alphonsine, who dresses the women in "skirts, heavy woolen stockings and rope-soled slippers [*espadrilles*]," while the men don slippers and clogs. "In this outfit Mme Rosémilly [Jean's future fiancée] looked altogether lovely, a loveliness that was unexpected, peasantish and bold," and the skirt, "saucily turned up and caught with a stitch . . . displayed her ankle and lower calf." Her appearance on this day is so enchanting that Jean decides to propose marriage.[20] Maupassant seemed to suggest that the free, spontaneous play that such an outing made possible, as well as the "pretty scene" the sea and landscape provided as a backdrop, permitted the expression of desires suppressed by the constraints of bourgeois daily life.

Flirting with the roles of fisherman and -woman was only one part of the city-dweller's fascination with this world. They were also interested in the drama of their nature-dependent lives. Novelists and painters fed the popular appetite for images of the struggle with nature throughout the century: it was a theme that lived on well past the heyday of Romanticism. Paintings of seafaring people tended to dwell on the potential for tragedy; they depicted the

Collection V. Faure

Arcachon. — Parqueuses

FIG. 26. Oyster-farming women. Collection of Richard Lahaye.

353 — ARCAC... Type de Pêcheur — ND Phot.

FIG. 27. Typical fisherman. Collection of Richard Lahaye.

fisherman's struggle with an angry sea, his wife's long periods of waiting, and her anxiety before the storm. The fishing community was seen as enacting an epic struggle with the elements, and this was read into the "tanned faces" of the old salts (men and women) who appeared in postcards.

In an interview in the October 1904 issue of *Le Figaro Illustré* devoted to the postcard, Humblot, one of France's most successful postcard publishers, claimed that "views" were more than "pieces of card upon which one writes a hurried word." The destruction of the "old," "picturesque" France meant that postcards "must have documentary value." They must "fix in our memory these things that will no longer exist in twenty years."[21] This archiving impulse fed the nostalgia for a world that appeared to be vanishing.

And yet, as we have already noted, this hardly applied to oyster farming, a relatively new industry on the Bassin. While the oystering community came, for the most part, from established fishing families, their work processes and their particular relationship with nature and with tourists were still being developed and negotiated. Oyster farming was becoming one of the most important industries on the Bassin. According to Lannoy in his 1900 guide, Arcachon was exporting two hundred million oysters; between 1875 and 1881, the number of oyster farms had jumped from 2,427 to 4,300, and in 1881 they occupied an area of ten thousand hectares (24,711 acres) on the Bassin.[22] This was no dying race exhibiting a lost art. A nostalgic perspective expressed in a picturesque framing could thus hide the lived experience—the changes, innovations, and new skills—of the people represented. Rehashing the same old themes of man against the sea or woman waiting for an uncertain return, or repeating motifs or symbols of authenticity, of tradition (such as the *benaize*), denied the role that that these communities played in an evolving coastal society. In tourist-oriented representations, they were stuck in a time warp in order to satisfy the desire for a reassuring image of France "as it always was." In a sense, by figuring them as belonging to another time, they came to represent a kind of otherness, not unlike the *types* in images from the colonies.

This kind of imagery also hid disputes between the fishing community and the promoters of bathing in Arcachon. While "traditional," artisanal sea workers were represented as fascinating figures in postcards, their access to the maritime domain was being threatened by the very people who bought these pictures. If we look closely, in a number of postcards we can see some evidence of work on the beach, for example nets hung out to dry in front of the Deganne Château—the nets that so offended foreshore proprietors and councillors. But many of these pictures seem to have been taken during the off-season, when only fishermen were present. On the whole, postcard images tended to show working fishermen and -women and oyster farmers as though they inhabited a world of their own, a space that Urbain calls "backstage" (*l'envers du décor*).[23] When they feature alongside bathers, it is either as helpers or guides to the newcomers, as distant figures sitting on their *pinasses* (perhaps waiting for clients?), or as performers. In the last case, visitors look on, often from the vantage point of a nearby jetty, as fishermen and -women "perform" their work, as in *On débarque le poisson* (Unloading the fish fig. 28). They might also perform in regattas, a popular spectacle for visitors.

But what of the visitors' own performances? Were postcard images of them different from those of the locals? Consider the postcard *Vue de la plage* (View of the beach fig. 29). Contrary to what one might expect, this is not a view of an expanse of sand. It focuses on three bourgeois women, in day dresses and decorated hats, perched on the edge of a beached wooden dinghy, each holding a parasol and looking out to sea. A young girl in a play smock and straw hat leans against the prow, also looking out toward the water, and a boatman in black, with a jaunty air, appears to be approaching them: perhaps it is his boat? A striped bathing tent directly behind the women enlivens the scene, echoing their verticality, and on either side of its umbrella-shaped top we see strolling men and women moving toward the camera.

The "view," then, is of the visitors who occupy the beach. The caption directs our gaze toward them. Although patches of sand and several boats moored just offshore are visible, the subject is the women in the foreground, who dominate the frame. While the view of the Bassin and the ocean was much commented on in guidebooks, and often represented in postcards, the (other) *gazers* were of equal interest. How does an image like this one (*Vue de la plage*) compare to those of working oyster-farming women? These bourgeois women were not so much objects of curiosity, or *types,* as signs of a resort that had established a particular social tone and that had something to offer this class of visitor. Their modesty and composure were reassuring signs of Arcachon's respectability; that is, the photographer asked the postcard reader or buyer to identify with these women. The beach was occupied by the sort of people with whom one might like to rub shoulders.

Postcards of visitors show us the ways these newcomers had occupied the sand: their tents and umbrellas—which Urbain calls the "totemic symbol of the tribe or clan"—were a very visible sign of their presence, while their bodily presence, their strength in numbers, was undeniable.[24] In *Arcachon—La Plage* (The beach fig. 30), postmarked 1904 but probably printed some years earlier, we see the beach at low tide, the broad sweep of glistening sand dotted

48 ARCACHON. — *On débarque le poisson.* — LL.

FIG. 28. Unloading the fish. Collection of Richard Lahaye.

ARCACHON — Vue de la Plage

FIG. 29. View of the beach. Collection of Richard Lahaye.

with barefoot, parasol-wielding women and children, men in boaters, excursion boats (converted *pinasses*), a donkey, bathers in striped outfits, and, in the background, the line of substantial hotels dominating the foreshore.[25] There is no doubt left in the mind of the viewer that the beach *belongs* to the visitors: they have made it their own.

Maupassant described the beach at Trouville in terms that might have been applied equally to Arcachon. From a distance, the crowd on the sand resembles "enormous bunches of flowers in an oversized meadow." Maupassant evokes the "continuous soft hubbub" of shouts and laughter, "which one breathed in with the almost imperceptible breeze"—an aural and sensual dimension that pictures fail to convey. This beach scene, relayed through his tormented character Pierre, is infused with a fit of misogyny brought on by Pierre's suspicion of his mother's adultery; he thus dwells on the exchange of glances, the flirtation that goes on in this licentious space: "So this wide strand was nothing but a market for love," Pierre thinks; he is witnessing "an immense flowering of female perversity."[26] While the story's tone lends an ugly edge to the beach scene, it also emphasizes the looking and being-looked-at, the awareness of bodies and all they might have to offer, that is such a powerful part of the vacationer's experience of life on the sands, which postcards could capture only partially.

On a lighter note, the joy of looking at others on the beach is expressed in a humorous guide called *Vingt-quatre heures à Arcachon* (Twenty-four hours in Arcachon), written in 1886 by Louis Branlat, director of the newspaper *La Vie Bordelaise*. He describes the beach scene as "the most bizarre and eventful spectacle you could imagine." Women are once again the central figures in his description of the gradual coming-to-life of the beach, as the incoming tide brings relief from the "implacable heat." The refreshing breeze draws people out of their lodgings and onto the sand. He focuses on "young and pretty women in fresh outfits, delicious under great white or pink umbrellas, holding a little piece of handiwork or a novel to be read," walking their children to the beach. He admires their "elegant casual wear so distinguished in its abandonment and its sea bathing simplicity."[27]

When it comes time to bathe, Branlat enjoys his status as a "*flâneur* [idler] smoking his pipe, nonchalantly stretched out on the sand in a strip of shade," passing comment on the hapless swimmers. He particularly enjoys the spectacle of young women hesitating to enter cold water, and "rubs his hands" upon their reemergence, when their wet bathing costumes cling to their bodies: "[W]ho wouldn't be crazy about them? After the modestly cut dresses [*demi-décolletés*] of winter evenings, the clinging revelation of the swim. Ravishing!"

FIG. 30. Arcachon beach. Collection of the author.

Ravishing!" He also pokes fun at the different ways that bathers of all shapes and sizes approach the water: some lower themselves in an abrupt movement, beating the wavelets with their hands; others slosh water onto themselves before diving in; while the "indolent" are carried in by bathing masters.[28]

What Branlat is describing is a theater of the sands: an endlessly entertaining spectacle tinged with eroticism, and a free one at that. The oyster farmers appear fleetingly in this panorama of the beach, when the *pinasses* arrive carrying "men and women in red trousers."[29] But they do not feature for long. Newfoundland dogs leaping into the sea after sticks are next on the list of performers, and the locals disappear from view. Branlat does discuss the oyster industry in a later section titled "Le Bassin," where he acknowledges that it constitutes, along with sardine fishing, "the commercial fortune of the entire Arcachon area, then La Teste and all the villages situated around the Bassin."[30] But this, as in most of the postcards, is a separate world; while it is of interest to the visitor, it is not central to his experience.

Postcards reveal much about the physical site and the look (both spontaneous and posed) of some of Arcachon's inhabitants and visitors, but they can gloss over the complexities and difficulties that exist in lived space. The moment captured has, more often than not, been carefully manufactured, directed by the photographer, and enacted by the subjects. So while it may have some basis in reality—in actual appearances, behaviors, and movements—it is nonetheless a performed moment, with a specific audience in mind. We might see postcards as the culmination of a century of efforts to circumscribe the fishing community, to keep them in their place: in the postcard, fishermen and -women are locked into a rectangle of appropriate space and behavior. Meanwhile, the beach—which, in reality, was perhaps more unsatisfactory than ever due to erosion, and crowding by uncouth Sunday picnickers and importunate oyster sellers—is represented in accordance with the desires of bourgeois escapees from urban suffocation.

Other Occupations

In the landes, the land is yours. Each creek, each little beach, each clearing,
belongs to you. The owner? Who is it? Where is he? Is it the State? The commune?
Bah! It's God. And what is God's belongs to every man."

—Henry de la Tombelle and Jean Samazeuilh, *Guide touristique Sud-Ouest:*
Cyclotourisme, canoë, camping, 1938

By the early 1900s, the bathers and promenaders had occupied the Arcachon beach. But this was not the end of the story. While it was during the nineteenth century that the essential spadework was done for the "pacification of the shore," there would be continued reworkings of the ways in which people used and represented the sand and sea over the ensuing decades. The twentieth century witnessed an intensification of the connection between the Bassin and the outside world, a connection that led, naturally, to further conflicts and negotiations over the use and understanding of the maritime zones: deeps, shallows, beach, and foreshore.

The process of industrialization of the fishing industry continued through the first part of the twentieth century, and by 1910, Arcachon was France's second biggest fishing port. The motorization of *pinasses,* experimental at the turn of the century, quickly became the norm, particularly for sardine fishing: by 1913, nearly every fishing *pinasse* had been motorized. From then on, much larger sardine *pinasses* were built, which could be manned by up to twelve fishermen, changing the way fishing crews organized themselves. The fishermen's relationship to the sea, their sense of control over the elements, must have been powerfully affected by these changes. The use of larger crews and the reliance on a motor also introduced a semi-industrial organization, bringing sardine fishing more into line with the trawler fishing regime.[1]

The expansion of sardine fishing and the canneries that grew up with it, as well as the Arcachon fishing companies' dispatch of cod-fishing trawlers to Newfoundland and Iceland, brought Breton families to work on the Bassin in increasing numbers. According to Noël Gruet and Pierre-Jean Labourg, the Bretons, unlike local fishermen, were prepared to man the vessels that would take them away from their new homes and families for months at a time.[2] The influx of fishing people from other regions of France—with their new skills, habits, and vocabulary—must have influenced the way Bassin residents saw themselves and their place in the world. At the same time, technological developments that facilitated longer absences (e.g., ice-making and eventually refrigeration) and the shipping of timber from the landes' forests to Great Britain in exchange for coal reinforced these links with other places.

With the intensification of production, the extension of canneries and workshops, and the organization of workers in larger groups came a consolidation of the urban division between eastern (industrial) and western (residential) quarters of Arcachon, as well as a growing awareness among the workers of their own class identity, or at least of their common grievances against employers and market forces. There were strikes in 1900, 1907, 1913, and 1936 by different sectors of the fishing industry, both in response to particular local grievances and, on occasion, tied in with national strike actions.

The industrialization of fishing occurred in tandem with the expansion of pleasure boating on the Bassin. Yachting had been an expensive and exclusive pursuit in the late 1800s. The invention of the monotype at the turn of the century, which made possible navigation without a crew, gradually opened up sailing to those who had been excluded from the sport. In 1907 the Touring Club of France created a nautical tourism committee, whose aim was to put "pleasure boating in reach of all classes of the population." This was an ambitious project given that most families could hardly afford a bicycle, let alone a boat.[3] But eventually, motorboats and yachts on the Bassin would far outnumber fishing vessels. Vacationers would occupy the surface of the water, pushing the fishing community to the margins, just as they had squeezed fishermen and -women, with their nets and paraphernalia, off the beaches in previous decades.

Motorization, of course, was not confined to the sea. On 13 April 1897, Arcachonnais saw the first automobile to drive through their town: a Panhard-Levassor. It took an hour and forty-six minutes to drive the sixty kilometers (37.2 miles) from Bordeaux.[4] Only the rich could afford to buy an automobile in the early years—only three hundred were on the road in 1895, jumping to three thousand in 1900—and driving was seen as a sport more than as a means of transport.[5] But the automobile would revolutionize the way people understood their environment and their relations with others. The railway had opened up regions and created a national network and market, but it confined its users to a fixed route and timetable, and to sitting for long periods beside strangers. With the automobile, "rich people of leisure" (re)discovered "absolute independence, . . . [and] the impression of being 'at home' maintained during the longest trips," as one journalist described it in 1909.[6] Drivers (and passengers) experienced the joys of an individualized itinerary and use of time, the possibility of stopping when and where one wished and exploring byways, and a new sense of the body moving rapidly through landscapes. While a certain freedom of movement had been won with the bicycle, riding was physically demanding, and one could not transport a whole family with luggage across the country.

Distances shrank between far-flung regions for those behind the wheel, and while it was not until the 1960s that most ordinary families could envisage buying a car, the early users formed strong lobby groups, provoking changes that would affect everyone: the creation of a new infrastructure (wider roads, signage, service stations, and garages) as well as improved hotels and inns that would not offend the urban bourgeois sensibility.[7] Arcachon's wealthy residents—of whom there were plenty—no doubt demanded changes to the town's organization to allow better access for automobiles. They also started to look beyond the Arcachon foreshore, which was, in the eyes of the *haute bourgeoisie,* suffering from the incursion of rowdy weekend crowds, and past the Ville d'hiver—tainted with the brush of tuberculosis—toward the as-yet-undeveloped, quiet and forested ocean coast: the Côte d'Argent (Silver Coast), as it had come to be known.[8]

In the prewar period, a struggle emerged over the identity of Arcachon—refuge for the sick, or holiday resort? Its reputation as a curative space for the terminally ill was becoming a burden in an era when bathing was moving away from a medicalized to a more pleasure-seeking model.[9] But on 14 July 1914, Arcachon was named a "climatic resort" by the government, meaning it would benefit from a tourist tax, and as tuberculosis was still a scourge, Arcachon's open sanatorium continued to appeal to the frail. The battle for a new, untainted image for Arcachon would continue for some time.[10]

The debate over Arcachon's future was put on hold by the Great War. There would be no turning away the thousands of sick and injured who streamed in over the next four years. Of the Bassin d'Arcachon's population of forty thousand, 9,000 were mobilized, of whom 2,360 were from Arcachon proper. Over 1,000 never returned.[11] When the Germans came frighteningly close to invading Paris in early September 1914, the French government relocated temporarily to Bordeaux. Ministers arrived with their public servants, ambassadors, the Paris press, and all their hangers-on, including many actresses—"the entire *Théâtre Français*" according to one journalist.[12] Bordeaux was transformed and decried as a party town where champagne flowed freely. Some of those who could not find accommodation in overflowing Bordeaux, including diplomats and politicians' mistresses, rented villas in Arcachon, mainly in the Ville d'hiver.

Journalists provoked a national scandal when they wrote about ministers living it up in their new home in the Southwest, gambling, drinking, and eating richly, at a time when thousands of Frenchmen were being slaughtered at the front. They described local women crying out with indignation at the thought of their sons going off to die while politicians enjoyed their safety so ostentatiously.[13] Michel Georges-Michel, in his book *Le bonnet rose,* described ministers spending their Sundays in Arcachon, enjoying the spectacle of "charming little Arcachonnaises, Arcochonnaises [a wordplay on pig—*co-chon*], as Mr Gallipaux [*sic*] calls them, walking on the beach in red pants and organizing tea parties where nothing is lacking."[14] So in 1914 the vision of women in pants was still seen as titillating. Ardoin Saint Amand notes that in Arcachon, the Belle Epoque lived on for four months longer than in the rest of the country. But when the Parisian circus returned to the capital in December, there was no time to contemplate the death of an extraordinary season.

Thousands of injured and sick soldiers had to be cared for, and the local economy kept alive in the absence of the young men. A Bordeaux newspaper reported in September 1914 that buyers were trying to purchase oysters in La Teste at "famine prices." The writer encouraged oyster farmers not to lower their prices and recommended they "wait, calm and confident, for the final success of the work of civilization that our allied armies are undertaking, at which point normal business will resume."[15] At this time the French envisaged a short war: no one could imagine how long the horror would drag on. Two days later, in the same newspaper, a correspondent wrote about the sardine season in Gujan-Mestras: "It is to be hoped that the fishing will be productive, for the sake of our sailors and also for the women of the area who work in the factories, because the oyster trade is in dire straits."[16] By the end of 1915, nearly all Arcachon's fishing trawlers had been requisitioned for dredging and mine-clearing operations in the Channel and elsewhere.[17]

Temporary military hospitals were set up in schools, sanatoria, and the casinos, as well as in the Grand Hotel, which was renamed "hospital number 23b" from 3 September and set up for surgery and radiography. It took in French, Senegalese, and Moroccan soldiers.[18] Its opening on the same day as the government's move from Paris to Bordeaux highlights the confusing nature of the times for Arcachon and its inhabitants. Adding to this sense of upheaval was the fact that, while Frenchmen were leaving the region in droves to fight, thousands of soldiers from other parts of the world were arriving on the Bassin. Nineteenth-century writers had described Arcachon's supposed "exoticism" and considered the opening up of the landes as a kind of colonization of wild deserts, but it was during the Great War that the region became connected in a real and unprecedented way with France's colonial empire.

In March 1916, up to twenty thousand Senegalese infantry (Tirailleurs Sénégalais)—who were not all from Sénégal but recruited (mostly by force) from many different parts of French West Africa—were posted to a purpose-built military camp in the landes, at Le Courneau, near Lake Cazaux, about seven kilometers (4.34 miles) south of La Teste (see fig. 31). For most, this was their first time away from their village. The men would spend several months there before being transported to the front. Sanitary conditions were poor, and many died of disease at Le Courneau—an estimated 1 percent of the men per month. The graves of nine hundred African soldiers can be found in the local cemetery.[19]

The location of this camp had been selected carefully for its mild climate (so the *tirailleurs* could adjust to the colder temperatures before going to the front) and for its isolation from the French civilian population. So the landes were still thought of by administrators as a kind of desert—although a desert accessible by train, facilitating the mass movement of troops to and from the front. Remember Jacques Arago in 1828: "I am only ten leagues from you, my friend, and yet deserts separate us. Deserts like those in Africa, with their loneliness, their sterility, their moving sands. I am a thousand leagues from civilized France." The irony is, of course, that African men were now living in that French "desert," and they probably felt the isolation and loneliness of their situation much more powerfully than Arago had, particularly as their contact with French civilians, and even soldiers, was deliberately restricted.[20]

The Tirailleurs Sénégalais were replaced in October 1917 by eight thousand

Tirailleurs au Campement

Photo Gaby Bessières, La Teste

FIG. 31. Infantrymen in camp (Senegalese soldiers stationed at Cazaux during World War I). Collection Jacques Clémens. Editions Alan Sutton, 1997. Reproduced with permission.

Russians (following the mutinies and split between loyalists and communists within the Russian brigades) and then in 1918 by fifteen thousand Americans. The Americans established a training school for pilots and a 960-bed hospital, as part of what came to be known as Camp Hunt. They also built an airship station at Gujan-Mestras and a radiotelegraphic station at Croix-d'Hins, and took over a seaplane station established by the French in late 1917 at Cap Ferret.[21] No part of the Bassin remained untouched. The American seaplanes were used for the surveillance of submarine activity along the Atlantic coast. The concept of invisible, underwater mechanical predators must have added a frightening new dimension to the fears provoked by the ocean, and fishermen were, of course, particularly vulnerable. As it turns out, in a year of surveillance the Americans reported not a single submarine sighting.[22]

The foreshore, beach, and water became, at least temporarily, a site for military exercises; soldiers' active and regimented bodies replaced the prewar bathers' tentative incursions into the water. Jean Cocteau, who was staying at Piquey on the Bassin peninsula in 1918, wrote that he envied the Americans: "bronze colossi, in pastry cook outfits, leaping across the water in glossy [*ripoliné*] tanks, all polished up, armed with machine guns and aeroplane propellers. He who hasn't seen their camp, hasn't seen It."[23] This new occupation of the shore, this testing out of human and mechanical domination over air and sea, may well have been seen by locals as a reassuring sign after years of stalemate on the western front.

A massive reconstruction effort followed the war. The fishing and tourism industries had to regroup, reequip, and refurbish. Fishing companies had new vessels built and extended their cod-fishing fleets. The industrial zone grew as associated trades developed: boat and engine builders, electricians, blacksmiths. Sardine fishing continued to expand, but the oyster industry faced difficult times.

Before the war there had been a serious decline in numbers of the local oyster species, *Ostrea edulis,* known more commonly as the flat oyster (*l'huître plate*). Competition from the "Portuguese" oyster, which had been introduced accidentally to the Charente coast (to the north) in the nineteenth century, began to cause concern. In 1914, the Portuguese oyster was banned from the Bassin! One cannot help make a connection between the fear—in this time of war—of this outsider species and that of the invading German forces. But in the early 1920s, the local flat oyster was almost wiped out by an epidemic, and oyster farmers had no choice but to embrace the Portuguese intruder—not without some reluctance. The industry's fortunes continued to fluctuate, and the golden age of the 1880s would never be recaptured. It would never be wiped out altogether, though: oyster farming is still a major part of the Bassin's economy today.[24]

Meanwhile, bathers flocked to the beaches through the 1920s and '30s and embraced new ways of using and presenting their bodies. Skimpier bathing suits, a new appreciation of tanned skin, and flirting were part of the process of trying to forget the dark years of the war. The evolution of beachgoers' behavior toward more permissive and ludic practices was still confined mainly to the wealthy elite, though an expanding middle-class of employees was beginning to enjoy the benefits of paid holidays (before 1936) and was thus coming into contact with this new playfulness.[25]

The shock effect of early tanners and wearers of body-hugging, revealing bathing suits should not be underestimated. Urbain argues that sunbathing was not embraced by the majority of beachgoers until after World War II. He analyses the progressive denuding of the bather's body as "the primordial dimension" of a new moral universe. The progressive stripping of the body followed the emptying of the shore and achieved the ultimate "harmonization of the site and the actor." A complete renewal seemed possible when the stripped body met the bare wave.[26]

Arcachon had already begun to burst at the seams in the prewar period. There was little room to move within the commune's boundaries, so developers began to look farther afield. The ocean coast to the south began to interest speculators. In the interwar period, a new estate called Pyla-sur-mer was created for an elite clientele. It lay between Arcachon's western end—the Moulleau quarter—and the Dune du Pyla, within La Teste's municipal boundaries. Its developer, Daniel Meller, imagined it as a Cannes for the Côte d'Argent.

Arcachon was beginning to fall out of fashion by this point. Its architecture, so cutting-edge in the previous century, seemed dated. The generous villas built at Pyla-sur-mer were in the Basque style; the architectural diversity and idiosyncrasies of the Ville d'hiver were no longer prized, it seems.[27] Pyla-sur-mer was the first of many developments radiating out from Arcachon and following the line of the ocean beaches over the ensuing decades. The building of new roads in response to the increasing use of the automobile was instrumental in this outgrowth: until this point, the placement of railway lines had dictated the shape and extent of development. A new consumption and representation of space was emerging.

In his report "1929–1935: Six Years of Municipal Progress," Arcachon's mayor Gounouilhou proudly reported the transformation of his town, in line with the vision of its first mayor, Lamarque de Plaisance, and his motto: "Yes-

ARCACHON. — Sa plage.

« Leo Neveu »

FIG. 32. Arcachon. The beach. Collection of the author.

terday solitude, today town, tomorrow city." The report featured a series of photographs, the captions of which were constructed according to the comparative model: "Yesterday . . . today . . ." Most of these illustrated a transformation of some aspect of the urban environment. For example, a line of spanking new buses, their drivers standing proudly beside them, the railway station visible in the background, was captioned: "Yesterday a wheezing tramway: today, comfortable Panhard-Levassor coaches and metered taxis await you at the station." Another image, of an urban street in the industrial quarter, showed a family standing beside a modest house: "Yesterday off-limits to cars, like so many other roads in the deprived Aiguillon quarter, the rue des Pêcheries [Fisheries Street] is now integrated into the vast network of Arcachonnais circulation."

Other photographs showed a new garbage service with "rapid and hygienic" trucks replacing "slow and dirty" tipcarts, and, especially noteworthy, a "New Beach" between the Thiers and Eyrac jetties, achieved, we must presume, by the importing of sand from other parts of the Bassin. Gounouilhou reported the removal of eight hundred tonnes of seaweed in 1934, which required the labor of twelve men over 120 days—something his predecessor Mauriac could only have dreamed of in the 1860s. We see here an abiding preoccupation with hygiene, which extended to the socioeconomic organization of the town: "No more poor quarters," the report announced in bold capitals, followed by a list of new or improved streets in the industrial areas to Arcachon's east. Perhaps promoting the town's modernity had become all the more essential because of serious competition from new developments farther south along the coast.

This opening up of Arcachon to circulation extended to other parts of the Bassin. In 1931 Meller built a road between La Teste and Pyla-sur-mer (the new residential development), and in 1929 a road was built to Cap Ferret, which hitherto had been accessible only by ferry, foot, or animal power. Arcachon, already tamed, would see a version of its former, uncivilized self take shape on the opposite shore—a place where wilderness would be valued and rampant development discouraged. Cap Ferret's comparative isolation and simplicity guaranteed its growing appeal, whereas the achievement of Lamarque's vision of Arcachon's progression from solitude to city would prove to be a burden.

In June 1936, a youth hostel (Auberge de Jeunesse) was opened at Pyla-sur-mer. Local poet Gilbert Sore recited a poem he had written that morning: "O Magnificent Bassin! O legendary land!" it began, and after describing an ancient and "harsh Pyla" rising like Lazarus with the coming of civilization, he went on:

Now, 'tis the influx of crowds onto our beaches,
The rich, the endowed have built ample nests,
Displaying to the sun their luxury without courage,
Burning their flesh and their faces
In a beaming farniente.

But the "lazy and serene" sea received the rich, "indifferent" to their "mon-eyed shame," just as it would welcome young people "simple and without riches," who stayed at the youth hostel. These last would be embraced by the country (*pays*) that would charm them with its beauty, declaring: "Bread, peace, liberty!"—the slogan of the recently elected Popular Front.[28]

This rather strained poem expresses the essence of the leisure philosophy of Léon Blum's Popular Front government. The establishment of youth hostels was part of a raft of measures—carried out mostly by regional organizations but with support from the government and in particular the Undersecretary of State for the Organization of Sport and Leisure, Léo Lagrange—designed to encourage those who had not previously had access to holidays to discover their own country and the recuperative benefits and simple pleasures of time off work. The Pyla hostel was opened six days after the famous *congés payés* legislation was promulgated, extending to all workers the benefit of two weeks' paid holidays. The following month, another youth hostel, "The Nest," was opened in Arès, on the Bassin, at whose opening the President of the Club of Friends and Users of Youth Hostels declared that the hostels would "teach young people solidarity and mutual love."[29]

While much has been made of the immediate impact of the Popular Front paid holiday legislation, with images of couples on tandem bicycles and fam-ilies camping by the sea, to the dismay of rich people forced to share their fa-vorite holiday spots, it actually took some time—decades—before most French families used their *congés payés* to leave home for anything more than day or weekend trips. France was just emerging from the Depression, so a lack of money was an obstacle for most, but it also has been argued that the working class had to develop its own culture of vacationing away from home. It was not until after World War II—when the economy strengthened, paid-leave provisions gradually expanded, and the automobile was democratized—that working-class French people left home *en masse* in the summer holidays.

Nevertheless, in the summer of 1936, the presence of people unfamiliar with, or dismissive of, the established etiquette of the seaside holiday had an impact on the Bassin's main resort. In August 1936, *La France de Bordeaux* re-ported a new municipal bylaw in Arcachon governing behavior in and around theaters. The bylaw included clauses requiring that queues be formed, that drunks be banned, and prohibiting the following activities: moving around with a pipe, cigar, or cigarette between one's lips, "even unlit"; introducing animals into the theater; "speaking, singing, yelling, whistling, making offensive comments or threats and noise of any kind, during the performances"; throwing objects; and spitting on the floor.[30]

This bylaw is reminiscent of the municipal efforts in the previous century to regulate behavior on and around the Eyrac beach and the nearby train station (discussed in chapter 6). The list of offenses also indicates that this was more than an accidental disturbance of bourgeois comfort by the newcomers. The strike wave of 1936—which did include the Bassin's fishermen and cannery workers from July, and possibly other employee groups—and the defiant tone of Gilbert Sore's ode to the Pyla-sur-mer youth hostel suggest that working-class visitors to the theaters may have been deliberately flouting convention, staking their claim to the territory of leisure.[31]

A much more frightening and damaging occupation of Arcachon's grand buildings, beach, and Bassin would soon eclipse anything that working-class vacationers could impose. In the spring of 1940, the French government moved south to Bordeaux once again, to escape the invading German army, who took possession of the national capital on 14 June. On 22 June the Armistice was signed, and Bordeaux, being part of the occupied zone, was no longer an appropriate home for the government, which then moved to Vichy. Arcachon, along with the rest of the Atlantic coast, became occupied territory and was declared a sensitive zone (*zone sensible*)—that is, vulnerable to attack. The German army took over the Grand Hotel and many villas; the beachfront casino (the Deganne Château) became their mess hall.[32] Their control extended to the hour: all clocks had to be set to Berlin time.

Once again Arcachon's trawlers were requisitioned for patrols and mine-clearing operations, and many were lost. Fishing activity was confined to fulfilling local subsistence needs and was closely monitored by the occupiers. Anxiety about mines, bombing, and strafing were added to the usual fears associated with confronting a changeable sea. Several vessels were sunk by mines, and others by British fighter pilots who mistook them for German vessels. Sixty-two sailors from Arcachon lost their lives in 1942 alone.[33]

From early 1942, the Gironde coastline was integrated into Hitler's defensive Atlantic Wall. Although the Germans considered the southwest coast overall as less vulnerable to attack than northern shores, they used forced labor to build fortified structures along the ocean shores, including camouflaged concrete pillboxes, known as *blockhaus,* from which the German army might fend off an Allied attack.[34] Alan Wilt alludes briefly to a conflict between the German army and navy over the way beach defenses were to be organized, arguing that their differences were to "hamper the effectiveness of the western defensive system for some time to come."[35] Once again that liminal zone, the point(s) where the sea and land meet, created difficulties for humans in their desire to define spheres of responsibility and control.

After the war, residents had to live with the litter of occupation. On 2 September 1944, the *Journal d'Arcachon* reported that mines had killed three people and injured three others in the previous week, and it warned children against "picking up grenades or bullets found on the beaches."[36] In 1950, newly emerging vacationers found semi-submerged *blockhaus* (some of which can still be seen today), artillery shells, and land mines hiding at the foot of the dunes.[37] The German occupiers had transformed the beach from a pleasure zone to a forbidding buffer zone; the fishing nets Johnston had complained about as an obstacle to free movement between water and sand were nothing compared to this.

The end of the war did not mean an end to the militarization of the Bassin region. The local Resistance took over the Grand Hotel in August 1944, keeping a number of Germans and Italians prisoner as well as storing arms in the basement.[38] Several hundred collaborators were held and questioned in barracks near the Ville d'hiver, known as the "Camp des Abatilles."[39] The arrests that took place after the Liberation were part of what the *Journal d'Arcachon* described, using climatotherapeutic vocabulary, as a "purification of 'the climate'" that would allow residents to "breathe freely" after four years of German intrusion.[40] In fact, the war was not over for the Gironde department until the Battle of the Pointe de Grave (at the mouth of the Gironde estuary, to Arcachon's north) was won in April of the following year, with a loss of four hundred Free French and six hundred German soldiers.[41]

In the final months of 1944, despite France's post-occupation devastation, the French army created an expeditionary corps of seventy-five thousand men destined for the Far East, to fight with the Allies in the Pacific. Arcachon was chosen as a training base for the Far Eastern Brigade, which was to prepare initially for the Pacific war and, after the Japanese surrender in August 1945, for amphibian conflict in French Indochina—for which the Bassin was thought to provide ideal conditions.[42] Once again we see the Bassin's connection with an "other," distant world. By May 1945, Arcachon had become an "important garrison town," with villas and hotels requisitioned for accommodation yet again. And, as in 1918, exercises were carried out on and around the Bassin: scaling of dunes, forest marches, camouflaged embarkations and land-

FIG. 33. Bathers standing on a semi-submerged German *blockhaus.* Collection Jacques Clémens. Editions Alan Sutton, 1997. Reproduced with permission.

ings. According to one veteran, Arcachon's residents and visitors were frequently surprised by trainees popping up from behind bushes. The Far Eastern Brigade left Arcachon in October 1945.[43] Finally, the town could begin to rebuild its identity as a holiday resort.

Although the postwar scarcity of resources and damaged transport infrastructure meant that vacationing could not immediately resume its momentum, it was not long before the French picked themselves up and threw themselves back into the sea. The 1950s and '60s saw an explosion in the numbers of French taking holidays, for longer periods. The car began to overtake the train as the main means of transport for vacationers, which, for Arcachon, reinforced the extension of development beyond the town limits.[44] La Teste and other Bassin communes benefited over this period, their populations increasing as Arcachon's declined. They had more space available to develop, meaning cheaper land on which middle-class families could build vacation homes.[45]

Arcachon, whose villas now seemed old-fashioned, had no room to grow outward, so many proprietors chose to demolish and rebuild. The "Thirty Glorious Years" saw the redevelopment of the foreshore in particular, with concrete blocks of holiday apartments replacing many of the ornate, single-family villas of earlier times. The Ville d'hiver was neglected, the owners of its mansions discouraged by the cost of maintenance.

Meanwhile, the ocean coast (within La Teste's boundaries) experienced a boom in camping, which Arcachon had never been willing or able to accommodate. Back in 1938, Jean Samazeuilh and Henry de la Tombelle, in a camper's guide to the Southwest, had declared that "a man must change his city skin for a newer, fresher, more airy, sporty one, for that of a man who does his own cooking and who carries his house on his back, on his bicycle or in his canoe."[46] This was a far cry from the civilized vacationing that Arcachon offered. Unlike Arcachon, the landes offered open spaces with an appeal similar to that the Eyrac beach had held for tourists in the early nineteenth century. "In the landes," Samazeuilh and de la Tombelle wrote, "the land is yours. Each creek, each little beach, each clearing, belongs to you. The owner? Who is it? Where is he? Is it the State? The commune? Bah! It's God. And what is God's belongs to every man. No cars to bother you. No whistling locomotives. No smells. Nothing but the perfume of the pines, the silence of the pines, the shade of the pines."[47] The landes and the ocean coast were there for the taking, according to him. No doubt there were local people (and other visitors) who would dispute this claim.

The debate over the status of the prés salés, a sore point for so much of the nineteenth century, was reignited in the postwar period. In 1951, whipped up by a great storm, the Bassin's waters broke through the seawalls surrounding the eastern prés salés in three places. While an association of proprietors in concert with the La Teste council applied for government funding to repair the walls, a handful of locals seized the opportunity to question the validity of the prés' status as private property. The old arguments were raised again, unleashing a series of new judgments, which favored their belonging to the public domain.[48] Various law courts also made conflicting decisions about the status of the western prés salés throughout the 1980s and 1990s.[49] So, the battle over definitions and usage continues on. Physical enclosure and legislation are no guarantee against change, particularly where the sea is concerned.

While the occupation of the landes and ocean coast proceeded apace, industrial fishing on the Bassin ended. Fisheries struggled to cope with the costs of fuel and of financing and maintaining their infrastructure, which was still privately owned. Companies moved their trawlers elsewhere or closed altogether.[50] The last cannery closed in 1964, and industrial buildings were torn down and redeveloped for hotels and apartments—they sat, after all, on the prized foreshore. Artisanal fishing continued on the Bassin, however, coexisting (though not always harmoniously) with the ever-expanding flotilla of pleasure vessels.[51]

Over the same period, a new appreciation of the ocean came into play. In the 1970 and '80s, surfers from Australia and North America began to make surfing pilgrimages to the Atlantic coast, which they considered undiscovered territory, peppered with exciting, secret "spots" where perfect waves unfurled their magic. French youth embraced the sport with enthusiasm in this period (though farther south, around Biarritz, some had taken it up in the 1960s). The surfers' way of approaching the sea, their eternal search for ideal conditions based on wind direction, swell size, and sandbar formation, is not unlike that of fishermen in that they must work with an ever-changing element and try to harness its energies. But the surfer's aim is different from the fisherman's: it is about experiencing intense bodily sensations, the pleasure of being at one with a wave. And the tribal culture that has developed around surfing, identifying its practitioners (truthfully or not) as intrepid misanthropes who refuse the trappings of "normal" life (work, a permanent home)—has not always encouraged sympathetic relations with fishing people or shore-bound bathers.

Bathers in nineteenth-century Arcachon had sought a beach free of obstacles, provoking the creation of zones for activities deemed incompatible. In the late twentieth century, the presence of surfers who covet the beach breaks preferred by swimmers—where waves break cleanly—and whose boards are seen as a physical threat, led to a division of the ocean beach into board-riding and swimming zones. Territories once again have had to be marked out, this time by movable flagpoles, and their limits are not always respected—by either group.

For surfers, the waves breaking in the Bassin's *passes* present, in the right conditions, an exciting challenge; for the fishing community, the primary concern is safety in an unstable zone that they must pass through in all conditions.[52] As it turns out, the reluctance of the fishing community to embrace engineering projects in the early to mid-1800s changed in the twentieth century to concerted calls for the dredging of the channels. Jacques Ragot relays that in 1969, an oyster farmer from Audenge, on the eastern shores of the Bassin, concerned about the northern channel becoming blocked and preventing the passage of plankton, proposed the sinking of car bodies weighed down by stones as a means of keeping the northern channel open. So the Baron d'Haussez's 1829 dream lived on, in a new form.[53]

In 1990, fishermen protested when the Société d'Etudes Hydrauliques declared that it would be useless to spend five to ten million francs (roughly $900,000 to $1.8 million) on dredging the channels; in response, the Union Intercommunal du Bassin d'Arcachon agreed to dredge the northern channel "when the morphology of the site proved favorable." Dissatisfied with this concession, the wives of the protesting fishermen took action: they wrote an open letter calling for an immediate dredging, listing recent deaths in the *passes* in support of their demand.[54]

Something had happened to change the way the fishing community understood the sea. Technological developments in navigation instruments, boat design, and fishing techniques had transformed the fishermen and -women's relationship with the Bassin and the ocean. Perhaps, having gained a certain amount of control over the elements, what lay underneath the water held less mystery, and the possibility of effecting change no longer seemed preposterous. We cannot overlook another important change: even though the women petitioners identified themselves as fishermen's wives, they were, unlike their predecessors a century before, literate and spoke directly to the administration, for themselves and their families.

Many of the issues causing tension in the 1800s were still alive a century later, in one form or another. This I discovered from speaking to oyster farmers, fishermen, and boat operators about their lives on the Bassin in the late 1990s.[55] Arcachon is still a contested space. The locals, whether they have become resort service providers or continue to fish and farm oysters, have an ambivalent attitude toward visitors to the Bassin. One oyster farmer complained to me about the way tourists behaved in their yachts and motorboats on the water; they showed no respect for the rules, for buoys, or for other sailors. Many wealthy out-of-towners, I heard, kept yachts in the marina and never used them—a waste of space and money. Theft of oysters from farms was also a problem. Vacationers rarely observed the legal limit on amateur shell fishing.

Another concern among local sailors was the effect of changing agricultural practices on the Bassin's water. The use of nitrogen to fertilize crops along the Leyre River was causing algal bloom and killing off fish stocks.[56] Relationships with outside authorities were strained, as ever. European regulations governing net sizes and hygiene (resulting in the demolition of old timber oyster huts) were unpopular with some fishermen and oyster farmers. Bigger outfits were squeezing smaller operators out, and, to make things worse, Atlantic fish stocks were diminishing.

The sleek Train à Grande Vitesse (High Speed Train) now comes as far as Arcachon during the summer months, bringing Parisians in less than four hours and visitors from all over Europe. A broad, fast freeway links the town to Bordeaux. And in the face of rampant overdevelopment and a suburbanization of the neighboring communes, visitors and locals alike are rediscovering the history of the Bassin. The Ville d'hiver, its old-world charms appreciated anew from the early 1980s, is a major attraction.[57] Even though most vacationers now carry their own videocameras, postcards still beckon from revolving stands outside news agencies, book shops, and cafés, including reprints of "old" postcards of Arcachon, once found only in collectors' albums.

The *types* fixed by the photographer's lens over a hundred years ago, the oyster farming women in their *benaizes,* the fishermen hauling up nets and cooking fish soup in their *chaloupes* and *pinasses,* stare out at passersby from their rectangles of cardboard. The people pictured are long dead and gone and, while their descendants may still be working on the Bassin, some in the same profession as their parents and grandparents, they no longer stake their claim to the beach in the same way. Their work activities are confined to zones removed from the center, and their tourist-oriented work is carefully organized in accordance with municipal regulations. The beaches belong to the bathers, the strollers, and the gazers.

ABBREVIATIONS

ADG   Archives Départementales de la Gironde
AN   Archives Nationales
BSHAA   *Bulletin de la Société Historique et Archéologique d'Arcachon*
DM   Délibérations Municipales
SHAA   Société Historique et Archéologique d'Arcachon

NOTES

Introduction

1. This imagined scene is based on contemporary descriptions by visitors and guidebook writers. See chapter 6 for more on the scene at the station.

2. "Ile aux Oiseaux" is the current spelling. In many pre–twentieth-century documents, it is called "Ile [or Isle] des Oiseaux." For consistency, I will follow current usage.

3. We might compare this to the renaming of Brighton, replacing the "humble" Brighthelmstone. Rob Shields, "The 'System of Pleasure': Liminality and the Carnivalesque at Brighton," *Theory, Culture, and Society* 7 (1990): 44. Note that Lamarque de Plaisance invented Arcachon's motto (see epigraph) in 1860, inspired by Monseigneur Donnet's inscription on the church bell of St. Ferdinand (Arcachon): "Nox heri, hodie aurora, cras lux" (Yesterday night, today dawn, tomorrow light). Michel Boyé, "Arcachon, 'la capitale' (1857–1906)," in *Une histoire du Bassin: Arcachon, entre landes et océan,* ed. Charles Daney and Michel Boyé (Bordeaux: Mollat, 1995), 167.

4. This interpretation is offered on a color brochure featuring the coat of arms, probably printed in the late 1990s by the city of Arcachon. No publication details supplied. Jacques

Ragot lists honey as one of the region's agricultural products in the 1700s—one of the only references I have found to honey in the local historiography. Jacques Ragot, "La vie et les gens pendant les siècles où La Teste de Buch vécut sous la menace des sables" (paper presented at the Cercle Universitaire d'Arcachon, 4 February 1970), 18.

5. City of Arcachon, coat of arms, n.d. (text on verso).

6. Alice Garner, "Floating Worlds: Conflicting Representations of Sea and Shore in Arcachon and La Teste, 1830–1910" (PhD diss., University of Melbourne, 2001).

7. The work of local historians and geographers Charles Daney, Michel Boyé, Robert Aufan, Eliane Keller, Noël Gruet, Micheline Cassou-Mounat, Fernand Labatut, Jacques Clémens, Jacques Ragot, Jacques Sargos, and many others has been indispensable. The Société Historique et Archéologique d'Arcachon publishes a rich and informative quarterly bulletin, *Bulletin de la Société Historique et Archéologique d'Arcachon* (hereafter *BSHAA*). See bibliography.

8. Anonymous, *Visite de Ll. Mm. L'Empereur et L'Impératrice et de S.A. le Prince Impérial à Arcachon, le lundi 10 Octobre 1859* (Bordeaux: Imp. de A.-R. Chaynes, 1859).

9. See the bibliography for references in these disciplines.

10. Henri Lefebvre, *La production de l'espace* (Paris: Editions Anthropos, 1974).

11. Alain Corbin, *The Lure of the Sea: The Discovery of the Seaside in the Western World 1750–1840,* trans. J. Phelps (Harmondsworth, U.K.: Penguin, 1994). Other works by this author that contributed to this book are *Les filles de noces: Misère sexuelle et prostitution (19e et 20e siècles)* (Paris: Aubier Montaigne, 1978); "Divisions of Time and Space," in *Realms of Memory: Rethinking the French Past,* ed. Pierre Nora (New York: Columbia University Press, 1992); and *The Foul and the Fragrant: Odour and the French Social Imagination,* trans. M. Koshan (London: Picador, 1994).

12. Jean-Didier Urbain, *Sur la plage: Mœurs et coûtumes balnéaires (XIXe–XXe siècles)* (Paris: Payot, 1994), 19. Note: An English translation of this title was published in 2003: *At the Beach,* trans. Catherine Porter (Minneapolis: University of Minnesota Press, 2003).

13. Urbain, *Sur la plage,* 74.

14. John K. Walton, "Consuming the Beach: Seaside Resorts and Cultures of Tourism in England and Spain from the 1840s to the 1930s," in *Being Elsewhere: Tourism, Consumer Culture, and Identity in Modern Europe and North America,* ed. Shelley Baranowski and Ellen Furlough (Ann Arbor: University of Michigan Press, 2001), 294–95.

15. For the history of the dunes and forests, see Jacques Sargos, *Histoire de la forêt landaise: Du désert à l'âge d'or* (Bordeaux: L'Horizon Chimérique, 1997); Fernand Labatut, "Le destin des dunes (3ème partie): Péripéties municipales," *BSHAA,* no. 108 (2001): 29–52; Fernand Labatut, "Préludes à l'ensemencement des dunes (suite)," *BSHAA,* no. 103 (2000): 68–94; Jacques Ragot, *Histoire de La Teste-de-Buch des origines à la fixation des dunes* (La Teste: J. Ragot, 1987); Robert Aufan, "Le Pays de Buch, de la lande aux forêts (XVIIIe et XIXe siècles)," *BSHAA,* no. 89 (1996): 1–40.

16. John Walton argues that historians of leisure have neglected the war years in seaside resorts "at their peril" in his "Leisure Towns in Wartime: The Impact of the First World War in Blackpool and San Sebastian," *Journal of Contemporary History* 31, no. 4 (1996): 603–18.

17. Alain Cabantous, *Les citoyens du large: Les identités maritimes en France (XVIIe–XIXe siècles)* (Paris: Aubier, 1995), 69.

18. The *Robert* defines the terms as follows (I provide only a brief version, with my English translation in brackets):

- *Lais:* "Terrains que les eaux de mer ou de rivière laissent à découvert en se retirant" [*Foreshore:* Territory or land that sea or river waters leave uncovered upon withdrawing].

- *Relais:* "Ce qui est laissé en arrière . . . terrain laissé à découvert par l'eau" [No equivalent English word: That which is left behind . . . land left uncovered by water].

- *Rivage:* "Zone soumise à l'action des vagues, et le cas échéant, des marées" [*Shore:* Zone subject to the action of waves and, in certain cases, of tides].

- *Grève:* "Terrain plat, formé de sables, de graviers, situé au bord de la mer ou d'un cours d'eau" [*Shore/Strand:* Flat terrain, formed of sand, gravel, situated beside the sea or water course].

- *Plage:* "I. Vx ou poét. Etendue de terre.—Par ext. *Plage de mer,* étendue de mer. Poét. (Encore au XIXe siècle). Contrée . . . II . . . 1. Vx. (Mar.) Rivage en pente douce dont les navires peuvent difficilement approcher . . . 2. (Répandu déb. XIXe). Mod. Endroit plat et bas d'un rivage où les vagues déferlent, et qui est constitué de débris minéraux plus ou moins fins (limon, sable, galets) . . . → Côte . . . Spécialt. Cet endroit, réservé à la baignade, aux loisirs" [*Beach.* I. Anc or poet. Stretch of land.—By ext. Sea beach, stretch of sea. Poetic (still in nineteenth century). Country . . . II . . . 1. Anc. (Mar.) Gently sloping shore that ships can approach only with difficulty . . . 2. (Widespread early nineteenth century). Mod. Flat and low part of a shore where the waves unfurl, and which is constituted by more or less fine mineral debris (lime, sand, pebbles) . . . → Coast. Esp. A place reserved for swimming, for leisure]. This last definition is particularly interesting; it points to the shift in understandings and usages that this book investigates.

Robert, Paul, and Alain Rey, eds. *Le grand Robert de la langue francaise: Dictionnaire alphabétique et analogique de la langue francaise.* 2nd ed. (Paris: Le Robert, 1986)(hereafter the *Robert*).

19. Villermé, *Tableau de l'état physique et moral des ouvriers,* Paris, 1840, quoted in Paul Louis, *Histoire de la classe ouvrière en France de la Révolution à nos jours: La condition matérielle des travailleurs, les salaires et le coût de la vie* (Paris: Librairie des Sciences Politiques et Sociales, Marcel Rivière, 1927), 67. Louis reproduces and analyses statistics from government and private sources from Paris and the departments from the Revolution of 1789 to the First World War.

20. Louis, 206–11.

1. Hideous Virginity, or Beautiful Maps on Annonay Paper

1. O. D., *Guide du voyageur à La Teste et aux alentours du Bassin d'Arcachon* (Bordeaux: P. Chaumas-Gayet, 1845), 17.

2. The *Petit Robert* defines *lande* as "Etendue de terre où ne croissent que certaines

plantes sauvages (ajonc, bruyère, genêt, etc.)" (Expanse of land where only certain wild plants grow [gorse, briar, broom, etc.]). Robert, Paul, Alain Rey, and J. Rey-Debove, eds. *Le petit Robert: Dictionnaire alphabetique et analogique de la langue francaise* (Paris: Le Robert, 1985)(hereafter the *Petit Robert*). Note the use of the lowercase for landes, to distinguish them from the department of the same name (always capitalized), which lies south of the Gironde department. The landes straddled the Gironde and Landes departments; this book concerns itself solely with the Gironde department.

3. The argument about the emptiness of the landes is made nicely by Marie-Dominique Ribereau-Gayon, in "Perceptions sensorielles et représentations des landes de Gascogne," in SHAA, ed., *Le littoral gascon et son arrière-pays (Moyen-âge, économie, Arcachon et le Bassin)* (Arcachon: Graphica/SHAA, 1993). The physiocrats' representation of communal lands, including the landes, is dealt with in Nadine Vivier, *Propriété collective et identité communale: Les biens communaux en France, 1750–1914* (Paris: Publications de la Sorbonne, 1998), chap. 1 and passim.

4. Baron de Mortemart de Boisse, *Voyage dans les Landes de Gascogne et rapport à la Société royale et centrale d'agriculture sur la colonie d'Arcachon,* Mémoires de la Société royale et centrale d'agriculture (Paris: L. Bouchard-Huzard, 1840), 147–48, 24.

5. See Jacques Sargos, *Histoire de la forêt landaise: Du désert à l'âge d'or* (Bordeaux: L'Horizon Chimérique, 1997), 409–27.

6. Jacques Arago, writing about the landes in 1829, described the shepherds as "savage beings, moronic men." Jacques Arago, *Promenades historiques, philosophiques et pittoresques, dans le département de la Gironde* (Bordeaux: Suwerinck, 1829), 9.

7. Mortemart de Boisse, *Voyage dans les Landes,* 146.

8. Ribereau-Gayon, "Perceptions sensorielles," 148–49.

9. See Sargos, *Histoire de la forêt landaise,* 327–48, for a comprehensive account of the canal projects in the landes, especially that of Claude Deschamps, who first showed interest in the area in 1810 and spent thirty years trying to realize his dream of a canal crossing the Grandes Landes.

10. I will henceforth refer to these respectively as the Compagnie des Landes and the Compagnie d'Arcachon.

11. Sargos, *Histoire de la forêt landaise,* 329, 350. Doudeauville was ministre de la maison du roi from 4 August 1824 to 2 June 1827. His son, Sosthène de la Rochefoucauld, also a director of the Compagnie d'Arcachon, had been director general of Beaux-Arts et Lettres. Benoit Yvert, ed., *Dictionnaire des ministres de 1789 à 1989* (Paris: Perrin, 1990), 127.

12. Hennequin, *Notice sur la Compagnie Agricole et Industrielle d'Arcachon, suivie de divers documents relatifs à ses opérations, ainsi qu'à la construction du canal et du chemin de fer qui faciliteront le transport de ses produits* (Paris: Imprimerie de Bourgogne et Martinet, 1838), 2.

13. Of course the noble settlers made sure their rural homes were as comfortable as they could be; Mortemart de Boisse described the Baron de Chabannes' "gracious house, whose interior would charm the most elegant Parisian woman." Mortemart de Boisse, *Voyage dans les Landes,* 124.

14. "Comité de colonisation, établi à La Teste de Buch, arrondissement de Bordeaux, par la Compagnie Agricole et Industrielle d'Arcachon" in Hennequin, *Notice,* 58.

15. Mareschal, "Journal du voyage fait en octobre 1833 dans les Landes de Bordeaux," 2 November 1833, in *Entreprise d'exploitation et colonisation des Landes de Bordeaux,* 1834.

16. We might ask what constituted the "original" state of the landes; despite appearances to the contrary, the land was being used, and changed, by its inhabitants. Shepherds burnt sections of the landes to promote plant growth. See Mortemart de Boisse, *Voyage dans les Landes,* 29–30.

17. Mortemart de Boisse, echoing Mareschal, writes of "lush vegetation coming after the desert of the Argentières" and of being "surprised and charmed to see life succeed nothingness." *Voyage dans les Landes,* 8, 10.

18. Mareschal, "Journal du voyage," 112.

19. Note that the *Petit Robert* defines *noyer* as both "tuer par asphyxie en immergeant dans un liquide" (to kill by suffocation caused by immersing in liquid) and "(XVIIe) faire absorber et disparaître dans un ensemble vaste ou confus" (to be absorbed and disappear into a vast or confused ensemble).

20. Mareschal, "Journal du voyage," 114.

21. O. D., *Guide du voyageur,* 24.

22. Mareschal, "Journal du voyage," 115.

23. DM La Teste, 3 March 1833.

24. Jacques Ragot informs us of the plans for the new town and port in *Histoire de La Teste-de-Buch des origines à la fixation des dunes* (La Teste: Ragot, 1987), 193.

25. James Scott discusses the exclusion of local knowledge as an important factor in the failure of state-sponsored social engineering projects in *Seeing Like a State: How Certain Schemes to Improve the Human Condition Have Failed* (New Haven: Yale University Press, 1998), 6 and chap. 9.

26. Justice of the Peace, La Teste, 2 December 1839. ADG, Series U (Annexe). Note that Gazaillan was also called Madame Bezian by Cazenave in one witness statement. On Boyer-Fonfrède's dismissal see Sargos, *Histoire de la forêt landaise,* 352.

27. Mareschal, "Journal du voyage," 116–17.

28. While Brémontier is the name most often credited with the creation of the forests, local historians have argued for recognition of his precursors, including the Amanieu de Ruats (La Teste's seigneurs from 1713), the Desbiey brothers, Jean-Baptiste Peyjehan de Francon, and the Baron Charlevoix de Villers, who were all instrumental in the first attempts at dune stabilization. See Sargos, *Histoire de la forêt landaise,* 261–66 on Brémontier's alleged subterfuge and also Robert Aufan, "La révolution forestière au début du XIXe siècle," in *Une histoire du Bassin,* ed. Daney and Boyé, 71–82.

29. Mareschal, "Journal du voyage," 132.

30. Ibid., 117.

31. Un Paysan des Landes, "Canal d'Arcachon," *Le Journal de la Guienne,* 18 July 1834.

32. The *Petit Robert* defines *faiseur* as "*Péj.* (déb. XIXe) N.M. Celui qui cherche à se faire valoir . . . Hâbleur. Homme d'affaires peu scrupuleux." (*Pejorative.* [Early nineteenth century] One who seeks attention . . . Boaster. Unscrupulous businessman.)

33. Un Paysan des Landes, "Industrialisme, nouveaux miracles, poudre d'or trouvée dans les sables des Landes," *Le Journal de la Guienne,* Tuesday, 24 June 1834.

34. Le Paysan des Landes, "Canalisation des Landes," *Le Journal de la Guienne,* 15 August 1834.

35. Sargos, *Histoire de la forêt landaise,* 340.

36. Lalesque père, "Canal d'Arcachon," *Journal de la Guienne,* Tuesday, 29 July 1834, 2; "Observations sur la critique du canal d'Arcachon," *Journal de la Guienne,* July 1834, 1.

37. Hennequin, *Notice sur la Compagnie Agricole et Industrielle d'Arcachon, suivie de divers documents relatifs à ses opérations, ainsi qu'à la construction du canal et du chemin de fer qui faciliteront le transport de ses produits* (Paris: Imprimerie de Bourgogne et Martinet, 1838), 5–6, 9.

38. Ibid., 5–6. The construction of the line had been authorized in July 1837 and the concession granted to the engineer Fortuné de Vergez in December of the same year.

39. Ibid., 7.

40. Ibid., 14.

41. Ibid., 8.

42. Bonneval, "Rapport au conseil d'agriculture," 15 November 1837, quoted ibid., 8.

43. "Comité de Colonisation établi à La Teste de Buch, arrondissement de Bordeaux, par la Compagnie Agricole et Industrielle d'Arcachon," in Hennequin, *Notice,* 62.

44. Compagnie Agricole et Industrielle d'Arcachon, *Assemblée Générale des Actionnaires et des Conseils d'Agriculture, d'Art et du Contentieux,* Paris, 25 February 1839, 38. See epigraph.

45. Mortemart de Boisse, *Voyage dans les Landes,* 113.

46. Mareschal, "Journal du voyage," 133.

47. See Alice L. Conklin and Ian Fletcher, eds., *European Imperialism, 1830–1930* (Boston: Houghton Mifflin, 1999), on the "mission civilisatrice," and James Scott, *Seeing Like a State,* 82.

48. Mortemart de Boisse, *Voyage dans les Landes,* 134.

49. O. D., *Guide du voyageur,* 14.

50. Sargos, *Histoire de la forêt landaise,* 428–30.

51. One example of the municipality's defense of usage rights in favor of a shepherd can be found in the records of the Juge de Paix, La Teste, 1838. ADG, Series U (Annexe). Nadine Vivier argues that historians often have assumed wrongly that access to communal lands benefited only the poor. In some regions only landowners, whether residents or not, were entitled to graze their livestock on *communaux,* while in others the landless were allowed to take a couple of head onto the shared pasture. Vivier, *Propriété collective,* 48–50. The sections of landes acquired by the Compagnies had belonged to the local seigneurs, a large section of which was leased to Daniel Nézer in 1766 on condition that he plant wheat and build mills but *not* plant trees, as this would violate the grazing rights of the inhabitants of the communes of La Teste, Gujan, and Cazaux, acknowledged in the *baillette,* or agreement between the seigneur and the communes, of 1550. See Sargos, *Histoire de la forêt landaise,* 433–39.

52. As James C. Scott puts it: "Telling a farmer only that he is leasing twenty acres of

land is about as helpful as telling a scholar that he has bought six kilograms of books." *Seeing Like a State,* 26.

53. Ragot, *Histoire,* 194–95.

54. See de Bonneval, principal director of the colonization committee, on the Spanish workers, reprinted as "1839, La main d'œuvre espagnole à La Teste," in *BSHAA,* no. 32 (1982): 44–45. From Comte André de Bonneval, *Tableau pittoresque et agricole des landes du bassin d'Arcachon* (Paris: Bourgogne et Martinet, 1839).

55. Arrêtés municipaux, La Teste, 28 March 1835.

56. Arrêtés municipaux, La Teste, 26 July 1839. Although the original documents use the word *passeport,* this may well have meant *livrets,* the identity booklets that all workers were required to carry and on which employers made notes on the worker's behavior. A worker without a *livret* was automatically suspect because it was likely his previous employers had either given him a poor report or kept the *livret.* Definition provided by French labor historian Charles Sowerwine.

57. "Incident causé à Cazaux par des ouvriers travaillant au canal," ADG 4 M 223, reprinted in *BSHAA,* no. 32 (1982): 46–47.

58. Ragot, *Histoire,* 198–99.

59. Ibid., 197.

60. Sargos, *Histoire de la forêt landaise,* 358; Michel Boyé, "Le temps des investisseurs (1820–1857)" in *Une histoire du Bassin,* ed. Daney and Boyé, 62.

61. Sargos, *Histoire de la forêt landaise,* 357–58.

62. Ragot, *Histoire,* 196.

63. The quote is from Mortemart de Boisse, *Voyage dans les Landes,* 11.

2. A Site of Contention

1. "Procès verbal de bornage," 28 January 1934. AN CC[5] 379.

2. Local geographer and historian Charles Daney uses the Dutch term *slikke* to define the prés salés, as well as the French term *mattes.* Daney, "Le Bassin, sables et marais," in *Une histoire du Bassin,* ed. Daney and Boyé, 25–26. The *Robert* defines *pré* as "terrain produisant de l'herbe destinée à la nourriture du bétail" (lands producing grass destined for livestock feed) and defines *prés salés* as the same, beside the sea. The *Petit Robert* defines *matte* as "(1627 . . .) *Techn.* Mélange de sulfures de fer et de cuivre, provenant de la première fusion d'un minerai sulfuré" (Mixture of sulphides of iron and copper, from the first fusion of a sulphurized ore).

3. Gujan is a commune on the southeast coast of the Bassin, between La Teste and the mouth of the Leyre River. Cameleyre's descendants would later establish a prominent cannery on the Bassin d'Arcachon. As for Ronveau: the first time his name appears in the report, it reads "Ronveau" in large type, but from then on it looks more like "Rondeau" (perhaps because they extend the right stem of the *v* upward and over the previous letter). I have chosen to read it as "Ronveau."

4. "La plantation des bornes qui doivent servir de limites entre les prés salés que possède

M. de Sauvage dans la commune de la Teste et le rivage du bassin d'Arcachon faisant partie du domaine de l'Etat." Procès verbal de bornage.

5. Emphasis in original. For more on the history of the enfeoffment, see Sargos, *Histoire de la forêt landaise,* 262–63, 276–77.

6. *Truc* (Gascon term) translates as *tertre, monticule* in French—hillock, or mound, in English. Charles Daney, *Dictionnaire de la Lande Française, du fond du Bassin au fin fond de la Lande* (Portet-sur-Garonne: Loubatières, 1992). I assume the dune lay *behind* the prés salés.

7. According to Franck Bouscau, author of a carefully researched law thesis on the status of the La Teste prés salés, Pierre Fleury was a brother of the mayor, Jean Fleury *fils aîné* (eldest son)—a delicate position to negotiate. Frank Bouscau, *Les prés salés de La Teste-de-Buch en Aquitaine: Contribution à l'histoire du domaine maritime de moyen-âge à nos jours* (Tours/Paris: Franck Bouscau, 1993), 329. Both Jean Fleury *fils aîné* (the mayor) and Jean Fleury *aîné père* appear in Soulignac's table of landowners whose cadastral revenue exceeded one thousand francs, but there is no mention of Pierre Fleury. Mayor Fleury was the wealthiest landowner in the commune, with over 600 hectares (1,482 acres) of land. Bernard Soulignac, "Aménagement agricole et évolution rurale de la Teste dans la première moitié du XIXe siècle" (master's thesis, Université de Bordeaux III, 1973), tables 8, 9.

8. Michel de Certeau discusses the bornage process, which requires, first, that the actors create a theater or field of actions: this entails "a renewal and a repetition of the originary founding acts, a *recitation* and a citation of the genealogies that could legitimate the new enterprise, and a *prediction* and a promise of success at the beginning of battles, contracts, or conquests." This follows the form of the Roman ritual of *fas.* Michel de Certeau, *The Practice of Everyday Life,* trans. S. Rendall (Berkeley: University of California Press, 1984), 123–24.

9. "Zone soumise à l'action des vagues, et, le cas échéant, des marées . . . Ce sens est le seul reçu en géographie et en droit." (Zone subject to the action of waves and, in some cases, of tides. This meaning is the only one accepted in geography and law.) The *Robert,* s.v. *rivage.* Note again the difficulty in translating the various French terms for shore, beach, etc.

10. The Cravey property contained "several scattered clumps of Pine, a little house and a lime kiln" (Procès verbal de bornage). If these were originally prés salés, they must at some time have been cut off from the sea by dikes.

11. My emphasis.

12. He bought them from Hiribarn, the ex-mayor of a neighboring commune, Andernos. Hiribarn had acquired them as *biens nationaux.* Fernand Labatut, "Les caractères originaux du Pays de Buch: Le Buch dans la période contemporaine," *BSHAA,* no. 96 (1998): 14.

13. Letter from Taffart to the prefect of the Gironde, 5 July 1831. ADG. Capitalization in original. In this passage he named "Croneau" as having abused his authority with respect to the municipal council. Croneau may have been the "subprefect" referred to in related accusations. The peer was most likely Sauvage's uncle, the Duc Decazes.

14. Jean-Baptiste Taffart, "Historique des faits qui ont précédé et déterminé la contestation," in "Mémoire rédigé par M. Taffart sur les prés salés pour l'Administration des Domaines contre les Sieurs Fleury jeune, Oxéda et Sauvage," DM La Teste, 1832, paragraph 1.

15. Taffart to prefect, 16 July 1831. Emphasis in original. We should note here that Jean-Baptiste Taffart was distantly related to the noble Taffard de la Ruade branch, whose heirs owned cultivated land that bordered the western end of the prés salés. This suggests another layer to the campaign, perhaps even a personal battle between prominent families? But it is probably of greater significance that Jean-Baptiste Taffart (born in 1767) had made a career in the domain and registration administration. He was fifty-three at the time of his campaign against Sauvage, and died the following year, in 1832. I thank M. Boyé for information about the Taffart family.

16. Vivier, *Propriété collective,* 222, 235.

17. *Padouens* was the Gascon term for pasture and *vacants* generally referred to seigneurial land on which locals could pasture animals, gather fuel, etc., in return for a levy.

18. In the original: "vrais seigneurs, utiles, paisibles possesseurs, comme de leur propre chose." Hameau, mayor of La Teste, to Dumon, minister for public works, 12 November 1846. AN Mar CC⁵ 379.

19. DM La Teste, 9 October 1831.

20. The local (Gascon) terms were *esteys*—natural saltwater channels—and *crassats*—sand- or mudbanks exposed at low tide. The quote is from the document outlining the terms of the leasing out of the island. Administrations de l'Enrégistrement et des Domaines, Département de la Gironde, Bureau de La Teste, "Isle des Oiseaux située dans le bassin d'Arcachon: Charges, clauses et conditions sous lesquelles il sera procédé, le 1er juillet 1806 . . . à la Réception des enchères et à l'adjudication à titre de bail de ferme . . . ," 20 June 1806, 1. See also "Mémoire des Marins du Quartier de Lateste [*sic*] Contre la mise en ferme de Lisle [*sic*] et Crassats du Bassin de Lateste, annoncée pour le 18 Juin 1806," La Teste, 1806. ADG S. Lotissements S 16 (Service Maritime). Emphasis in original. For a thorough account of the battle over the Ile aux Oiseaux lease, see Garner, *Floating Worlds,* chap. 2, and Bouscau, *Les prés salés,* 325–30.

21. Taffart, *Mémoire,* DM La Teste, 1832, paragraph 2. Capitalization in original. The *Robert,* s.v. *grève:* "(V. 1140, du lat. pop. grava 'gravier') 1. Terrain plat, formé de sables, de graviers, situé au bord de la mer ou d'un cours d'eau" ("[C. 1140, from the popular Latin 'grava'] Flat terrain, formed of sand, gravel, situated beside the sea or a watercourse."). For *rivage* see n. 9, this chapter. Emphasis in original.

22. Taffart, *Mémoire.* Capitalization in original.

23. "Sera réputé bord et rivage de la mer, tout ce qu'elle couvre et découvre pendant les nouvelles et pleines lunes, et jusques où le grand flot de mars se peut étendre sur les grèves." Quoted in Bouscau, "La curieuse histoire des prés salés de La Teste de Buch (1)," *BSHAA,* no. 40 (1984): 3.

24. DM La Teste, 9 October 1831. Emphasis in original.

25. Dumora took on the lease in 1792, according to article 6 of Taffart's report.

26. Corbin, *Lure of the Sea,* 273.

27. Gairal, "Consultation faite par l'Administration des domaines de la Couronne pour savoir si l'Administration doit prétendre à la propriété des prés salés," 8 June 1833. AN Mar CC^5 379.

28. The *Petit Robert* defines a *perche* as a measurement equivalent to one hundredth of an *arpent,* while an *arpent* was roughly equivalent to an acre, or a *journal* (I thank Peter McPhee for this explanation).

29. Hameau, mayor of La Teste, to Dumon, minister for public works, 12 November 1846. AN Mar CC^5 379. Capitalization in original.

30. Gairal, "Consultation."

31. Scott, *Seeing Like a State,* 35.

32. James Scott notes the "gulf between land tenure facts on paper and facts on the ground." *Seeing Like a State,* 49.

33. DM La Teste, séance extraordinaire, 16 February 1838. Léon Rémy de Brandos, Marquis de Castéja, bought the prés salés for 200,000 francs, according to Soulignac, "Aménagement agricole," 85.

34. Juge de paix, La Teste canton, 4 October 1838. ADG, Série U (Annexe).

35. Juge de paix, La Teste canton, 16 and 18 March 1839.

36. "Mémoire des marins."

37. Mortemard [*sic*] de Boisse, *Extrait d'un rapport adressé le 4 Juin 1849 au Ministre de la Marine par M. Mortemard, Capitaine de frégate,* 4 Juin 1849. AN Marine CC^5 379. My emphasis. Note the different spelling of his name. In the text, I have kept to the spelling that appeared in documents referred to in chapter 1, for the sake of consistency.

38. Cabantous, *Les citoyens du large,* 51, 72, 78.

39. Mortemard de Boisse, *Extrait.* Capitalization in original. It is significant that women were recognized as taking part in fishing; this was not the case in all regions in France. The *chaloupe* was a vessel with sails but no deck, usually manned by twelve rowing fishermen.

40. Bouscau, *Les prés salés,* 363–64.

41. Comte d'Armaillé bought the prés salés in 1845 from Etienne de Verneuil, who had bought them from Léon Rémy de Biaudos, Marquis de Castéja, in 1840. Ibid., appendix PJ 15. D'Armaillé is spelled differently by different people; I have used the spelling that appears most often in La Teste's council minutes.

42. Hameau, mayor of La Teste, to Dumon, minister for public works, 12 November 1846. AN Mar CC^5 379.

43. Extract from DM La Teste, 20 Avril 1854. AN Marine CC^5 379.

44. Bouscau, *Les prés salés,* 365–66.

45. For example, on 24 February 1855, the naval commissioner in La Teste, M. Duchesne, wrote to the mayor of La Teste informing him that the minister for the navy and colonies had refused to authorize d'Armaillé's fish farms on the prés salés, in accordance with article 271 of the imperial decree of 4 July 1853, which dealt with coastal fishing in the 4th arrondissement and "formally declared his opposition to any enclosure works on this PART

OF THE PUBLIC MARITIME DOMAIN." *Procès des prés-salés de La Teste* (Bordeaux: Imprimerie Générale d'Emile Crugy, 1875), 10–11. Capitalization in original.

46. Bouscau, "Curieuse histoire," 6.

47. Bouscau, *Les prés salés,* 500, n. 166.

3. To Suspend the Ocean

1. Jules Taffard, *Mémoire sur la navigation du Bassin d'Arcachon,* 8 October 1810. AN 3 JJ Marine 171, pièce 35. Capitalization in original.

2. M. P. Monnier, *Rapport sur le Bassin d'Arcachon,* 1835. ADG 6 J 42.

3. Mareschal, "Journal du Voyage," 117.

4. "Not a single one of the projects under consideration was carried out, except for improvements in the placement of markers" (beacons, buoys etc). Catherine Bousquet-Bressolier, "Les projets d'aménagement de l'entrée du Bassin d'Arcachon (1768–1864). Une lecture rationelle des mouvements de la nature," in *L'aventure maritime du Golfe de Gascogne à Terre-Neuve,* ed. Comité des Travaux Historiques et Scientifiques (Paris: Editions du Comité des Travaux Historiques et Scientifiques, 1993), 90.

5. As Denis Cosgrove expresses it: "The map excites imagination and graphs desire, its projection is the foundation for and stimulus to projects." Denis Cosgrove, ed., *Mappings* (London: Reaktion Books, 1999), 15.

6. Certeau, *Practice of Everyday Life,* 92. See also Scott, *Seeing Like a State,* 3, 12–15, 76.

7. Peter Gould, *The Geographer at Work* (London: Routledge and Kegan Paul, 1985), 191.

8. Catherine Bousquet-Bressolier, *Les aménagements du Bassin d'Arcachon au XVIIIe siècle* (Dinard: Laboratoire de Géomorphologie, Ecole Pratique des Hautes Etudes, 1990), 108.

9. Gould, *Geographer at Work,* 145.

10. James C. Scott makes similar observations about cadastral maps, which "may freeze a scene of great turbulence." *Seeing Like a State,* 46.

11. Mark Monmonier, *How to Lie with Maps* (Chicago: Chicago University Press, 1991), 25.

12. Certeau, *Practice,* 97.

13. M. P. Monnier, *Etat dans lequel M. P. Monnier Ingénieur Hydrographe de la Marine a trouvé les Passes et la Rade intérieure du Bassin d'Arcachon dans les mois de Juin et Juillet 1835,* ADG 6 J 42.

14. AN F⁷ 7252, dossier 12 (1868).

15. Letter to Billaudel, chief engineer, Ponts et Chaussées, Bordeaux, 12 June 1830. ADG 6 J 42.

16. Bousquet-Bressolier, "Projets d'aménagement," 90.

17. *Mémoire sur la navigation des Vaisseaux à la Coste d'Arcasson [sic]: Observations sur le Port d'Arcasson et l'avantage de sa position,* art. 4 [1768]. ADG 6 J 42. Kearney's name is not recorded in the *Mémoire* itself: Jules Taffard referred to the 1768 survey of the Bassin as Kearney's, and others seem to have followed suit, including Bousquet-Bressolier, "Projets d'aménagement," 91. I refer to this hereafter as Kearney, *Mémoire.*

18. Bousquet-Bressolier, "Projets d'aménagement," 91. Note: Kearney called the bay "Arcasson"; I have maintained this spelling in my translation of his report. Capitalization in original.

19. Kearney, *Mémoire,* art. 3.

20. Ibid. Capitalization in original.

21. Consider Cosgrove's observation of the "social and environmental exclusions involved in European colonial mapping . . . whose claims to objective knowledge practiced a double denial of their selectivity, first of their often considerable dependance upon information supplied by non-European [in our case, local or peasant] inhabitants of the territories mapped, and second of the physical and social landscapes as occupied and understood by those inhabitants themselves." *Mappings,* 11.

22. Kearney, *Mémoire,* art. 1.

23. Certeau, *Practice of Everyday Life,* 93, 117.

24. Michel Mollat, *Europe and the Sea,* trans. Teresa Lavender Fagan (Oxford: Blackwell, 1993), 95.

25. Taffard, *Mémoire sur la Navigation,* 1810. Unless otherwise specified, all quotations from Taffard are from this source. He was a distant cousin of Jean-Baptiste Taffart, who defended the Testerins against Sauvage over the prés salés. Jules was born in 1784 to Pierre Taffard de Laruade and Jeanne Marie Julie Pic de Blais de la Mirandole. See Pierre Labat, "Les Taffard de La Teste," *BSHAA,* no. 116 (2003): 21–40; "Nicolas Taffard et sa descendance," *BSHAA,* no. 117 (2003), 29–46; and his forthcoming article in *BSHAA.* I thank Michel Boyé for explaining the Taffard family connections to me.

26. He used the word "*état,*" which I take to mean *métier* and have translated as "craft."

27. Jean-Marie Bouchet, "Evolution du Bassin d'Arcachon et des conditions de navigation," in *Le littoral gascon et son arrière-pays: mers, dunes, forêt,* ed. SHAA, 1990, 76. The Dune du Pilat is Europe's highest sand dune: it is approximately 105 meters (115 yards) high, but it has measured up to 114 meters (125 yards). In 1855, it was only 35 meters (38 yards) high. *Arcachon Magazine,* Office Municipal de Tourisme, 1996, 22.

28. It was the hydrographer Caspari who, in 1872, recognized the cyclical nature of the Bassin's shifting contours. Bousquet-Bressolier, "Projets d'aménagement," 90, 92, 98.

29. Ibid., 93.

30. Taffard, *Description du Bassin d'Arcachon* [1810]. AN 3 JJ Marine 171, pièce 35bis.

31. Ibid.

32. Lefebvre, *Writings on Cities,* trans. Eleonore Kofman and Elizabeth Lebas (Cambridge, Mass.: Blackwell, 1996), 191.

33. Lettre à Son Excellence Monseigneur le Baron d'Haussez, Ministre de la Marine et des Colonies (from a member of the commission appointed to investigate the improvement of the passes, possibly its president, M. Billaudel), 25 May 1830. ADG 6 J 42. The members of the Commission were Messrs Billaudel, Beautemps-Beaupré, Le Saulnier de Vaubelle, Sauvage, Legallais and Clémenceau. Jacques Ragot, "Projets successifs d'amélioration des passes du Bassin d'Arcachon" in SHAA, ed., *Le littoral gascon et son arrière-pays (mer, dunes, forêt),*" n. 10.

34. Baron d'Haussez, *Notice sur les avantages que présente le changement de la passe de la baie d'Arcachon et sur les moyens d'y opérer cette amélioration,* 1829, AN 3 JJ marine 171, pièce 43. Quoted in Bousquet-Bressolier, "Projets d'aménagement," 94. Ragot, "Projets successifs," 94.

35. Billaudel to d'Haussez, 25 May 1830. ADG 6 J 42.

36. Sauvage, *Rapport,* 26 May 1830. (Reply to the commission's questions concerning the likely success of d'Haussez's proposals). ADG 6 J 42.

37. *Rapport sur la notice relative au bassin d'Arcachon adressée à son Excellence le ministre de la Marine par Monsieur le baron d'Haussez par Beautemps-Beaupré,* daté du 8 mai 1829, AN 3 JJ Marine 171, pièce 44. Cited by Bousquet-Bressolier, "Projets d'aménagement," 94 n. 19.

38. Letter from a member of the commission (probably Billaudel) to Baron d'Haussez, 25 May 1830.

39. Sauvage, *Rapport.* My emphasis.

40. Letter from Billaudel to prefect, 8 February 1831. ADG 3 S/Cô 17.

41. Letter from Chef Maritime to prefect, 22 February 1831. ADG 3 S/Cô 17.

42. In 1830, M. Sauveroche, sent to La Teste to investigate the state of the *passes,* spent two days looking for sailors who could read and write, an almost impossible task given that they were nearly all "out of La Teste, fishing." Letter to Billaudel, chief engineer, Ponts et Chaussées, Bordeaux, 12 June 1830. ADG 6 J 42.

43. Bousquet-Bressolier, "Projets d'aménagement," 95.

44. Monnier, *Rapport sur le Bassin d'Arcachon,* based on his May 1835 survey, published 1836. ADG 6 J 42.

45. Ibid., 3.

46. Ibid., 4.

47. Ibid., 9.

48. Ibid., 5. Capitalization in original.

49. DM La Teste, 3 March 1833.

50. Wissocq, *Mémoire sur les travaux à exécuter pour améliorer l'entrée du Bassin d'Arcachon* (Paris: Imprimerie Porthmann, 1839). The title translates as "Report on the work to be executed for the improvement of the entry to the Bassin d'Arcachon."

51. One of his partners in the Compagnie d'Arcachon, the Saint-Simonian Pierre-Euryale Cazeaux, was involved in the financing of the railway line. Institut Français d'Architecture, ed., *La Ville d'hiver d'Arcachon* (Paris: Institut Français d'Architecture, 1983), 38.

52. Wissocq, *Mémoire,* 20–21.

53. Ibid., 20.

54. Ibid., 19.

55. Bousquet-Bressolier, "Projets d'aménagement," 102–5. James C. Scott analyzes the high modernist ideology of state planners, who "tend to see rational order in remarkably visual aesthetic terms. For them, an efficient, rationally organized city, village or farm was [one] that *looked* regimented and orderly in a geometrical sense." *Seeing Like a State,* 4, 6.

56. Johnston quoted in Ragot, *Histoire de La Teste-de-Buch,* 175. Letter from Ingénieur Ordinaire to Ingénieur en Chef, Ponts et Chaussées, 29 May 1850. AN F[14] 7252.

57. Postscript to Taffard's *Description,* by his father, Laruade Taffard. Michel Boyé supplied the name of the vessel (personal communication).

4. Océano Nox

1. Gendarmes' report, 10th legion, Gironde, March 1836. AN F^7 4013 (Prolongée).

2. Letter from B. Marichon, the mayor of Mios, to the prefect of the Gironde, 1 April 1836. ADG 1N 404.

3. Letter from Fleury *fils aîné,* mayor of La Teste, to the prefect of the Gironde, 1 April 1836. ADG 1N 404.

4. "Lou Gran Malhour" is the Gascon term; it is most commonly referred to in contemporary texts in French, as "Le Grand Malheur" (this is the term I will use).

5. Report by Verrière, Commis Principal de la Marine, chargé des armements et des classes, La Teste, addressed to the Commissaire Général de la Marine in Bordeaux, 24 April 1818.

6. Figure given by Captain Allègre in a letter to the general councillors (*conseillers généraux*) of the Gironde, 15 September 1842. Reprinted in Michel Boyé, "A propos du Grand Malheur (II)," *BSHAA,* no. 99 (1999): 20.

7. Séance de la Commission des Secours du 4 mai 1831. DM La Teste. To illustrate the high death rates for men in maritime communities, Cabantous notes figures from Dunkerque, 1740–80: the sailor's (*gens de mer*) average age at death was 35, compared to the day-laborer's 45 and merchant's 56 ½. Cabantous, *Les citoyens du large,* 128.

8. Mortemart de Boisse, *Voyage dans les Landes,* 25–27.

9. See Louise A. Tilly and Joan W. Scott, *Women, Work, and Family* (New York: Routledge, 1978), 12, on "family economy."

10. Elisée Reclus, "Les plages et le Bassin d'Arcachon," *Revue des Deux Mondes* 48 (15 November, 1863). Quoted by Jacques Plantey, "Les hommes et leur langue," in *Une histoire du Bassin,* ed. Daney and Boyé, 53.

11. Noël Gruet and Pierre-Jean Labourg, "La vie maritime du bassin d'Arcachon," *Le Chasse-Marée: Histoire et Ethnologie Maritime,* no. 41 (1989): 23, 33. Wooden nails were made for the *pinasses;* no metal was used in their construction. The pine was from the La Teste forest: the inhabitants of the southern coast of the Bassin had communal rights to timber for boat and house building on the basis of a sixteenth century agreement with their seigneur, the Captal de Buch. This communal *droit d'usage* is still in force today in parts of the forest.

12. Kearney, *Mémoire,* 3.

13. It seems that women had been abandoning their agricultural labor—work that Testerin men shunned—for ocean fishing, thereby threatening the commune's capacity to subsist in wartime. DM La Teste, 16 November 1793 (25 brumaire, an II). Quoted in Jacques Ragot, *Les pêcheurs du Bassin d'Arcachon au temps des chaloupes* (Bordeaux: Ulysse, 1983), 21.

14. Mareschal, "Journal du Voyage," 118.

15. Capt. David Allègre, *De la pêche dans le Bassin et sur les côtes d'Arcachon: Moyen de la pratiquer sans danger et avec profit* (Bordeaux: Imprimerie de Suwerwinck, 1836), 19.

16. Ibid., 20–21.

17. Ibid., 8.

18. Ibid., 11.

19. Ibid., 11–12.

20. In the original French, to describe the locals' fear for their lives, the signatories used a phrase that is more expressive than my translation: they spoke of sailors "dont la vie se passe dans les alarmes." Allègre, *De la pêche dans le Bassin,* 23–24.

21. Ibid., 18. Note: The mayor of La Teste's account claimed that only two crews returned safely in March 1836. There are slight variations among reports of the disaster.

22. Rôles d'armement au cabotage et à la (petite) pêche, 1836–38. Archives Maritimes 12 P 3 12. Rochefort. Note: tonnage is metric (1 metric tonne = 1.10 tons).

23. This information given by the prefect of the Gironde, Baron Sers, in a letter to the minister for the interior, 8 April 1843, reprinted in Boyé, "A propos," 24.

24. Noël Gruet, "Les chaloupes de pêche de La Teste, 1816 à 1880. Première partie: 1816–1845," *BSHAA,* no. 101 (1999): 38.

25. Michel Boyé and Noël Gruet, "La pêche industrielle: Petite histoire des chalutiers d'Arcachon," in *Une histoire du Bassin,* ed. Daney and Boyé, 97.

26. David Allègre, *De la pêche dans le Bassin et sur la côte extérieure d'Arcachon,* 1841, reprinted in Boyé and Gruet, "La pêche industrielle," 99.

27. Victor Hugo noted the suspicious reaction of the people of Guernesey to the introduction of steam-powered vessels in the 1820s: "To the good fishermen of the time, previously Catholic and more recently Calvinists, always bigots, it seemed to be a piece of hell afloat. . . . In the presence of the steamer, the religious point of view was this:—water and fire are divorced. This divorce is ordered by God . . . one mustn't unite what God has disunited.—The peasant's point of view was this: it scares me." Hugo, *Les travailleurs de la mer* (Garnier-Flammarion, 1980 [1866]), 135–37.

28. From Bernardeau, "Tablettes contemporaines, historiques et cryptographiques de l'Ecouteur Bordelais ou Mémoires secrets pour servir à l'histoire anecdotique du temps qui court," quoted in Jean-Philippe Dubourg, "Histoire de la pêche au chalut, dans le bassin d'Arcachon: Une épopée d'un siècle," *BSHAA,* no. 16 (1978): 7.

29. Lhotellerie to de Prigny, 17 March 1842, reprinted in Boyé, "A propos," 14–15.

30. Allègre to Conseillers Généraux, 15 September 1842, reprinted in Boyé, "A propos," 20. Consider also a letter dated 13 July 1842 from Eugène Dignac to the prefect concerning the mayor, Soulié, who had replaced Fleury in June 1840. Dignac alleged that Soulié, supposedly close to the naval commissioner (Commissaire de la Marine), was threatening fishermen with naval service if they did not use him as their notary (rather than Dignac who had set up practice in Gujan). This is strong evidence of locals' fear of being pressed into service. ADG 3 M 550.

31. Ragot, *Histoire de La Teste-de-Buch,* 235.

32. Prefect to minister of interior, 8 April 1843, reprinted in Boyé, "A propos," 24.

33. Allègre's claim, in Boyé, "A propos," 21.

34. P. M. Tardis, *Organisation de la Compagnie Générale de Pêche et de Salaison du littoral d'Arcachon* (Bordeaux: Imprimerie de Lanefranque, successeur de Ragle, 1843), 7.

35. Oscar Dejean, *Arcachon et ses environs* (Paris: Res Universis, 1992 [1858]).

36. This figure supplied in Bruno Labarbe and Alain Pujol, *Les caprices du Bassin* (Villandraut: Editions de la Palombe, 1998), 113.

37. Cabantous, *Citoyens du large,* 142–44.

38. In 1626, the cardinal-archbishop of Bordeaux, de Sourdis, accorded an indulgence to all those who visited the chapel of Notre-Dame on 25 March. Jacques Clémens, *Le Bassin d'Arcachon* (Joué-lès-Tours: Alan Sutton, 1997), 95.

39. Arago, *Promenades historiques,* 63.

40. Cabantous, *Citoyens du large,* 149.

41. Ibid., 147.

42. Mortemart de Boisse, *Voyage dans les Landes,* 117.

43. ADG 2V 150. Letter reprinted in *BSHAA,* no. 30 (1981): 37. Only the year of the letter provided. Emphasis in original.

44. B. Peyrous, "La vie religieuse autour du bassin d'Arcachon durant l'épiscopat du Cardinal Donnet (1836–82)," in *Arcachon et le Val d'Eyre: Histoire, art, economie,* ed. Fédération Historique du Sud-Ouest (Bordeaux: Biscaye Frères, 1977), 122. Cabantous describes missions as "massive spiritual investments during which, over several weeks, a team of priests made a parish into an intensive site of retreats, exhortations, confessions and processions." He also notes that sailors' wives, generally considered more pious than their husbands, were expected to continue the priests' good work after their departure. *Citoyens du large,* 137, 152. On missions, see also Peter McPhee, *A Social History of France, 1780–1880* (London: Routledge, 1992), 158.

45. Une Testerine, *La fête de la chapelle d'Arcachon, offert par une Testerine à Madame la Préfète et aux dames bordelaises* (Bordeaux: Chaumas-Gayet, libraire, 1849), title page.

46. Ibid., 2, 22. Emphasis in original.

47. Ibid., 6, 12.

48. Mareschal, "Journal du Voyage," 117.

49. Hugo, "Océano Nox," in *Œuvres complètes: Poésie,* vol. 1, ed. Jean Gaudon (Paris: Laffont, 1985), 1034–35.

50. Corbin, *Lure of the Sea,* 244, 245. He discusses this obsession under the heading "Shipwrecks on the Sand" in his chapter "Pathos of the Shore," 242–49.

51. Allègre, *De la pêche dans le Bassin,* 1836, 10.

5. An Emotional Tableau

1. Jacques Arago, *Promenades historiques, philosophiques et pittoresques, dans le département de la Gironde* (Bordeaux: Suwerinck, 1829), 16, 29. Emphasis in original. Jacques was the brother of the famous scientist François Arago.

2. Anonymous, "Une saison chez Legallais: 5 août—15 août 1825," pt. 1, *BSHAA,* no. 76 (1993): 53. Royan is a resort town at the mouth of the Gironde River and a competitor with Archachon from the mid-nineteenth century on.

3. Arago, *Promenades*, 17.

4. Robert Aufan, "La naissance d'Arcachon," in *Une histoire du Bassin,* ed. Daney and Boyé, 85. It is possible that the creators of these establishments were motivated in part by the presence of the directors of the investment companies, which set up in the area in the 1830s.

5. Out of 1,935 visitors in 1854, 1,356 rented rooms in private residences. Aufan, "La naissance," 86.

6. Corbin suggests that the northern European beaches, the first bathing sites, were "much too closely involved in the conflict to allow a true holiday bathing industry to develop"; the absence of English visitors added to their decline over this period. *Lure of the Sea,* 257.

7. Ibid., 257, 270, and 261–62.

8. Ibid., 262.

9. *Guide du voyageur à La Teste,* quoted in Patrick Chadeyron, "La mode et la renommée," in *Une histoire du Bassin,* 140.

10. Ernest Laroche, *A travers le vieux Bordeaux: Récits inédits, légendes, études de moeurs, portraits, types, monuments, reconstitution des quartiers pittoresques* (Bordeaux: Editions de la Grande Fontaine, 1890), 115–16.

11. Exploring this further, see Douglas Mackaman, *Leisure Settings: Bourgeois Culture, Medicine, and the Spa in Modern France* (Chicago: Chicago University Press, 1998), 2, 124–25, and passim on guidebooks and spa novels as "scripts" for a bourgeoisie in the process of developing leisure practices as an integral part of their identity formation.

12. Patrick Chadeyron tells us that Dr. Buchan's guide, written in 1804, was first translated for Boulogne bathers in 1812 and then by Bordelais doctors in 1824. Its French title was *Observations sur l'usage des bains de mer.* Chadeyron, "La mode et la renommée," 141.

13. Anonymous, "Une saison," pt. 1, 47.

14. For biographical information on Legallais, see Aufan, "La naissance," 85. He married into the Taffard family in 1811, and his wife Marie-Angélique inherited the property at Eyrac. A seigneurial document of 1785 claims that a Monsieur Dumora had built "an edifice or building divided into several rooms for bathing and treatment of invalids" (well before Legallais' arrival). Later sources show no evidence of this structure, suggesting either that it was never built or that it was demolished or left to the mercy of the elements. Robert Aufan, *La naissance d'Arcachon (1823–1857): De la forêt à la ville* (Arcachon: SHAA, 1994), 55. However, the fact that it was mentioned suggests that Laroche was right about sea bathing having been practiced earlier, then abandoned—perhaps due to the revolutionary wars? See also Chadeyron, "La mode et la renommée," 139.

15. "Bains de Mer à La Teste: Etablissement Legallais, à Bel-Air" in *Le Mémorial Bordelais,* 3 July 1830, reprinted in *BSHAA,* no. 19 (1979): 42–43.

16. Louis, *Historie de la classe ouvrière,* 67.

17. Anonymous, "Une saison," pt. 2, *BSHAA,* no. 77 (1993): 49.

18. For a description of *pêche à la senne,* see chapter 4.

19. Corbin, *Lure of the Sea,* 251–52.

20. This cultivated leisure involved "perfecting one's culture, enjoying one's collections, and perfecting the art of conversation." See Corbin, "Du loisir cultivé à la classe de loisir," in Alain Corbin, ed., *L'avènement des loisirs, 1850–1960* (Paris: Aubier-Flammarion, 1995), 58.

21. J. P. P., "Une visite à La Teste du [*sic*] Buch à travers les Grandes Landes": Extract from a letter published in *Le Glaneur* of Bazas on 17 September 1837, addressed to "Mme Elisa P." Reprinted in *BSHAA,* no. 37 (1983): 45. According to André Sapaly, who published this letter in *Les Cahiers du Bazadais,* no. 52 (1981), J. P. P. was Jacques Paulin Polhe, a municipal councillor born in Bazas in 1787. Armide was a sorceress who lived in an enchanted palace, in a much-loved opera, *Armide* (1686) by French composer Jean-Baptiste Lully and librettist Philippe Quinault. The story of Armide, based on a section of *Gerusalemme liberata,* a popular epic poem by the Italian poet Torquato Tasso, was also dramatized in operas by composers Antonio Salieri, Christoph Willibald Gluck, Joseph Haydn, Gioachino Rossini, and Antonín Dvořák.

22. Corbin, *Lure of the Sea,* 279, 164.

23. J. P. P., "Une visite à La Teste," 43–46.

24. Anonymous, "Une saison," pt. 1, 51–52.

25. Ibid., 53; ibid., pt. 2, 46.

26. Ibid., 56. Jacques-Benigne Bossuet was a celebrated French bishop, pulpit orator, and poet (1627—1704).

27. Ibid., 55–56.

28. Ibid., pt. 2, 60–61.

29. Arago, *Promenades,* 5–6, 20.

30. Ibid., 23.

31. "Salut, gouffre sans fond, magnifique Océan/ De la grandeur de Dieu noble et sublime image!" J. P. P., "Une visite à La Teste," 45.

32. Ibid., 44–45.

33. Chateaubriand, "René," in *Œuvres romanesques et voyages,* ed. Maurice Regard (Paris: NRF/Gallimard, [1802]); Lord Byron, *Childe Harold's Pilgrimage: A romaunt; and other poems,* 9th ed. (London: printed for John Murray, 1815).

34. Anonymous, "Une saison," pt. 1, 52, 59. About Byron's *Childe Harold,* Corbin writes: "The poem speaks of a sensitivity to the alternation between silence and the loud crash of the breakers, and of an ear for the music of 'the roaring ocean' or the babble of the wavelets on the water's fringe. It also speaks of pleasure in the contact with the salty wind that penetrates one's skin and ruffles one's hair." *Lure of the Sea,* 175–76.

35. J. P. P., "Une visite à La Teste," 44–45.

36. Arago, *Promenades,* 28, 34. Capitalization in original. Twenty years later an anonymous Testerin woman would give a more Romantic slant to a similar walking experience, in her description of Testerin pilgrims arriving by foot at the Arcachon chapel: "As the dawn rose, through the dew and the brush, up to the thighs, in the moving sand." Une Testerine, *La fête de la chapelle d'Arcachon,* 5.

37. Arago, *Promenades,* 15, 17, 63.

38. Ibid., 9.

39. Arago, *Promenades,* 17. In 1823 Arago had published a *Narrative of a Voyage round the World, in the 'Uranie' and 'Physicienne' Corvettes, commanded by Captain Freycinet, during the years 1817–1820* (London: Treuttel and Wurtz, 1823).

40. Ibid., 10. Marie-Noëlle Bourguet, in her study of the Napoleonic departmental statistical inquiries, notes the problem raised by the regional reports' picture of an extreme variety of cultures within French national borders. How could a nation be forged out of such difference? She also claims that the approach of these departmental investigators, even after the national project was abandoned, influenced the later writings of travelers, administrators, and geographers about rural France. Bourguet, *Déchiffrer la France: La statistique départementale à l'époque napoléonienne* (Paris: Editions des Archives Contemporaines, 1989), 306–9.

41. Arago, *Promenades,* 27, 12.

42. Anonymous, "Une saison," pt. 2, 48; J. P. P., "Une visite à La Teste," 45. Thirty years later, Oscar Dejean, in his local history, *Arcachon et ses environs,* also imagined Arcachon as "a sort of French Oceania. It is a Tahiti a few kilometers from Bordeaux, life in the wild only a gunshot away from the center of civilization." Quoted in *La Ville d'hiver,* 60.

43. "Je voulus la sonder, je voulus en toucher / Le sable, y regarder, y fouiller, y chercher, / Pour vous en rapporter quelque richesse étrange, / Et dire si son lit est de roche ou de fange." Hugo, *Œuvres complètes: Poésie,* vol. 1, 631–34.

44. Anonymous, "Une saison," pt. 2, 57.

45. Ibid., 55.

46. Ibid., pt. 1, 56–58.

47. Compare this to Chateaubriand: "Happy Savages! Oh! If only I could enjoy the peace that accompanies you always." Chateaubriand, "René," 125.

48. "Plus les peuples avancent en civilisation, plus cet état du vague des passions augmente." Ibid., preface.

49. J. P. P., "Une visite à La Teste," 45.

50. Ibid., 46.

6. Movement and Life

1. A grassy verge is a strip of grass planted alongside the pavement—or down the center of a road.

2. J. Brenot, *Cent cinquante ans de chemin de fer de Bordeaux à La Teste et à Arcachon* (Bordeaux: Le Bouscat, 1991), 49–51.

3. Isaac and Emile Pereire, bankers from Bordeaux, were to have an enormous influence on the later development of Arcachon, after their absorption in 1852 of the Bordeaux–La Teste line by their Compagnie du Midi and their creation in the 1860s of the Ville d'Hiver. G. Bouchon, *Historique du chemin de fer de Bordeaux à La Teste et à Arcachon* (Bordeaux: G. Gounouilhou/L'Esprit du Temps, 1991 [1891]), 73.

4. Quoted in Bouchon, *Historique du chemin de fer,* 20–21.

5. A limited company was constituted in December 1837: Its members were Aristide-Louis Pereyra, Henri-Nicolas Hovy, Walter and David Johnston, Henri Cart, Mestrezat (member of the initial commission of enquiry), the brothers Louis Pereyra, Nathaniel Johnston and son (who were involved in reintroducing steam-powered fishing vessels to Arcachon later in the century), Jacques Galos and son, David-Frédéric Lopès-Dias, de Vergez, Ferdinand-Jean Bayard de la Vingtrie, and Charles Bayard de la Vingtrie (engineers). Its bankers were the Rothschild brothers. Bouchon, *Historique du chemin de fer,* 24.

6. Extract from prospectus quoted in Bouchon, *Historique du chemin de fer,* 24–25. Capitalization in original. Note: Bouchon does not provide sources.

7. Quoted in Bouchon, *Historique du chemin de fer,* 38–39. "Tillots" should be "tilloles"—this was probably the journalist's mistake.

8. Arrêtés municipaux, La Teste, 4 July 1841.

9. Quoted in Bouchon, *Historique du chemin de fer,* 41.

10. Quoted in ibid., 42.

11. Ibid., 46.

12. Brenot, *Cent cinquante ans,* 49–51.

13. Baron Mortemart de Boisse noted the resignation on the part of Testerins who had dreaded the coming of the railway as though it were a calamity. Mortemart de Boisse, *Voyage dans les Landes,* 114–15.

14. Schivelbusch notes that "regions lost their temporal identity in an entirely concrete sense: the railroads deprived them of their local time." Wolfgang Schivelbusch, *The Railway Journey: The Industrialization of Time and Space in the Nineteenth Century* (Berkeley: University of California Press, 1986), 42–43. See also Donald M. Lowe, *History of Bourgeois Perception* (Brighton: Harvester Press, 1982), 37–38.

15. "Représentation au gouvernement de la situation de la contrée." DM La Teste, 27 May 1846 (extraordinary meeting).

16. Scott Lash and John Urry, *Economies of Signs and Space* (London: Sage, 1994), chap. 10.

17. Une Testerine, *La fête de la chapelle d'Arcachon,* 1.

18. Ibid., 3.

19. Quoted in Bouchon, *Historique du chemin de fer,* 54–55.

20. Peter Quennell, ed., *Memoirs of William Hickey* (London: Century Publishing, 1984), 195–96. I thank Elizabeth Graham for drawing my attention to this passage.

21. Ragot, *Histoire de La Teste-de-Buch,* 195.

22. Quoted in Aufan, *La naissance d'Arcachon,* 51.

23. Anthelme Roux, "Fanelly aux bains d'Arcachon," in *La poitrinaire de Nice, suivi de Fanelly aux bains d'Arcachon* (Bordeaux: Imprimerie de Justin Dupuy et Cie, 1853). Roux's book appears to have been modeled on the "spa novel," a genre of promotional literature that burgeoned after mid-century. Usually pitched at women readers, it provided a coded "script" or guide to appropriate behavior for first-time visitors. Mackaman, *Leisure Settings,* 124–25.

24. Roux, "Fanelly," 41–42.

25. Arrêtés municipaux, La Teste, 22 July 1841. Capitalization in original.

26. Chadeyron, "La mode et la renommée," 148–50.

27. Arrêtés municipaux, La Teste, 8 August 1841.

28. Walton, "Consuming the Beach," 282–83.

29. Corbin, *Lure of the Sea,* 278, n.109.

30. Articles 6 and 7, arrêtés municipaux, La Teste, 15 July 1847. Capitalization in original.

31. Anonymous, "Une saison," pt. 2, 47.

32. Victor Hugo, "Biarritz, 25 July," in "Voyage aux Pyrénées, 1843," (published 1890) in Victor Hugo, *Oeuvres complètes,* vol. 6, ed. Jean Massin (Paris: Club Français du Livre, 1968), 855.

33. Arrêtés municipaux, La Teste, 15 July 1847.

34. Quoted in Bouchon, *Historique du chemin de fer,* 53.

35. Roux, "Fanelly," 2–3.

36. Schivelbusch, *Railway Journey,* 33–37.

37. DM La Teste, 3 March 1833.

38. DM La Teste, 2 March 1847 (extraordinary meeting).

39. DM La Teste, 15 November 1845 and 2 September 1846.

40. DM La Teste, 3 November 1847. Capitalization in original.

41. Aufan, *La naissance d'Arcachon,* 111–12.

42. Henry Ribadieu, *Un voyage au Bassin d'Arcachon* (Paris: J. Tardieu, 1859). Quoted in Aufan, *La naissance d'Arcachon,* 136.

43. DM La Teste, 9 October 1847 (extraordinary meeting).

44. DM La Teste, 23 March 1846.

7. The Pacific Conquests of Hygiene

1. The region of Guienne, in the eighteenth century, covered the present-day departments of Gironde, Dordogne, Lot, Lot-et-Garonne, and Aveyron and most of Tarn-et-Garonne. It lay under the jurisdiction of the *parlement* of its capital city, Bordeaux.

2. ADG C 1830 (years 1744–49), in Jacques Ragot, "Rôle joué par les effluves 'térébenthines' des pins dans le développement d'Arcachon," in *Le Corps et la Santé: Actes du 110è Congrès National des Sociétés Savantes* (Montpellier, 1985), 57.

3. Jacques Latrille, "Un savant girondin oublié, sinon méconnu: Le docteur Jean Hameau," *BSHAA,* no. 94 (1997): 10. Latrille cites Albert Rèche, *Plaisirs et amours du Bordeaux romantique,* for this claim.

4. In "Un savant girondin oublié," Latrille traces the history of Hameau's manuscript, *Réflexions sur les virus,* which he addressed to the Société Royale de Médecine de Bordeaux in 1837, to a dampening reception, and to the Académie de Médecine in Paris in 1843, where it was lost (or ignored) by the allocated reader until 1850. By this time Hameau's cause had been taken up by Théophile Roussel, whose article in the *Revue médicale* jolted the Académie reader's memory. The value and precocity of Hameau's work was not recognized until the year of his death.

5. Jean Hameau, *Quelques avis sur les bains de mer* (Bordeaux: Lavigne Jeune, 1835), 5.

6. Dr. F.-A. Lalesque, *Topographie médicale de la Teste de Buch, département de la Gironde, suivie de considérations hygiéniques applicables aux pays marécageux* (Bordeaux: Lavigne Jeune, 1835), 3. Marie-Noëlle Bourguet discusses the prevalence of the "hippocratic metaphor, which sees man as a reflection of the environment, air, and soil" in her study of Napoleonic departmental statistics; this clearly applies here. Bourguet, *Déchiffrer la France: La statistique départementale à l'époque napoléonienne* (Paris: Editions des Archives Contemporaines, 1989), 238.

7. Corbin, *Lure of the Sea*, 208. In 1776–78, the Société Royale de Médecine called on all French doctors to contribute to a "topographical and medical map of France in which the temperament, constitution, and illnesses of the inhabitants of each province or canton would be considered in relation to the nature and the exploitation of the land." Drs. Hameau and Lalesque were indebted to the tradition of medical writing that developed out of this ongoing inquiry. Bourguet, *Déchiffrer la France*, 39–40.

8. Arago, *Promenades*, 60.

9. Lalesque refers to *marins*, which is normally translated as "sailors." While all Testerin fishermen were enrolled in the navy and had to serve when called on, they were first and foremost fishermen rather than sailors, in the sense that their livelihood depended on fishing and their service to the navy was secondary to this. Unlike professional sailors, they stayed closer to home and were generally healthier because less often exposed to the unhealthy environments of ships' holds and port cities. The difference is important, as Alain Cabantous explains in *Les citoyens du large*, 58–61.

10. Lalesque, *Topographie*, 34, 29.

11. *Concise OED*, 6th ed., s.v. *sanguine* and *bile*. See also *The New Columbia Encyclopedia*, s.v. *humors*.

12. Lalesque, *Topographie*, 60–61.

13. Ibid., 30–35.

14. Hameau, *Quelques avis*, 16.

15. Dr. Fernand Lalesque, *La cure marine de la tuberculose pulmonaire sur le bassin d'Arcachon* (Paris: Masson et Cie, 1900), 2–3. See chapter epigraph.

16. Hameau, *Quelques avis*, 8.

17. O. D., *Guide du voyageur à La Teste*, 38.

18. Hameau, *Quelques avis*, 8–9. O. D.'s advice was nearly identical: O. D., *Guide du voyageur à La Teste*, 38. This raises the question once again as to whether the locals knew how to swim or not. This suggests they could, even though reports of drownings sometimes implied that fishermen could not swim. It is possible, of course, that by "diving," Hameau meant wading in deep, fully clothed, without a second thought, as fishermen had to do to reach their boats anchored offshore. See chapter 5.

19. See Mackaman, *Leisure Settings*, 88, 101, and passim.

20. Hameau, *Quelques avis*, 8–9.

21. Ibid., 7.

22. Ibid., 13. Capitalization in original.

23. Ibid., 15, 21.

24. O. D., *Guide du voyageur à La Teste,* 37. St. Vitus's dance is known as "danse de St. Guy" in French.

25. *Album illustré des villes d'eaux et de bains de mer: Guide spécial (divisé par régions)* (Paris: G. Le Couturier et L. Souberbielle, 1896), 29, 111.

26. Abbé Véchambre, *Bains maritimes d'Arcachon* (Bordeaux: Justin Dupuy et Cie, 1853), 27.

27. Dominique Rouillard, *Le site balnéaire* (Liège: P. Mardaga, 1984), 39–42, 65–67.

28. Jules Mareschal, *De la mise en valeur des Landes de Gascogne* (Paris: Poussielgue, Masson et Cie, 1853), 72.

29. Anonymous, *Visite de LL. MM. l'Empereur et l'Impératrice et de S.A. le Prince Impérial à Arcachon, le lundi 10 Octobre 1859* (Bordeaux: Imp. de A.-R. Chaynes, 1859), 32, 25, 11–12, 23.

30. Robert Fleury claims that Dr. Emile Pereira (the name is spelled differently in different texts), medical inspector of baths (*médecin-inspecteur des bains*), was the Pereires' cousin, while Roger-Henri Guerrand identifies him as the brother of one of the founders of the Bordeaux–La Teste railway. It is possible that he was both. Robert Fleury, "Médecines et médecins en Arcachon," in *Une histoire du Bassin,* eds. Daney and Boyé, 121. Roger-Henri Guerrand, "La Ville dont les princes furent des médecins," in *La Ville d'hiver,* 59.

31. Bernard Marrey, "Arcachon ou le levier de l'idée," in *La Ville d'hiver,* 38–40.

32. Ibid., 40–46.

33. Guerrand, "La Ville," 59. Guerrand quotes from Pereyra's writings: (1) *Du traitement de la phtisie pulmonaire, quelques réflexions sur les phtisiques observés à l'hôpital Saint-André de Bordeaux,* 1843, and (2) *Des bains de mer d'Arcachon. De l'influence des bords de ce bassin sur les tubercules pulmonaires et les maladies du cœur, et de l'habitation de cette plage pendant l'hiver par les personnes atteintes de maladies chroniques,* 1853.

34. Dr. Isidore Sarraméa, *Un regard sur Arcachon* (Bordeaux: Mme. Crugy, 1860), 6–7.

35. Jacques Léonard, *La médecine entre les savoirs et les pouvoirs: Histoire intellectuelle et politique de la médecine française au XIXe siècle* (Paris: Aubier Montaigne, 1981), 173.

36. Sarraméa, *Un regard,* 5.

37. Sarraméa, *Un regard,* 14–15.

38. The paper, appearing between May and October 1880, was edited *and* financed by Eugène Faure *fils.* It seems unlikely that Faure was an oyster farmer himself; the name Faure is not one that appears in Testerin archives. His family may have been Bordelais. The page numbering relates to a collated volume of all the issues, held by the Société Historique et Archéologique d'Arcachon.

39. *Le Détroqueur,* Friday, 23 July 1880 (no. 12), 94–95.

40. The defamation case was covered in *Le Détroqueur,* 22 October 1880 (no. 25), 98.

41. Fleury, "Médecines et médecins en Arcachon," 124. He gives no source for this claim.

42. Jacques Gubler, "Entre mer et forêt: La ville aux balcons d'argent," in *Ville d'hiver,* 90–91. See also Mackaman, *Leisure Settings,* 138–40, on spa parks, whose meandering paths encouraged romantic encounters.

43. Roux, "Fanelly aux bains d'Arcachon," 11.

44. P. A. de Lannoy, *Guide aux plages girondines* (Bordeaux: G. Delmas, 1900), 118.

45. Louis Branlat, *Vingt-quatre heures à Arcachon* (Bordeaux: G. Gounouilhou, 1886), 15–16.

46. For the "tambour" (or town crier) complaint, see DM Arcachon, *voeu* of M. Millien, 23 February 1891, and Lafon, 14 June 1893. On the St. Ferdinand church, letter from curé Largeteau to Arcachon council, discussed in DM Arcachon, 7 January 1892, and the budget forecasts for Notre Dame (20,092 francs) and St. Ferdinand (4,999 francs) in DM Arcachon, 7 June 1893. On the tramway, DM Arcachon, 29 December 1894 (extraordinary session), 9 April 1895, 13 November 1895, 5 and 23 June 1896 and 19 February 1897. The tramline opened in August 1911 and closed in 1932, to be replaced by a bus service. Claude Robin, "Les transports sur rail à Arcachon," *BSHAA,* no. 112 (2002): 29–66.

47. DM Arcachon, 13 June 1891.

48. David S. Barnes, *The Making of a Social Disease: Tuberculosis in Nineteenth-Century France* (Berkeley: University of California Press, 1995).

49. Eliane Keller, "La ville d'hiver d'Arcachon," in *Une histoire du Bassin,* eds. Daney and Boyé, 165. Keller does not give the source of her claim, but it seems credible given the ensuing boom in hygienic villa construction.

50. Barnes, *Social Disease,* 41, 29, 81–85, 115.

51. The municipal disinfection service was established in 1903. Fleury, "Médecines et médecins," 127.

52. Barnes, *Social Disease,* chap. 5.

53. Ibid., 100.

54. Dr. Fernand Lalesque, *Le climat d'Arcachon étudié à l'aide des appareils enrégistreurs* (Paris: Octave Doin, 1890), 8.

55. Dr. Henri Lamarque, *De quelques abus de bains de mer et des cures marines, en particulier dans le Sud-Ouest . . . Communication faite au congrès de thalassothéraphie de Biarritz (avril 1903)* (Bordeaux: Gounouilhou, 1903).

56. Dr. Fernand Lalesque, *Climathérapie française: La cure libre de la tuberculose pulmonaire (Conférence publique faite le 4 juin 1899)* (Bordeaux: Gounouilhou, 1899), 13, 5; Lalesque, *La cure marine,* 2.

57. Lalesque, *Climathérapie française,* 7.

58. Ibid., 8. See Mackaman, *Leisure Settings,* 101–6, on the "intensely close relationship between doctor and patient" in spa towns.

59. Lalesque, *Climathérapie française,* 14–16.

60. In French: "l'être reprend conscience de lui-même." Lannoy, *Guide aux plages girondines,* 120.

61. Corbin, *Lure of the Sea,* 87–88.

62. Lalesque, *La cure marine,* 4.

63. Ibid., 6–8.

64. Ibid., 8.

65. Lalesque, *Climathérapie française,* 19.

66. Lalesque, *La cure marine,* 9.

67 . L. de P., *Arcachon et ses environs* (Arcachon: Librairie Editions Bon, 1901), 20.

68. Paul Joanne, *De la Loire aux Pyrénées* (Paris: Hachette, 1908), 35, 369.

8. Whistles and Pickets, or "Dejecta of All Sorts"

1. Noël Gruet, "Les bateaux de service du bassin d'Arcachon," *Le Chasse-Marée: Histoire et Ethnologie Maritime,* no. 116 (1998): 51–52. On the northwest coast of the Bassin, in Cap Ferret and nearby beaches (opposite Arcachon), these inhabited pontoons would lay the foundation for the development of fishing villages.

2. Mairie d'Arcachon, "Procès-verbaux," (report, signed by Mauriac, 27 July 1872). ADG S Domaine Maritime 10. For a full discussion of the role of the harbormaster and the Arcachon council's campaign to counter the power of the La Teste representative and bolster the new town's status by having their own official appointed, see Garner, *Floating Worlds,* 227–35. On the Grand Hotel, see Eliane Keller, "Le Grand Hôtel d'Arcachon," *BSHAA,* no. 109 (2001): 57.

3. 30 July 1872; note in margins signed "G." ADG S Domaine Maritime 10. Autran's full title was Commissaire Général, Chef du Service de la Marine.

4. Urbain, *Sur la plage,* 55. He quotes Corbin, *Lure of the Sea,* 263.

5. See Rob Shields' analysis of the beach as "a necessary counter-space free of the built-in cues and spatialization of 'normal,' workaday life in nineteenth-century towns." In order to become this, it "had to be territorialized as a site fit for leisure." Shields, "The 'System of Pleasure,' " 41.

6. DM La Teste, 23 March 1846.

7. Héricart de Thury to prefect of the Gironde, 20 July 1866. ADG S Domaine Maritime 10. Capitalization in original.

8. *Notice sur la pêche dans le quartier de la Teste,* 1866, 49–50. AN Marine CC^5 580.

9. Mairie d'Arcachon, "Procès-verbaux," 27 July 1872. ADG S Domaine Maritime 10.

10. Walton, "Consuming the Beach," 285.

11. Since the creation of the system of naval classes under Colbert, reinforced by the introduction of naval registration in 1795, fishermen had to be enrolled with the navy to be eligible for a navigating and fishing permit. Cabantous, *Les citoyens du large,* 78.

12. Mayor (Mauriac) to prefect, 24 July 1871. ADG S Domaine Maritime 10.

13. 29 October 1872. ADG S Domaine Maritime 10.

14. Lalesque to prefect, 29 October 1872. ADG S Domaine Maritime 10. For more on the rivalry between Arcachon and her "mother" commune, La Teste, see Garner, *Floating Worlds,* 231–34.

15. Mauriac to prefect, 23 November 1872. ADG S Domaine Maritime 10.

16. Mauriac to prefect, 26 November 1872. ADG S Domaine Maritime 10. Capitalization in original.

17. Extract from DM Arcachon, 19 May 1873. Quotes prefectorial council decision of 24 January 1873. ADG S Domaine Maritime 10.

18. Corbin, *Filles de noces,* 8.

19. In *Filles de noce,* 15, Corbin explains the parallels that Parent-Duchâtelet, a doctor who carried out an in-depth inquiry into Parisian prostitution in the early 1800s, drew between prostitutes and sewers: by channeling men's overflowing desires, they acted as a safety valve for their society. How revealing, then, that Mauriac should have been responsible, as mayor, for the construction of Arcachon's main sewer! Appendix ("Biographies"), in *La Ville d'hiver,* 230.

20. Mairie d'Arcachon, "Procès-verbaux" (6 August 1873). ADG S Domaine Maritime 10.

21. Urbain, *Sur la plage,* 129.

22. John M. Merriman, *The Margins of City Life: Explorations on the French Urban Frontier, 1815–1851* (New York: Oxford University Press, 1991), 62.

23. *Notice sur la pêche,* 72.

24. Gironde prefecture, statistics on prostitution. La Teste, 6 June 1879. ADG 4 M 337.

25. 3 July 1874. ADG S Domaine Maritime 10.

26. Procès-verbal d'enquête de commodo et incommodo, Boulevard de la Plage, 18 November 1872. ADG Domaine Maritime S 11.

27. Letter from H. S. Johnston to prefect, Bordeaux, 3 December 1872. ADG Domaine Maritime S 11 (Boulevard inquiry folio). All quotes from the inquiry are from this ADG Domaine Maritime S 11 folio. Harry Scott Johnston (1834–1918) was the second son of Nathaniel Johnston and Charlotte Scott. The Johnstons were a wealthy family of Protestant merchants, whose forebears had migrated from Scotland to Bordeaux in the 1700s. They became one of Bordeaux's prominent Chartrons families. Harry Scott was a director of the family company, the Maison Nathaniel Johnston et fils, and married Anna de Galz de Malvirade in 1857. *Dictionnaire biographique et album Gironde,* vol. 2 (Paris: E. Flammarion, n.d.); Paul Butel, *Les dynasties bordelaises de Colbert à Chaban* (Paris: Perrin, 1991).

28. ADG Domaine Maritime S 11 (Boulevard inquiry folio). My emphasis. Moureau was described as a proprietor in Arcachon. He appeared before Gaussens on 29 November 1872. He might have agreed with Victor Hugo, who expressed his hatred for "all this stonework with which the sea is trimmed. In the maze of piers, moles, dikes, jetty heads," he wrote, "the ocean disappears like a carthorse under the harness." Quoted in Corbin, *Lure of the Sea,* 197.

29. Statement by O. Lafon, an Arcachon property owner and retired coastal navigator who appeared on 30 November 1872.

30. M. Alfred Guérard wrote a letter to the inquiry; he also stated that the inquiry was not valid because the council had failed to convene a committee to study the project after its initial meeting on 12 August 1872.

31. Cabanne and Durand both presented on 30 November 1872.

32. Letter from the board of Société Immobilière d'Arcachon to prefect, 24 September 1873. Signed by Labouris, Johnston, Galen, Durant, Bertin, Higaneau, Léon. ADG S Domaine Maritime 10.

33. 5 March 1869. Ingénieur Ordinaire's report in response to mayor's demands. ADG S Domaine Maritime 10.

34. *Careening* is the practice of turning a boat onto its side for repairs or cleaning.

35. Prefectorial *arrêté* naming members of committee, 22 December 1873, ADG S Domaine Maritime 10. Other members: Constant, prefectorial councillor (*conseiller de préfecture*) and committee president; Amédée Pilloton, registration department officer or rates collector (*Receveur de l'enregistrement*), La Teste. Johnston formed the Compagnie des Pêcheries de l'Océan with Léon Lesca in 1866. F. Montigaud, *Arcachon, statistique générale et notes historiques,* 2nd ed. (Bordeaux: Gounouilhou, 1905), 115.

36. He was referred to as "Président du Conseil d'administration de la Société Immobilière" in DM Arcachon, 29 December 1894, session on the tramway concession. His prés salés purchase is discussed in Bouscau, *Les prés salés de La Teste,* 479–80.

37. Adalbert-Alexandre Deganne was a civil engineer from the Marne who moved to the Bassin to work on the Bordeaux–La Teste railway line and later supervised the extension of the line to Arcachon. He was mayor of Arcachon from November 1870 to April 1871, and October 1876 to March 1880, and was responsible for the creation of some of the town's grandest avenues. Appendix ("Biographies"), *La Ville d'hiver,* 228.

38. Ponts et Chaussées, Service Maritime de la Gironde, 3rd arrondissement, Subdivision d'Arcachon, M. Laran, Modification à l'arrêté du 29 Janvier 1896 (Conductor's report), 19 August 1902. ADG: 3 S/Cô 17.

39. Urbain, *Sur la plage,* 74–75. Urbain does not acknowledge the hiccups in this industrialization process.

40. *Notice sur la pêche;* Pérotin, *Chalutage,* 70.

41. René Pérotin, *Le chalutage à vapeur à Arcachon* (Bordeaux: Y. Cadoret, 1911), chap. 2, "Le personnel et les salaires."

42. Rougerie, *Arc 280* [*Lou chalutayre*], 1939, in Puig, "De l'ethnologie comme matériau littéraire: L'exemple du Bassin d'Arcachon et des pratiques de pêche durant la première moitié du XXè siècle chez E. Barreyre et R. Rougerie," in *La littérature régionale en langue d'oc et en français à Bordeaux et dans la Gironde,* ed. Centre d'Etudes des Cultures Aquitaines et d'Europe du Sud and Université de Bordeaux III (Bordeaux: CECAES & Université de Bordeaux III, 1989), 275–76; Pérotin, *Chalutage,* 99.

43. Pérotin, *Chalutage,* 96.

44. *Ligue Maritime,* June 1911, quoted in Pérotin, *Chalutage,* 30. Italics in original.

45. *Notice sur la pêche,* 49.

46. ADG S Domaine Maritime 10, 5 September 1883. While there were no *X*s in lieu of signatures, some of the signatures appear to be in the same handwriting, suggesting that not all the petitioners were literate. It is difficult to ascertain where these men stood in the social hierarchy because apart from a Maucouvert, who noted he was a mariner and municipal councillor, none of those who signed gave his professional status (e.g., *capitaine au long cours, patron,* or *matelot*).

47. *Petit Robert,* s.v. *Jésuite:* "2. *Péj.* (A cause de la casuistique des moralistes jésuites).

Personne qui recourt à des astuces hypocrites." (Pejorative. [Due to the casuistry of the Jesuit moralists]. Person who resorts to hypocritical tricks).

48. The *baleinière* was a vessel in use on the Bassin, though apparently not for whaling. Gruet, "Les bateaux de service," 53–54.

49. *Le Détroqueur,* Friday, 14 May 1880 (no. 2): 13–14. Note: at this time, there was already a grand casino operating in Arcachon, the Casino Mauresque. In 1903 the Chateau Deganne would be converted into a beachfront casino.

50. Ingénieur Ordinaire's report concerning the Ramond, Sentout, and Lacaze hot baths. Ponts et Chaussées, Service Maritime, 1st arrondissement, Bordeaux, 3 April 1885. ADG S non coté S Domaine Maritime 11.

51. 20 April 1883, ADG S non coté S Domaine Maritime 11. Signed by Drs. Rougier and Hameau.

52. Letter from Marie Ramond, married name Sentout, to the prefect, La Teste, 29 March 1885. Note: There is some confusion about identities. Is this Marie, who claims to be caring for her mother "afflicted by mental alienation," the sister-in-law of Marie Lacaze, daughter of Gérard Lacaze, who refers to Pierre Ramond as her brother-in-law and whose February letter to the prefect (i.e., before the storm) requested a renewal of her father's concession? It is unclear whether these women were competing for the concession or working together. ADG S non coté S Domaine Maritime 11.

53. Letter from Ramond Père to prefect, La Teste, 22 March 1865. ADG S non coté S Domaine Maritime 11.

54. Pétition des habitants d'Eyrac. DM Arcachon, 18 June 1892.

55. Demande Repetto. DM Arcachon, 7 June 1892. The threatening reputation of the *banlieue* (outer suburbs), is the fascinating subject of Merriman, *Margins of City Life.*

56. DM Arcachon, 18 June 1891.

57. DM Arcachon, 18 February 1891. Councillor Couilleau.

58. Procès-verbal d'Enquête de Commodo et incommodo, sur le projet de règlement de la police du port d'Arcachon: Harry Johnston, Directeur des Pêcheries de l'Océan, domicilié à Bordeaux, propriétaire à Arcachon. 22 August 1891. ADG 3 S/Cô 17. Capitalization in original.

59. Règlement proposé par les ingénieurs du Service Maritime (Police du Port), 14 April 1891. ADG 3 S/Cô 17.

60. Montigaud's statistics on railway passenger numbers do show that some ten thousand fewer passengers bought tickets in 1896 than in the previous year, although it is difficult to draw accurate conclusions from the figures because from 1892, the Compagnie du Midi no longer kept records of passenger numbers by station. The statistics are for numbers of passengers "dispatched" and "received" each year: their destination is not signaled. Montigaud, *Arcachon, statistique générale,* 140.

61. DM Arcachon, 7 September 1892.

62. Ponts et Chaussées, Service Maritime de la Gironde, 3rd arrondissement, Subdivision d'Arcachon, M. Laran, Modification à l'arrêté du 29 Janvier 1896 (Conductor's report), 19 August 1902. ADG 3 S/Cô 17.

63. Letter from deputy mayor of Arcachon to prefect of the Gironde, 15 July 1902. ADG 3 S/Cô 17. My emphasis.

64. Extrait du registre des délibérations, Chambre de Commerce de Bordeaux (Extract from minutes of Bordeaux Chamber of Commerce), 9 August 1905. ADG 3 S/Cô 17.

65. "On beautiful summer nights, there is nothing more curious than seeing the flame fishermen's many fires drifting over the calm waters of the Bassin." De Gabory, *Guide d'Arcachon* (Arcachon: Mme. Delamare, 1896), 54–55.

9. A Magnificent Panorama

1. *69 Arcachon. La jetée devant le Casino.—C.B.* Lahaye collection. No postmark, but probably dates from 1890s. See chapter 10 for an in-depth discussion of postcard imagery.

2. Dominique Rouillard, *Le site balnéaire* (Liège: P. Mardaga, 1984), 139. See Vanessa Schwartz on *flânerie* as a "positionality of power—one through which the spectator assumes the position of being able to be part of the spectacle, and yet command it at the same time." *Spectacular Realities: Early Mass Culture in Fin-de-Siècle Paris* (Berkeley: University of California Press, 1998), 10.

3. DM La Teste, 9 October 1847, extraordinary session on the extension of the Eyrac Road. Note the councillors' use of the phrase, "movement and life," which they also used in May 1846 to describe the impact of the railway line.

4. *Arcachon.—La Place Thiers Coll. V. Faure.* Lahaye collection.

5. Letter from Baron Michel to prefect of the Gironde, 5 December 1881. The Baron had a Parisian address. ADG S non coté S Domaine Maritime 14.

6. In my notes taken from his letter, he requested an area of Bassin of eight thousand square meters (8000m² [86,112 square feet]), but that cannot possibly be right—eighty square meters (80m² [861 square feet]) seems more likely.

7. The term "architecture of pleasure" comes from John Urry, *The Tourist Gaze: Leisure and Travel in Contemporary Societies* (London: Sage, 1990), 35.

8. John K. Walton, *The English Seaside Resort: A Social History, 1750–1914* (Leicester: Leicester University Press; New York: St. Martin's Press, 1983), 173–74.

9. Gabory, *Guide d'Arcachon,* 30–31. The *Encyclopedia CD-Universalis* notes that Semiramis was incorrectly credited—originally by the Greeks—with the creation of the famous hanging gardens of Babylon, one of the Seven Ancient Wonders of the World. The gardens were in fact a gift from Nebuchadnezzar II (BC 604–562) to his wife Amyitis.

10. Ibid., 30–31.

11. Bernard Marrey, "Arcachon ou le levier de l'idée," in *La Ville d'hiver,* 51.

12. Jacques Gubler, "Entre mer et forêt," in *La Ville d'hiver,* 92.

13. Urbain, *Sur la plage,* 280.

14. Arago, *Promenades.* Joanne (the French equivalent of Baedeker) compared Arcachon, with its "*cachet* of strangeness and exoticism," to "the empty and indecisive lands of certain Asian archipelagos, of the Sunda islands." Paul Joanne, *De la Loire aux Pyrénées* (Paris: Hachette, 1908), 368.

15. Advertisement for the Grand Hôtel des Pins et Continental in Joanne, *De la Loire aux Pyrénées*. Capitalization in original. Note: this was not the Grand Hotel on the beachfront.

16. Mackaman discusses the casino and its multiple entertainment functions in *Leisure Settings*, 129–33.

17. Monsieur le Baron Michel, "Projet d'un Etablissement de Bains-promenade à créer sur le bassin d'Arcachon. Mémoire explicatif," 24 October 1882. ADG S non coté S Domaine Maritime 14.

18. Mauriac's pseudonym for Arcachon, "Gravette," was taken from the local species of oyster. He also described the forest "where doubtful consumptives in their never-disinfected chalets come to give a definitive character to their sickness." François Mauriac, *Les préséances* 2nd ed. (Paris: Flammarion, 1928), 40–41. I thank Charles Daney and Jacques Bernard for drawing my attention to this text and for alerting me to the fact that in later editions, the passages relating to Arcachon were toned down.

19. Michel, "Projet d'un Etablissement."

20. Urbain notes the fear of a "loss of social identity, the hell of mixing and the confusion of classes" that arose as beaches became increasingly crowded. *Sur la plage*, 210–12.

21. Note that in September 1904, fishermen petitioned the La Teste council, objecting to the construction of a new jetty that would prevent them from fishing on the "best and most productive" beach. Although the jetty in question was probably within the boundaries of La Teste (and so not the Jetée Thiers), this indicates that jetties did not always serve the fishing population as their builders (like the Baron Michel) claimed. Jacques Ragot, *Le Cap-Ferret de Lège à La Pointe* (Arcachon: Imprimerie Graphica, 1982), 66.

22. Michel, "Projet d'un Etablissement." The estimated cost was one million francs, with an eighty-year concession.

23. The dossier for the Lawson project is in ADG S non coté S Domaine Maritime 14. St. Clair proposal: DM Arcachon, 9 February 1891; favorable response from council; letter accompanying pilot study dated 27 April 1891, addressed to prefect of Gironde, ADG S non coté S Domaine Maritime 14. Brisson et Delamare et Cie: project mentioned in DM Arcachon, 16 February 1891.

24. Enquête administrative, Mairie d'Arcachon: Jetée-Promenade, Procès-verbal et Avis du Commissaire enquêteur, 7 June 1883. ADG S non coté S Domaine Maritime 14.

25. Ibid.

26. Letter from John Lawson to prefect, 15 July 1892. ADG S non coté S Domaine Maritime 14. For a picture of the Nice jetty-promenade, see Bernard Toulier, "L'architecture des bains de mer: un patrimoine marginalisé," *Revue de l'Art*, no. 101 (1993): 33.

27. DM Arcachon, extraordinary session on the stabilization of the beach and the construction of two jetties and breakwaters, 16 December 1899.

28. DM Arcachon, 3 December 1898.

29. The Central Bureau of Meteorology was created in 1871, and in 1886 an international conference on hydrology and climatology was held in Biarritz, at which the merits of various resorts were debated by doctors and climatologists. Chadefaud, *Aux origines du*

tourisme, 83–87. The earliest use of the term *climatothérapie* is dated 1876 in the *Grand Robert,* while the word *aérothérapie,* defined as "traitement de diverses maladies . . . par des cures au grand air" (treatment of various illnesses . . . by fresh air cures), appeared in 1865. The local newspaper *L'Avenir d'Arcachon* reported the installation of an Institut d'Aérothérapie in the Villa Esterhazy on 13 January 1895.

10. Posing for Posterity

1. In this way, the visitor might experience what James Buzard calls "sublime synthesis," which occurs when stored images match an encountered scene. Buzard, *The Beaten Track: European Tourism, Literature, and the Ways to Culture, 1800–1918* (Oxford: Oxford University Press, 1993), 196.

2. Aline Ripert and Claude Frère, *La carte postale: Son histoire, sa fonction sociale* (Paris: Editions du Centre National de la Recherche Scientifique, 1983), 17–18, 23, 42–43. The national census of 1906 recorded a population of 39,252,245.

3. Urry lists anticipation, fed by the forces that construct the tourist gaze, as one of his nine "minimal characteristics" of tourism. Urry, *Tourist Gaze,* 3.

4. *73.—ARCACHON.—Côte d'Argent. Parqueurs et Parqueuses au travail—BR—576.* Lahaye collection.

5. P. Kauffmann, "Le Parqueur d'Arcachon," *L'Illustration: Journal Universel* (30 January 1892): 91–94.

6. Charles Daney, *Dictionnaire de la Lande française,* 42–43. In Grasset de Saint Sauveur's series *Estampes* from 1806, a "Femme parée des environs de la tête [*sic*] de Buch Landes de Bordeaux" (Woman dressed from the environs of La Teste de Buch, Landes of Bordeaux) wears a *benaize*-like headpiece, although the long piece of fabric sits at the front and a shorter piece at the back. Reprinted in Frédéric Maguet, "De la série éditoriale dans l'imagerie: L'exemple des costumes régionaux," in "Usages de l'Image," special issue, *Ethnologie française* 24, no. 2 (1994): 231. In a private communication (3 January 2000), Daney noted that headwear similar to the *benaize* appeared on different parts of the Atlantic coast, including Brittany, while the black straw hat was prevalent in the Landes until the late nineteenth century. This prompts the question: did the Breton women who came to Arcachon with their husbands to fish for sardines at the turn of the century have an influence on the local costume?

7. Catherine Bertho Lavenir makes a similar observation in her discussion of late-nineteenth-century railway posters, in which Breton and Niçois women were depicted in hats decorated with mimosa, a plant that had only recently been introduced to the coast; this was understood to represent the "charm and picturesque qualities of the country." Catherine Bertho Lavenir, *La roue et le stylo* (Paris: Editions Odile Jacob, 1999), 34.

8. Aline Valette, "Le Travail des Femmes," *La Fronde,* Sunday, 19 June 1898, 1. Women were paid 1 franc 50 to men's 3 francs for one tide (*marée*) and 2 francs for a full day (13 hours) to men's 3 francs 50.

9. Buzard, *Beaten Track,* 188.

10. P. Kauffmann, "Le Parqueur d'Arcachon," 91–94. *Patins* were wooden boards, strapped to the soles of one's shoes, which prevented sea workers from sinking into the Bassin's mud flats.

11. Full titles: *La Côte d'Argent (131) Arcachon. Le "Quart de Bain," Débarcadère.* ND Phot. Lahaye collection.

12. Roux, "Fanelly aux bains d'Arcachon," 39.

13. The card with the masculine noun was titled: *58 Arcachon— Parqueurs se rendant au travail.— C.C.* Reprinted in Clémens, *Le Bassin d'Arcachon,* 81.

14. Griselda Pollock, " 'With My Own Eyes': Fetishism, the Labouring Body and the Colour of Its Sex," *Art History* 17, no. 3 (1994): 348, 358. Arthur J. Munby was a Victorian poet, barrister, and civil servant who recorded his meetings with thousands of working women in Victorian Britain, France, Belgium, Germany, and Switzerland, in sketches, photographs, and detailed written notes. The collection, held at Trinity College, Cambridge, covers the period from 1850 to 1910.

15. Undated postcard from Lahaye collection.

16. On *scènes et types* in French postcard sets of Algerians, see David Prochaska, "The Archive of *Algérie Imaginaire,*" *History and Anthropology* 4 (1990): 373, 407, 416. He argues that postcard collecting was an "ordering, disciplining activity" along the lines of classificatory crazes like phrenology. Frédéric Maguet notes the role of the series in fixing stereotypes of regional figures, which would become "indefinitely recyclable," while Alain Corbin has written about the role of *ethnotypes* in the working up of an essential and enduring cultural differentiation between Paris and the provinces. Maguet, "De la série éditoriale dans l'imagerie," 228. Corbin, "Divisions of Time and Space," 438–439 and passim. See also Marie-Noëlle Bourguet, "Race et folklore: L'image officielle de la France en 1800," *Annales,* no. 31 (1976).

17. Drawing of Testerine by Comte Gustave de Galard, 1814, reproduced in Clémens, *Le Bassin d'Arcachon,* 21. Note also a drawing of "Femmes de La Teste" by Ed. Servrin, dated 1836, reproduced in Roger Galy, *Histoire du Bassin d'Arcachon des origines à nos jours: Les événements, les lieux et les hommes* (Gradignan: Princi Nègre, 1998), 101.

18. Reproduced in Jacques Baschet, *Le Panorama Salon, d'après les clichés photographiques de Neurdein frères* (Paris: Ludovic Baschet, 1901). *Panorama Salon* is a book of photographs of popular Salon paintings.

19. While the Aquitaine experienced a strong rural exodus overall (Peter McPhee notes that Bordeaux's population increased by 69 percent between 1851 and 1881, to the detriment of the provinces), Fernand Labatut's demographic study of the Bassin d'Arcachon shows that its population was growing strongly over the nineteenth and twentieth century. Peter McPhee, *A Social History of France, 1780–1880* (London: Routledge, 1992), 197–98, 225. Fernand Labatut, "Esquisse de l'évolution démographique dans le pays de Buch depuis la Révolution Française (suite)," *BSHAA,* no. 70 (1991): 33–38.

20. Guy de Maupassant, *Pierre et Jean,* in *Oeuvres complètes* (Paris: Maurice Gonon and Albin Michel, 1969 [1888]), 332.

21. Quoted in Ripert and Frère, *La carte postale,* 76.

22. Lannoy, *Guide aux plages girondines,* 101. In 1905, F. Montigaud claimed that overproduction was causing a slump in prices. *Arcachon, statistique générale,* 107.

23. Urbain, *Sur la plage,* 70.

24. Urbain writes about umbrellas in a section called "The rites of installation," *Sur la plage,* 267.

25. Produced by Neurdein Frères. Author's own collection.

26. Maupassant, *Pierre et Jean,* 314–15. Note that the Goncourts were also disgusted by the feminine presence on the beach; their misogyny was explicit. Describing Trouville in 1864, they wrote: "Motherhood displays itself here, . . . animalistic and chooklike [*poussinière*]," while sea baths were an "honest and disgusting site of reproductivity, a place where one brings one's wife to pullulate." Quoted in Urbain, *Sur la plage,* 198.

27. Louis Branlat, *Vingt-quatre heures à Arcachon* (Bordeaux: G. Gounouilhou, 1886), 31–32.

28. Ibid., 32–33.

29. Charles Daney notes in a private communication (3 January 2000) that the red pants of Arcachonnais fishing people may have been made with the remnants of army-issue fabric from the 1870 war. Whatever their origin, they became fashionable among yachtsmen, and still are. The Arcachon boat drivers' uniform today includes bright red trousers.

30. Branlat, *Vingt-quatre heures,* 35.

Epilogue

1. Gruet and Labourg, "La vie maritime," 34, 38; Puig, "Un exemple d'ethnographie maritime," 16.

2. Gruet and Labourg, "La vie maritime," 38; L. H. Roblin, "Les forçats de la mer," *L'Humanité,* Saturday, 19 October 1907, 1.

3. Lavenir, *La roue et le stylo,* 296, 90.

4. Clémens, *Le Bassin d'Arcachon,* 71.

5. Lavenir, *La roue et le stylo,* 158; André Rauch, *Vacances en France de 1830 à nos jours* (Paris: Hachette, 1996), 85.

6. Pierre Nolay, "Les Routes Françaises: Leur Révélation par l'Automobile," *La Petite République,* Friday, 27 August, 1909, 1.

7. See Lavenir, *La roue et le stylo,* chap. 9, "Réformer l'hôtellerie."

8. The name was coined by the publicity-savvy writer Maurice Martin, to compete with the Côte d'Azur, in 1906. Lavenir, *La roue et le stylo,* 215; Fernand Labatut, "Esquisse de l'évolution démographique dans le Pays de Buch depuis la Révolution Française (suite)," *BSHAA,* no. 70 (1991): 43.

9. Rauch, *Vacances,* 28–29; Urbain, *Sur la plage,* 123.

10. Fleury, "Médecines et médecins," 127–29.

11. Ibid., 127; Clémens, *Bassin d'Arcachon,* 112. On the need for historians of tourism and leisure to investigate the impact of war on resorts, see Walton, "Leisure Towns in Wartime," 603–4, 615.

12. Emmanuel Brousse, "A Bordeaux," *L'Indépendant des Pyrénées-Orientales,* no. 251, Sunday, 13 September 1914. Quoted in Jean-Pierre Ardoin Saint Amand, "Nelly Béryl ou la fin de la Belle Epoque à Arcachon," *BSHAA,* no. 102 (1999): 59. Ardoin Saint Amand notes that *L'Indépendant* was suspended for a month (subsequently reduced to two weeks) for printing demoralizing material, by the commandant général of the 16th region (ibid., 60).

13. Brousse, "A Bordeaux." A grandson of the great Radical politician Georges Clemenceau (who would begin his second stint as prime minister in 1917) remembered his grandfather as being furious about the minister for the interior, Louis-Jean Malvy, who "spent the best part of his time in Arcachon with his mistress Nelly Béryl, a flashy former *demi-mondaine* [woman from the fringes of respectable society]. She kept an open house, for meals and poker, and they drank champagne joyously." Georges Gatineau-Clemenceau, *Des pattes du Tigre aux griffes du destin* (Paris: Les Presses du Mail, 1961), 148. Quoted in Ardoin Saint Amand, "Nelly Béryl," 61.

14. Michel Georges-Michel, *Le bonnet rose* (Paris: L'édition, 1920), 29. Quoted in Ardoin Saint Amand, "Nelly Béryl," 56. A Web search gives the full title as *Le bonnet rose: Cahiers d'une comédienne—Bordeaux, Paris, Deauville, Rome, Petrograd, Espagne, Riviera, 1914/1918.* Mr. Galipaux was a popular actor and writer.

15. *La France de Bordeaux,* Wednesday, 9 September 1914, 4.

16. *La France de Bordeaux,* Friday, 11 September 1914, 4.

17. Gruet, "La pêche industrielle après 1914," 209–10.

18. Eliane Keller, "Le Grand Hôtel d'Arcachon" in *BSHAA,* no. 109 (2001): 60.

19. Joe Lunn, *Memoirs of the Maelstrom: A Senegalese Oral History of the First World War* (Portsmouth, N.H.: Heinemann, 1999), 106. According to Lunn (p. 1), over 140,000 West Africans were recruited to fight at the western front between 1914 and 1918. See also Clémens, *Le Bassin d'Arcachon,* 113.

20. Lunn, *Memoirs,* 163.

21. Luc Dupuyoo, "Projet de sanatorium au Camp Américain du Cap-Ferret," *BSHAA,* no. 114 (2002): 35.

22. Jacques Ragot and Max Baumann, *La presqu'île Lège Cap-Ferret: Évocation historique* (Marguerittes, France: Equinoxe, 1992), 104–5.

23. Quoted in Clémens, *Le Bassin d'Arcachon,* 114.

24. Jean-Pierre Deltreil, "L'âge d'or et les crises de l'ostréiculture dans le Bassin d'Arcachon," in SHAA, ed., *L'ostréiculture arcachonnaise: Actes du colloque organisé par la Société Historique d'Arcachon, tenu à Gujan-Mestras les 15 et 16 octobre, 1994* (Arcachon: Graphica, 1994), 55.

25. Jean-Claude Richez and Léon Strauss, "Un temps nouveau pour les ouvriers: Les congés payés (1930–1960)," in *L'avènement des loisirs, 1850–1960* (Paris: Aubier-Flammarion, 1995), 376–78.

26. Urbain, *Sur la plage,* 143–45, 136.

27. Cassou-Mounat, "La vie humaine," 350–51, 355.

28. *La France de Bordeaux,* Sunday, 28 June 1936, 6.

29. *La France de Bordeaux,* Friday, 26 July 1936, 5. On the Popular Front, youth hostels, and paid holidays, see Julian Jackson, *The Popular Front in France: Defending Democracy,*

1934–1938 (Cambridge: Cambridge University Press, 1988); Lavenir, *La roue et le stylo,* chap. 14; Ellen Furlough, "Making Mass Vacations: Tourism and Consumer Culture in France, 1930s to 1970s," *Comparative Studies in Society and History,* no. 40 (1998): 247–86; Gary Cross, "Vacations for All: The Leisure Question in the Era of the Popular Front," *Journal of Contemporary History* 24, no. 4 (1989): 599–621. This is a small sample of English-language references, within what is an impressively broad literature on the period.

30. *La France de Bordeaux,* Saturday, 15 August 1936, 5.

31. The local weekly newspaper *Le Phare d'Arcachon* reported on strikes hitting the fishing fleets and canneries, on 17 July 1936 (p. 2), 24 July (pp. 1–2) and 31 July (p. 1).

32. Alain Pujol, "Chronique des années 50," *Arcachon Magazine* (1996): 46.

33. Gruet, "La pêche industrielle après 1914," in *Une histoire du Bassin,* 214.

34. For the design of pillboxes, see George Forty, *Fortress Europe: Hitler's Atlantic Wall* (Surrey: Ian Allan, 2002). Forty also discusses the use of forced labor for the construction of the Atlantic Wall, as does Alan Wilt in *The Atlantic Wall: Hitler's Defenses in the West, 1941–1944* (Ames: Iowa State University Press, 1975). Laborers conscripted by Organisation Todt (a German construction and engineering group named after its founder) were used on the Bassin according to Francis Magne de la Croix, "La Brigade Marine d'Extrême-Orient à Arcachon, 1945," *BSHAA,* no. 88 (1996): 46.

35. Wilt, *Atlantic Wall,* 35.

36. Michel Boyé, "Arcachon et le Bassin sous l'Occupation (2)," *BSHAA,* no. 84 (1995): 51–52.

37. Pujol, "Chronique des années 50."

38. Keller, "Le Grand Hôtel d'Arcachon," 61.

39. Magne de la Croix notes that the Camp des Abatilles was built originally in 1938 to house refugees from Spain and then accommodated people fleeing eastern France, followed by Organisation Todt laborers. "La Brigade Marine," 46.

40. "A propos des arrestations," *Journal d'Arcachon,* 2 September 1944, quoted by Boyé, "Arcachon et le Bassin sous l'Occupation (2)," 52–53, n.10.

41. Dominique Lormier, *Bordeaux pendant l'Occupation* (Bordeaux: Sud-Ouest, 1992), 148.

42. Magne de la Croix, "La Brigade Marine."

43. Ibid., 56, 60.

44. For succinct coverage of the postwar development of mass tourism in France, see Rauch, *Vacances,* 129–55.

45. Labatut, "Esquisse de l'évolution démographique dans le pays de Buch depuis la Révolution Française (suite et fin)," *BSHAA,* no. 74 (1992): 41.

46. Henry de la Tombelle and Jean Samazeuilh, *Guide touristique Sud-Ouest: Cyclotourisme, canoë, camping* ([Bordeaux]: Editions Delmas, c.1938), 61–62.

47. Tombelle and Samazeuilh, *Guide touristique,* 16.

48. Bouscau, "Curieuse histoire," 7–9.

49. Bouscau, *Les prés salés de La Teste,* PJ 16 (Chronologie de l'affaire des prés salés), iv–v.

50. Gruet, "La pêche industrielle," 216.

51. Gruet and Labourg, "La vie maritime," 39.

52. On surfing the Bassin's *passes,* see Fiona Capp, *That Oceanic Feeling* (Crows Nest, NSW (Australia): Allen and Unwin, 2003), 245.

53. Ragot, "Projets successifs," 101–3.

54. Ibid.

55. Author interviews (1996 and 1998) with Eugène ("Gégène") Picard, "Bicou" Marsan, Guy Brouchet, Michel Fourton, François Fadeuilhe, Gérard Gentil, M. Lagauzère, Jean-Louis Castaing, Laurent Malrieux, Michel Martin, André Darbo, and Hugues Teyssier. I thank Jean-Louis Castaing and Jean Hourtané for arranging these meetings.

56. Michel Boyé, "La place de l'ostréiculture arcachonnaise," in SHAA, ed., *L'ostréiculture arcachonnaise,* 112.

57. Keller, "La ville d'hiver d'Arcachon," in *Une histoire du Bassin,* 166.

BIBLIOGRAPHY

PRIMARY SOURCES

ARCHIVES NATIONALES
Fonds de la Marine (Séries modernes)
Série CC Personnel

CC⁴ Navigation commerciale (1730–1912)

44 Inscription maritime et police de la navigation, 1836

974 bis Police de la navigation et des pêches maritimes: enregistrement de la correspondence adressée aux ports, 1818–37

2073 Naufrages, sauvetages, 1806–36

CC⁵ Pêches (an IX-1908)

151 and 151 bis Mémoires statistiques sur le commerce, les pêches et l'inscription maritime, 1834–35

374 Législation sur les pêches, 1681–1861

379 Bassin d'Arcachon. Réservoirs à poisson dans le bassin d'Arcachon, 1830–70
394 La Teste: huîtres, pêcheries, crassats, affaires diverses, 1854–86
579 Pisciculture maritime; police et justice, 1859–67
580 Situation des pêches côtières et maritimes, rapports etc, 1862–68
588 Littoral de la Manche et de l'Atlantique: pêcheries, huîtres etc 1885–92
632–33 Secours aux pêcheurs; congrès maritimes etc., 1842–1906

Série DD Matériel
DD² Travaux maritimes (1676–1939)
799 Bassin d'Arcachon, an VII-1858
1007 Dossiers des travaux portuaires et non-maritimes du littoral: Arcachon, 1855–80
1069–70 Travaux effectués dans les ports secondaires, 1837–83

Série GG Documents divers
GG¹ Mémoires et projets (1689–1882)

Série F Versements des ministères et des administrations qui en dépendent
F⁷ Archives de la Police
4013–14 Police générale: Rapports de gendarmerie. Gironde, 1828–44
7252 dossier 12 (1868)

F¹² Commerce et industrie
2624 Pêche maritime
4847 Pêche 1900 (sardine)

F¹⁴ Travaux publics: Chemins de fer, ports maritimes
1462 Phares et balises
7252 Classement départemental de ports maritimes: Bassin d'Arcachon, 1830–68

ARCHIVES DÉPARTEMENTALES DE LA GIRONDE
Série J: Dons et acquisitions
Autres fonds (conservés à titre de dépôt): Inscription maritime de Bordeaux, XVIIIè s.-
    1954

6 J 1–III Fonds Billaudel (Ponts et Chaussées), 1746–XIXe
42 Navigation du Bassin d'Arcachon: plans, mémoires etc.

Série M: Administration générale du département et économie depuis 1800

1M Administration générale an VIII-1940 (correspondence, événements politiques, associations, syndicats, fêtes et cérémonies)

212 Troisième division (travaux publics, police administrative), 8/1–17/8/1836

314 Canton d'Arcachon: Érection d'Arcachon en chef-lieu de canton (loi du 17 avril 1906), 1898–1906

351 Rapport du préfet, des sous-préfets, renseignements statistiques fournis par les sous-préfets; rapports du maire de Bordeaux . . . sur l'esprit public, 31/7/1830–1836

412 Rapports mensuels du préfet et des sous-préfets sur la situation politique, économique, 1889–1908; rapports divers, 1902–12

673 Usines (1936–38)

3M Plébiscites, élections

550 Dossiers par commune: Listes d'électeurs, renseignements sur les membres du conseil municipal, procès-verbaux d'élections, procès-verbaux d'installation: Electeurs à La Teste.

4M Police et sûreté générale 1790–1940

176 Police: Rapports périodiques Arcachon 1890–1900

180 Police: Rapports périodiques La Teste, 1890–1900

222–225 Procès-verbaux et rapports particuliers de gendarmerie, procès-verbaux de maires, rapports de commissaires de police . . . 1829–1907

237–238 Procès-verbaux de gendarmerie . . . 1890; 1896–97

244 Naufrages, incendies, ouragans, accidents de chemin de fer, 1814–1938

337 Police des moeurs, prostitution; instructions, correspondance, arrêtés municipaux, 1851–1919

373 Casinos des stations balnéaires: Arcachon, Casino de la Plage, surveillance, rapports . . . 1882–1906

426 Sociétés de fêtes de quartiers et fêtes locales, 1863–1929

463 Bals: instructions, correspondance, 1863–1919

5M Santé publique

113 Rapports des médecins des épidémies . . . 1880–1900

316–17 Etablissements classés dangereux, insalubres . . . dossiers d'établissements: Arcachon: Johnston et cie: dépôt de pétrole et fabrique de conserves (1878–89); Haentjens: atelier de salaison et fab. de conserves (1897); Duvergier, atelier de construction d'articles de pêche (1900)

6M Population, affaires économiques, statistique
1338 Statistique par commune (La Teste, Gujan, 1827)

10M Travail et main d'oeuvre; chômage, syndicats
157 Syndicats professionnels: inscrits maritimes, marins, pêcheurs, 1873–1903

Série N: Administration et comptabilité départementales depuis 1800
1N Conseil général, délibérations . . .
404 Subventions pour les veuves et les orphelins du naufrage de 6 chalutiers de La Teste le
28 mars 1836 faisant 78 victimes

Série R: Affaires militaires et organismes de temps de guerre (1800–1940)
7R Marine et garde côtes
1 Circulaires et instructions, 1814–1906
6 Personnel: demandes de secours et d'emploi et interventions diverses, an IX-1909

Série S: Travaux publics et transports 1800–
2 S Chemins de fer et transports 1831–XXe siècle
2 S/M Compagnie du Midi
2 S1/M 2 Projet—Enquête—procès-verbal de la Commission—Réception-Expropria-
tions—Cessions de terrains—Alignements, 1835–1856

3 S Navigation, an X-1930
3 S/Cô Côtes
17 Bassin d'Arcachon—ports, 1829–1921
20–21 Cabestans, pêche: La Teste, 1818–1847
22 Amélioration du port de La Teste, 1869–82
3 S1 1 Bateaux à vapeur
3 S1 1 Ordonnances, instructions, 1822–1906; permis de navigation

S 16 Domaine maritime 1860–
Pêches fluviales (Service maritime)

S 121
S non côté
S.—Domaine Maritime
10 Arcachon: Affaires diverses, police de la plage
11 Etablissements de bains chauds
12 Enlèvement de 4 cabanes au quartier d'Eyrac, Etablissement d'une jetée-promenade,
1894

14 Affaires générales intéressant la Commune, 1858–1895 (jetées-promenades)
120 Ile des Oiseaux: Contestation entre la Commune de La Teste et l'Etat. Demande concession Sauvage, 1823–1830

S. Lotissements
S 16 (Service Maritime) La Teste: Mémoire des Marins de La Teste contre la mise en ferme
de l'Isle et brassats du Bassin, 1806; Réclamations, 1829–1830

Série U: Justice
Juge de paix de La Teste, 1833, 1838–40, 1844 (Annexe)

Newspapers
Le Journal de la Guienne, 1834

ARCHIVES MARITIMES, ROCHEFORT
Sous-série 12 P Quartier d'Arcachon
2/46 Officiers mariniers et matelots (La Teste et Arès)
2/51 Marins étrangers au quartier, 1836–54
3/12 Rôles d'armement au cabotage et à la (petite) pêche, 1836–38

ARCHIVES MUNICIPALES DE LA TESTE
Délibérations municipales 1829–48; 1895–1903
Arrêtés municipaux 1828–42; 1847–1848
1J 1 Police locale, 1837–1843 (1837–40: période des grands travaux)

ARCHIVES MUNICIPALES D'ARCACHON
Délibérations municipales 1858–68; 1877–79; 1889–1900

BIBLIOTHÈQUE MUNICIPALE D'ARCACHON
Newspapers
Le Détroqueur: Revue Hebdomadaire, Politique, Littéraire, Satirique, Incisive et Burlesque,
1880
L'Avenir d'Arcachon
Postcard collection (deposited by SHAA)
Local history collection: pamphlets, reports, memoirs

BAILLIEU LIBRARY, UNIVERSITY OF MELBOURNE
Newspapers
La France de Bordeaux, 1906–07, 1914, 1936
La Fronde

L'Humanité, 1880–1914, 1936

La Petite République, 1880–1914, 1936

PRIVATE COLLECTIONS
Collection Jacques Clémens

Collection Lahaye (postcards)

SECONDARY SOURCES

Album illustré des villes d'eaux et de bains de mer: Guide spécial (divisé par régions). Paris: G. Le Couturier et L. Souberbielle, 1896.

Allègre, Capt. David. *De la pêche dans le Bassin et sur les côtes d'Arcachon: Moyen de la pratiquer sans danger et avec profit.* Bordeaux: Imprimerie de Suwerwinck, 1836.

Allen, James Smith. *Popular French Romanticism: Authors, Readers, and Books in the Nineteenth Century.* Syracuse, N.Y.: Syracuse University Press, 1981.

Amanieu, C., P. Capdeville, B. Quessard, and C. Sausset. "Traitement préventatif et curatif de la tuberculose pulmonaire à Arcachon entre 1850 et 1940." *BSHAA,* no. 91 (1997): 1–31.

Anonymous. *Visite de LL. MM. l'Empereur et l'Impératrice et de S.A. le Prince Impérial à Arcachon, le lundi 10 Octobre 1859.* Bordeaux: Imp. de A.-R. Chaynes, 1859.

———. "Une saison chez Legallais: 5 août—15 août 1825." Pts. 1 and 2. *BSHAA,* no. 76 (1993): 45–60; no. 77 (1993): 46–61.

Arago, Jacques. *Promenades historiques, philosophiques et pittoresques, dans le département de la Gironde.* Bordeaux: Suwerinck, 1829.

Arcachon, guide annuaire. Arcachon: n.p., 1903.

Arcachon Magazine. Toulouse: Ici et Là, 1996–98.

Ardoin Saint Amand, Jean-Pierre. "Nelly Béryl ou la fin de la Belle Epoque à Arcachon" *BSHAA,* no. 102 (1999): 49–89.

Aufan, Robert. *La naissance d'Arcachon (1823–1857): De la forêt à la ville.* Arcachon: SHAA, 1994.

———. "La naissance d'Arcachon." In *Une histoire du Bassin: Arcachon, entre landes et océan,* edited by Charles Daney and Michel Boyé, 83–94. Bordeaux: Mollat, 1995.

———. "Le Pays de Buch, de la lande aux forêts (XVIIIe et XIXe siècles)." *BSHAA,* no. 89 (1996): 1–40.

Augustin, Jean-Pierre, ed. *Surf atlantique: Les territoires de l'éphémère.* Talence: Maison des sciences de l'homme d'Aquitaine, 1994.

Auzac de Lamartine, Gilles d', and Charles Daney. *Bassin d'Arcachon: Mer Fertile.* Mérignac: Editions Premiers Pas, 1995.

Bachelard, Gaston. *L'eau et les rêves: Essai sur l'imagination de la matière.* Paris: Librairie José Corti, 1942.

———. *La poétique de l'espace.* Paris: Presses Universitaires de France, 1957.

Bailhé, Claude, and Paul Charpentier. *La côte atlantique de Biarritz à La Rochelle au temps des guides baigneurs.* Toulouse: Editions Milan, 1983.

"Bains de Mer à La Teste: Etablissement Legallais, à Bel-Air." In *Le Mémorial Bordelais,* 3 July 1830, reprinted in *BSHAA,* no. 19 (1979): 42–43.

Bainbridge, Cyril. *Pavilions on the Sea: A History of the Seaside Pleasure Pier.* London: R. Hale, 1986.

Baranowski, Shelley, and Ellen Furlough, eds. *Being Elsewhere: Tourism, Consumer Culture, and Identity in Modern Europe and North America.* Ann Arbor: University of Michigan Press, 2001.

Barnes, David S. *The Making of a Social Disease: Tuberculosis in Nineteenth-Century France.* Berkeley: University of California Press, 1995.

Baschet, Jacques. *Le Panorama Salon, d'après les clichés photographiques de Neurdein frères.* Paris: Ludovic Baschet, 1901.

Baumann, Max, and Jacques Ragot. *La presqu'île Lège Cap-Ferret: Lège, Claouey, Les Jacquets, Piquey, Piraillan, Le Canon, L'Herbe.* Marguerittes, France: Equinoxe, 1992.

Baurein, Abbé. *Variétés bordelaises, ou Essai historique et critique sur la topographie ancienne et moderne du diocèse de Bordeaux.* Bordeaux: Chez les frères Labottière, 1784–1786.

Bénichou, Paul. *Les mages romantiques.* Paris: Gallimard, 1988.

Benoît, Patrice. "Les premières tentatives de création de chemin de fer en Gironde (1830–1837)." *BSHAA,* no. 80 (1994): 34–44.

Bernard, Jacques. "Les Gascons et la mer (XIVe–XVIe siècle)." In *Sociétés et groupes sociaux en Aquitaine et en Angleterre: Actes du Colloque franco-britannique tenu à Bordeaux du 27 au 30 septembre 1976,* edited by Fédération Historique du Sud-Ouest, 141–56. Bordeaux: Centre National de la Recherche Scientifique, 1979.

Béteille, Roger. "Le paysage, le mythe et le tourisme." *Acta Geographica* 99, no. 3 (1994): 35–41.

Bishop, Michael. *Nineteenth-Century French Poetry.* New York: Twayne Publishers, 1993.

Boisgontier, Jacques, ed. *Bordelais, Gironde.* Paris: Editions Bonneton, 1990.

Bonneval, Comte André de. *Tableau pittoresque et agricole des landes du bassin d'Arcachon.* Paris: Bourgogne et Martinet, 1839.

Bouchet, Jean-Marie. "Evolution du Bassin d'Arcachon et des conditions de navigation." In *Le littoral gascon et son arrière-pays (mer, dunes, forêt): Actes du colloque de la Société Historique d'Arcachon et du Pays de Buch, Arcachon, 27–28 octobre 1990,* edited by SHAA, 69–89. Arcachon: Graphica, 1990.

Bouchon, G. *Historique du chemin de fer de Bordeaux à La Teste et à Arcachon.* Bordeaux: G. Gounouilhou/L'Esprit du Temps, 1891 [1991].

Bouneau, Christophe. "Chemins de fer et développement régional en France de 1852 à 1937: La contribution de la Compagnie du Midi." *Histoire, Economie et Société* 9, no. 1 (1990): 95–112.

Bourdieu, Pierre. *Distinction: A Social Critique of the Judgement of Taste.* Cambridge, Mass.: Harvard University Press, 1984.

Bourgeois, Claude, and Michel Melot. *Les cartes postales (nouveau guide du collectionneur).* Paris: Editions Atlas, 1984.

Bourguet, Marie-Noëlle. *Déchiffrer la France: La statistique départementale à l'époque napoléonienne.* Paris: Editions des Archives Contemporaines, 1989.

——. "Race et folklore: L'image officelle de la France en 1800." *Annales,* no. 31 (1976): 802–23.

Bouscau, Franck. "Recherches sur la cartographie des prés salés de La Teste." *BSHAA,* no. 36 (1983): 94–100.

——. "La curieuse histoire des prés salés de La Teste de Buch (1)." *BSHAA,* no. 40 (1984): 1–12.

——. *Les prés salés de La Teste-de-Buch en Aquitaine: Contribution à l'histoire du domaine maritime du moyen-âge à nos jours.* Tours/Paris: Franck Bouscau, 1993.

Bousquet-Bressolier, C. *Les aménagements du Bassin d'Arcachon au XVIIIe siècle.* Dinard: Lab. de Géomorphologie, Ecole Pratique des Hautes Etudes, 1990.

——. "Les projets d'aménagement de l'entrée du bassin d'Arcachon (1768–1864). Une lecture rationele des mouvements de la nature." In *L'Aventure maritime du Golfe de Gascogne à Terre-Neuve,* edited by Comité des Travaux Historiques et Scientifiques, 89–104. Paris: Editions du Comité des Travaux Historiques et Scientifiques, 1993.

Boyé, Michel. "Arcachon, 'la capitale' (1857–1906)." In *Une histoire du Bassin: Arcachon, entre landes et océan,* edited by Charles Daney and Michel Boyé, 167–75. Bordeaux: Mollat, 1995.

——. "Arcachon et le Bassin sous l'Occupation (2)." *BSHAA,* no. 84 (1995).

——. "A propos du Grand Malheur (II)." *BSHAA,* no. 99 (1999): 1–27.

——. "La place de l'ostréiculture arcachonnaise." In *L'ostréiculture arcachonnaise: Actes du colloque organisé par la Société Historique et Archéologique d'Arcachon, tenu à Gujan-Mestras les 15 et 16 octobre, 1994,* edited by SHAA, 105–14. Arcachon: Graphica, 1994.

——. "Le temps des investisseurs (1820–1857)." In *Une histoire du Bassin: Arcachon, entre landes et océan,* edited by Charles Daney and Michel Boyé, 59–64. Bordeaux: Mollat, 1995.

Boyé, Michel, and Noël Gruet. "La pêche industrielle: Petite histoire des chalutiers d'Arcachon." In *Une histoire du Bassin: Arcachon, entre landes et océan,* edited by Charles Daney and Michel Boyé, 95–106. Bordeaux: Mollat, 1995.

Branlat, Louis. *Vingt-quatre heures à Arcachon.* Bordeaux: G. Gounouilhou, 1886.

Brenot, J. *Cent cinquante ans de chemin de fer de Bordeaux à La Teste et à Arcachon.* Bordeaux: Le Bouscat, 1991.

Briffaud, Serge. *Naissance d'un paysage: La montagne pyrénéenne à la croisée des regards : XVIe–XIXe siècle.* Tarbes, Toulouse: Association Guillaume Moran, Archives des Hautes-Pyrénées; C.I.M.A.-C.N.R.S., Université de Toulouse II, 1994.

Brissonneau-Steck, Gilles. "Le Casino de la Plage d'Arcachon—Le procès (1904–1914)." *BSHAA,* no. 88 (1996): 61–66.

Brombert, Victor. *The Hidden Reader: Stendhal, Balzac, Hugo, Baudelaire, Flaubert.* Cambridge, Mass.: Harvard University Press, 1988.

———. *The Romantic Prison: The French Tradition.* Princeton, N.J.: Princeton University Press, 1978.

Brousse, Emmanual. "A Bordeaux." *L'Indépendant des Pyrénées-Orientales,* no. 251, Sunday, 13 September 1914.

Brunet, R. "Analyse des paysages et sémiologie. Eléments pour un débat." *L'Espace Géographique,* no. 2 (1974): 120–26.

Bureau de la recherche architecturale. *L'architecture des villes d'eaux en France.* Paris: Direction de l'Architecture, 1983.

Butel, Paul. *Les dynasties bordelaises de Colbert à Chaban.* Paris: Perrin, 1991.

Buzard, James. *The Beaten Track: European Tourism, Literature, and the Ways to Culture, 1800–1918.* Oxford: Oxford University Press, 1993.

———. "Forster's Trespasses: Tourism and Cultural Politics." *Twentieth-Century Literature* 34, no. 1 (1988): 155–79.

Cabantous, Alain. "Apprendre la mer: Remarques sur l'apprentissage des mousses à l'époque moderne." *Revue d'Histoire Moderne et Contemporaine* 40, no. 3 (1993): 415–22.

———. *Les citoyens du large: Les identités maritimes en France (XVIIe–XIXe siècle).* Paris: Aubier, 1995.

———. *Les côtes barbares: Pilleurs d'épaves et sociétés littorales en France, 1680–1830.* Paris: Fayard, 1993.

———. *Dix mille marins face à l'océan, les populations maritimes de Dunkerque au Havre aux XVIIe et XVIIIe siècles (vers 1660–1794): Étude sociale.* Paris: Editions Publisud, 1991.

Cabaud, Michel, and Ronald Hubscher, eds. *1900, la Française au quotidien (cartes postales).* Paris: A. Colin, 1985.

Calhoun, Craig, Edward LiPuma, and Moishe Postone. *Bourdieu: Critical Perspectives.* Cambridge: Polity, 1993.

Capizzi, Virginie. "La naissance de la commune d'Arcachon." *BSHAA,* no. 103 (2000): 22–67.

Capp, Fiona. *That Oceanic Feeling.* Crows Nest, NSW (Australia): Allen and Unwin, 2003.

Carter, Paul. "Dark with Excess of Bright: Mapping the Coastlines of Knowledge." In *Mappings,* edited by Denis Cosgrove, 125–47. London: Reaktion Books, 1999.

———. *The Lie of the Land.* London: Faber and Faber, 1996.

Casey, Edward S. *The Fate of Place.* Berkeley: University of California Press, 1997.

Cassou-Mounat, Micheline. "La vie humaine sur le littoral des Landes de Gascogne." Thèse d'Etat, Université de Bordeaux III, 1975.

Castandet, Léo. *La Hume et le tourisme 1834–1997.* La Hume: Maison du Tourisme, 1997.

Cazenave, Sylvain, and Gibus de Soultrait. *L'homme et la vague.* Guéthary, Biarritz: Vent de Terre/Surf Session, 1995.

Certeau, Michel de. *The Practice of Everyday Life.* Translated by S. Rendall. Berkeley: University of California Press, 1984.

Chadefaud, Michel. *Aux origines du tourisme dans les pays de l'Adour, du mythe à l'espace: Un essai de géographie historique.* Pau: Département de Géographie et d'Aménagement de l'Université de Pau et des Pays de l'Adour, Centre de Recherche sur l'Impact Socio-Spatial de l'Aménagement, 1987.

Chadeyron, Patrick. "La mode et la renommée." In *Une histoire du Bassin: Arcachon, entre landes et océan,* edited by Charles Daney and Michel Boyé, 139–52. Bordeaux: Mollat, 1995.

Chambre de commerce et d'industrie de Bordeaux. *Atlas commercial du Bassin d'Arcachon.* Bordeaux: Chambre de Commerce et d'Industrie, 1987.

Charles, A. "Le développement de la station balnéaire d'Arcachon sous le Second Empire." *Revue Historique de Bordeaux* (1953): 239–49.

Chateaubriand. "René." In *Œuvres romanesques et voyages,* edited by Maurice Regard, 103–46. Paris: NRF/Gallimard, [1802].

Chatelin, Y., and G. Riou, eds. *Milieux et paysages: Essai sur diverses modalités de connaissance.* Paris: Masson, 1986.

Clary, Daniel. *Le tourisme dans l'espace français.* Paris: Masson, 1993.

Clémens, Jacques. *Le Bassin d'Arcachon.* Joué-lès-Tours: Alan Sutton, 1997.

———. "La première vue du Bassin d'Arcachon (1684–1817)." *BSHAA,* no. 90 (1996): 4–16.

Collectif. *Le Pilat, la grande dune et le pays de Buch.* Arcachon: Arpège, 1983.

Comité d'études sur l'histoire et l'art de Gascogne. *Mémoire des Landes: Dictionnaire biographique.* Mont-de-Marsan: Comité d'Etudes sur l'Histoire et l'Art de Gascogne, 1991.

Comité des travaux historiques et scientifiques. *L'aventure maritime, du Golfe de Gascogne à Terre-Neuve.* Paris: Editions du Comité des Travaux Historiques et Scientifiques, 1993.

———. *Le corps et la santé: Actes du 110e Congrès National des Sociétés Savantes,* Paris: Vente directe, Documentation française, 1985.

Congrès d'études régionales, ed. *Arcachon et le Val de l'Eyre: histoires, art, économies: Actes du XXVIème congrès.* Bordeaux: La Fédération Historique du Sud-Ouest, 1977.

Conklin, Alice L., and Ian Fletcher, eds. *European Imperialism, 1830–1930.* Boston: Houghton Mifflin, 1999.

Corbin, Alain. "Divisions of Time and Space." In *Realms of Memory: Rethinking the French Past,* edited by Pierre Nora, 427–446. New York: Columbia University Press, 1992.

———. *Les filles de noces: Misère sexuelle et prostitution (19e et 20e siècles).* Paris: Aubier Montaigne, 1978.

———. *The Foul and the Fragrant: Odour and the French Social Imagination.* Translated by M. Koshan. London: Picador, 1994.

———. *The Lure of the Sea: The Discovery of the Seaside in the Western World 1750–1840.* Translated by Jocelyn Phelps. Harmondsworth, U.K.: Penguin, 1994 [1988].

——. *Le territoire du vide: L'Occident et le désir du rivage (1750–1840)*. Paris: Aubier, 1988.

——, ed. *L'avènement des loisirs, 1850–1960*. Paris: Aubier-Flammarion, 1995.

Cosgrove, Denis. *Social Formation and Symbolic Landscape*. London: Croom Helm, 1984.

——, ed. *Mappings*. London: Reaktion Books, 1999.

Cross, Gary. "Vacations for All: The Leisure Question in the Era of the Popular Front." *Journal of Contemporary History* 24, no. 4 (1989): 599–621.

Daney, Charles. *Dictionnaire de la Lande Française, du fond du Bassin au fin fond de la Lande*. Portet-sur-Garonne: Loubatières, 1992.

Daney, Charles, and Michel Boyé, eds. *Une histoire du Bassin: Arcachon, entre landes et océan*. Bordeaux: Mollat, 1995.

Dejean, Oscar. *Arcachon et ses environs*. Paris: Res Universis, 1992 [1858].

Delano-Smith, Catherine. "Art or Cartography? The Wrong Question." *History of the Human Sciences* 2, no. 1 (1989): 89–93.

Deltreil, Jean-Pierre. "L'âge d'or et les crises de l'ostréiculture dans le Bassin d'Arcachon." In *L'ostréiculture arcachonnaise: Actes du colloque organisé par la Société Historique et Archéologique d'Arcachon, tenu à Gujan-Mestras les 15 et 16 octobre, 1994*, edited by SHAA, 51–66. Arcachon: Graphica, 1994.

Derek, Gregory. *Geographical Imaginations*. Cambridge: Basil Blackwell, 1994.

Desbiey, Guillaume. *Trois mémoires d'un precurseur landais méconnu*. Arcachon: SHAA, 1991.

Deschamps, Claude. *Des travaux à faire pour l'assainissement et la culture des Landes de Gascogne et des canaux de jonction de l'Adour à la Garonne*. Paris: Carillan-Gœury, 1832.

Désert, Gabriel. *La vie quotidienne sur les plages normandes du Second Empire aux Années folles*. Paris: Hachette, 1983.

Desplantes, Anne. "Les chemins de fer et l'essor du tourisme de masse en France, 1900–1939." *Revue de l'Histoire des Chemins de Fer*, no. 9 (1993): 93–102.

Dictionnaire biographique et album Gironde, vol. 2. Paris: E. Flammarion, n.d.

Dubourg, Jean-Philippe. "Histoire de la pêche au chalut, dans le bassin d'Arcachon: Une épopée d'un siècle." *BSHAA*, no. 16 (1978): 1–24.

Duncan, James, and David Ley, eds. *Place/Culture/Representation*. London: Routledge, 1993.

Dupuyoo, Luc. "Projet de sanatorium au Camp Américain du Cap-Ferret." *BSHAA*, no. 114 (2002): 35–39.

Féret, Edouard. *Statistique générale du département de la Gironde*. Vol. 3: *Biographies*. Bordeaux: Féret, 1889.

Fleury, Robert. "Arcachon, ville de santé." In *Le littoral gascon et son arrière-pays (Moyen-âge, économie, Arcachon et le Bassin): Actes du deuxième colloque de la Société Historique et Archéologique d'Arcachon et du Pays de Buch, Arcachon, 17–18 octobre, 1992*, edited by SHAA, 187–202. Arcachon: Graphica/SHAA, 1993.

——. "Médecines et médecins en Arcachon." In *Une histoire du Bassin: Arcachon, entre landes et océan*, edited by Charles Daney and Michel Boyé, 119–37. Bordeaux: Mollat, 1995.

Forty, George. *Fortress Europe: Hitler's Atlantic Wall.* Surrey: Ian Allan, 2002.

Foucault, Michel. "Questions on Geography." In *Power/Knowledge: Selected Interviews and Other Writings 1972–1977,* edited by C. Gordon, 63–77. Translated by C. Gordon. Brighton, Sussex: Harvester Press, 1980.

Furlough, Ellen. "Making Mass Vacations: Tourism and Consumer Culture in France, 1930s to 1970s." *Comparative Studies in Society and History,* no. 40 (1998): 247–86.

Gabory, de. *Guide d'Arcachon.* Arcachon: Mme. Delamare, 1896.

Gairal. "Consultation faite par l'Administration des domaines de la Couronne pour savoir si l'Administration doit prétendre à la propriété des prés salés." AN Mar CC^5 379, 1833.

Galy, Roger. *Le Bassin d'Arcachon: . . . à la recherche de la lumière de l'aube pâle au rayonnant crépuscule [ou] La laca d'Arcaishon: . . . en cèrca de la lutz de l'aubina avant dinc'a las arrajantas so-vaguèiras.* Gradignan: Princi Negre, 1995.

———. *Histoire du Bassin d'Arcachon des origines à nos jours: Les événements, les lieux et les hommes.* Gradignan: Princi Nègre, 1998.

Garner, Alice. "Floating Worlds: Conflicting Representations of Sea and Shore in Arcachon and La Teste, 1830–1910." PhD diss., University of Melbourne, 2001.

———. "Une forêt de piquets: Le désir de rivage à Arcachon, 1866–1902." In *Le littoral gascon et sa vocation balnéaire: Actes du colloque de la Société Historique d'Arcachon et du Pays de Buch, Cap-Ferret, juin 1999,* 15–29. Arcachon: SHAA, 1999.

Gatineau-Clemenceau, Georges. *Des pattes du Tigre aux griffes du destin.* Paris: Les Presses du Mail, 1961.

Gavignaud, Geneviève. *Les campagnes en France au XIXème siècle (1780–1914).* Paris: Ophrys, 1990.

Geiger, Reed G. *Planning the French Canals: Bureaucracy, Politics and Enterprise under the Restoration.* Cranbury, N.J.: University of Delaware Press, 1995.

Gerbod, Paul. *Voyages en histoire.* Paris: Les Belles-Lettres, 1995.

Goujon, Paul. *Cent ans de tourisme en France.* Paris: Le Cherche Midi, 1989.

Gould, Peter. *The Geographer at Work.* London: Routledge and Kegan Paul, 1985.

Green, Nicholas. *The Spectacle of Nature: Landscape and Bourgeois Culture in Nineteenth-Century France.* Manchester: Manchester University Press, 1990.

Gregory, Derek, and John Urry, eds. *Social Relations and Spatial Structures.* New York: St. Martin's Press, 1985.

Grew, Raymond. "Picturing the People: Images of the Lower Orders in Nineteenth Century French Art." *Journal of Interdisciplinary History* 17, no. 1 (1986): 203–31.

Gruet, Noël. "Les bateaux de service du bassin d'Arcachon." *Le Chasse-Marée: Histoire et Ethnologie Maritime,* no. 116 (1998): 48–59.

———. "Les chaloupes de pêche de La Teste, 1816 à 1880. Première partie: 1816–1845." *BSHAA,* no. 101 (1999): 33–40.

———. "La pêche industrielle après 1914." In *Une histoire du Bassin: Arcachon, entre landes et océan,* edited by Charles Daney and Michel Boyé, 209–16. Bordeaux: Mollat, 1995.

Gruet, Noël, and Pierre-Jean Labourg. "La vie maritime du bassin d'Arcachon." *Le Chasse-Marée: Histoire et Ethnologie Maritime,* no. 41 (1989): 22–39.

Gubler, Jacques. "Entre mer et forêt: La ville aux balcons d'argent." In *La Ville d'hiver d'Arcachon,* edited by Institut Français d'Architecture, 75–110. Paris: Institut Français d'Architecture, 1983.

Guerrand, Roger-Henri. "La Ville dont les princes furent des médecins." In *La Ville d'hiver d'Arcachon,* edited by Institut Français d'Architecture, 59–74. Paris: Institut Français d'Architecture, 1983.

Guillaume, Pierre. *Du désespoir au salut: Les tuberculeux aux XIXe et XXe siècles.* Paris: Aubier, 1986.

———. *Le rôle social du médecin depuis deux siècles: 1800–1945.* Paris: Association pour l'Etude de l'Histoire de la Sécurité Sociale, 1996.

Hameau, Jean. *Quelques avis sur les bains de mer.* Bordeaux: Lavigne Jeune, 1835.

Hennequin. *Notice sur la Compagnie Agricole et Industrielle d'Arcachon, suivie de divers documents relatifs à ses opérations, ainsi qu'à la construction du canal et du chemin de fer qui faciliteront le transport de ses produits.* Paris: Imprimerie de Bourgogne et Martinet, 1838.

Herbert, Robert L. *Manet on the Normandy Coast: Tourism and Painting, 1867–1886.* New Haven: Yale University Press, 1994.

Hobsbawm, Eric, and Terence Ranger. *The Invention of Tradition.* Cambridge: Cambridge University Press, 1983.

Hugo, A. *France pittoresque ou, Description pittoresque, topographique et statistique des départements et colonies de la France.* 3 vols. Paris: Delloye, 1835.

Hugo, Victor. ———. *Œuvres complètes: Poésie.* Edited by Jean Gaudon. Paris: Laffont, 1985.

———. *Les travailleurs de la mer.* Paris: Garnier-Flammarion, 1980 [1866].

———. "Voyage aux Pyrénées, 1843." In *Œuvres completes,* vol. 6, edited by Jean Massin, 854–58. Paris: Club Français du Livre, 1968.

Hyde, Ralph. *Panoramania!: The Art and Entertainment of the "All-Embracing" View.* London: Trefoil, 1988.

Ikni, Guy. "Sur les biens communaux pendant la Révolution Française." *Annales Historiques de la Révolution Française,* no. 54 (1982): 71–94.

Institut Français d'Architecture. *Villes d'eaux en France.* Paris: Institut Français d'Architecture, 1984.

———, ed. *La Ville d'Hiver d'Arcachon.* Paris: Institut Français d'Architecture, 1983.

J. P. P. [Jacques Paulin Polhe] "Une visite à La Teste du [*sic*] Buch à travers les Grandes Landes [1837]." Reprinted in *BSHAA,* no. 37 (1983): 43–46.

Jackson, Julian. *The Popular Front in France: Defending Democracy, 1934–1938.* Cambridge: Cambridge University Press, 1988.

Jardin, André, and André-Jean Tudesq. *Restoration and Reaction, 1815–1848.* Translated by Elborg Forster. Cambridge: Cambridge University Press/Paris: Editions M.S.H., 1983.

Joanne, Paul. *Arcachon et la Côte d'Argent.* Paris: Hachette et Cie, 1917.

———. *De la Loire aux Pyrénées.* Paris: Hachette, 1908.

Jouannet, François Vatar de. *Département de la Gironde.* Paris: Res Universis, 1986 [1837–43].

Juret, Pierre-Marie. *Le domaine public maritime.* Paris: Dalloz, 1964.

Kauffmann, P. "Le Parqueur d'Arcachon." *L'Illustration: Journal Universel* (30 January 1892): 91–94.

Kearney. *Mémoire sur la navigation des Vaisseaux à la Coste d'Arcasson [sic]: Observations sur le Port d'Arcasson et l'avantage de sa position,* art. 4 [1768]. ADG 6 J 42.

Keller, Eliane. *Arcachon.* Marguerittes, France: Equinoxe, 1992.

———. *Arcachon: Villas et personnalités.* Marguerittes, France: Equinox, 1994.

———. "Le Grand Hôtel d'Arcachon." *BSHAA,* no. 109 (2001): 57–65.

———. *Le Sud Bassin: Arcachon—La Teste—Gujan-Mestras. Petite histoire maritime et balnéaire.* Barbantane: Equinoxe, 1997.

Kern, Stephen. *The Culture of Time and Space, 1880–1918.* Cambridge, Mass.: Harvard University Press, 1983.

Konvitz, Josef W. "Changing Concepts of the Sea." *Terrae Incognitae* 11 (1979): 1–17.

L. de P. *Arcachon et ses environs.* Arcachon: Librairie Editions Bon, 1901.

La Blanchère, H. de. *La pêche aux bains de mer.* Paris: Firmin-Diderot et Cie, 1894.

Labarbe, Bruno, and Alain Pujol. *Les caprices du Bassin.* Villandraut: Editions de la Palombe, 1998.

Labat, Pierre. "L'accès à la mer et le passage sur les digues." *BSHAA,* no. 45 (1985): 10–28.

———. "Nicolas Taffard et sa descendance," *BSHAA,* no.117 (2003): 29–46.

———. "Les Taffard de La Teste," *BSHAA,* no. 116 (2003): 21–40.

Labatut, Fernand. "Les caractères originaux du Pays de Buch: le Buch dans la période contemporaine." *BSHAA,* no. 96 (1998): 1–33.

———. "Le destin des dunes (3ème partie): Péripéties municipales." *BSHAA,* no. 108 (2001): 29–52.

———. "Esquisse de l'évolution démographique dans le pays de Buch depuis la Révolution Française." *BSHAA,* no. 67 (1991): 49–54; no. 68 (1991): 40–61; no. 70 (1991): 31–54; no. 72 (1992): 24–43; no. 74 (1992): 33–56.

———. "Préludes à l'ensemencement des dunes (suite)." *BSHAA,* no. 103 (2000): 68–94.

Laborde, Pierre. *Biarritz, huit siècles d'histoire, 200 ans de vie balnéaire.* Biarritz: Ferrus, 1984.

Lacou, Jean. *Examen critique sur le Bassin d'Arcachon.* Bordeaux: Métreau et Cie, 1865.

———. *Guide historique, pittoresque et descriptif du voyageur aux bains de mer d'Arcachon.* Bordeaux: Mme. Crugy, 1856.

La Harpe, Dr. de. *Formulaire des stations d'hiver, des stations d'été et de la climatothérapie.* Paris: J.-B. Baillère et Fils, 1895.

Lahaye, Richard. *Andernos.* Marguerittes, France: Equinox, 1995.

Lalaing, Madame de. *Les Côtes de la France de Saint-Nazaire à Biarritz par la plage.* Paris-Lille: J. Lefort, 1898.

Lalesque, Dr. F.-A. *Topographie médicale de la Teste de Buch, département de la Gironde, suivie de considérations hygiéniques applicables aux pays marécageux.* Bordeaux: Lavigne Jeune, 1835.

Lalesque, Dr. Fernand. *Arcachon, ville d'été, ville d'hiver, topographie et climatologie médicales.* Paris: G. Masson, 1886.

———. *Le climat d'Arcachon étudié à l'aide des appareils enrégistreurs.* Paris: Octave Doin, 1890.

———. *Cure d'air et de repos dans ses rapports avec les pesées des tuberculeux.* Bordeaux: Gounouilhou, 1889.

———. *Cure marine de la phtisie pulmonaire.* Paris: Masson, 1897.

———. *Climathérapie française: La cure libre de la tuberculose pulmonaire (Conférence publique faite le 4 juin 1899).* Bordeaux: Gounouilhou, 1899.

———. *La cure marine de la tuberculose pulmonaire sur le bassin d'Arcachon.* Paris: Masson et Cie, 1900.

———. *La suraération en cure libre.* Bordeaux: G. Gounouilhou, 1902.

Lamarque, Dr. Henri. *De quelques abus de bains de mer et des cures marines, en particulier dans le Sud-Ouest . . . Communication faite au congrès de thalassothéraphie de Biarritz (avril 1903).* Bordeaux: Gounouilhou, 1903.

Lannoy, P. A. de. *Guide aux plages girondines.* Bordeaux: G. Delmas, 1900.

Laroche, Ernest. *A travers le vieux Bordeaux: Récits inédits, légendes, études de moeurs, portraits, types, monuments, reconstitution des quartiers pittoresques.* Bordeaux: Editions de la Grande Fontaine, 1890.

Lash, Scott, and John Urry. *Economies of Signs and Space.* London: Sage, 1994.

Latéoule, Robert. "L'économie testerine au milieu du 19ème siècle." In *Le littoral gascon et son arrière-pays (mer, dunes, forêt): Actes du colloque de la Société Historique d'Arcachon et du Pays de Buch, Arcachon, 27–28 octobre, 1990,* edited by SHAA, 239–47. Arcachon: Graphica, 1990.

La Tombelle, Henry de, and Jean Samazeuilh. *Guide touristique Sud-Ouest: Cyclotourisme, canoë, camping.* Bordeaux: Editions Delmas, 1938.

Latour, Bruno. *Les microbes: Guerre et paix, suivi de Irréductions.* Paris: A. M. Metailié and Association Pandore, 1984.

Latrille, Jacques. "Un savant girondin oublié, sinon méconnu: Le docteur Jean Hameau." *BSHAA,* no. 94 (1997): 1–32.

Lavenir, Catherine Bertho. *La roue et le stylo.* Paris: Editions Odile Jacob, 1999.

Leclercq, Yves. "L'état, les entreprises ferroviaires et leurs profits en France, 1830–60." *Histoire, Economie, Société* 9, no. 1 (1990): 39–63.

Lefebvre, Henri. *La production de l'espace.* Paris: Editions Anthropos, 1974.

———. *Writings on Cities.* Translated by Eleonore Kofman and Elizabeth Lebas. Cambridge, Mass.: Blackwell, 1996.

Lencek, Lena, and Gideon Bosker. *The Beach: The History of Paradise on Earth.* New York: Viking, 1998.

Léonard, Jacques. *La médecine entre les pouvoirs et les savoirs: Histoire intellectuelle et politique de la médecine française au XIXe siècle.* Paris: Aubier Montaigne, 1981.

Léonard, Martine. "Photographie et littérature: Zola, Breton, Simon (Hommage à Roland Barthes)." *Etudes Françaises* (Canada) 18, no. 3 (1983): 93–108.

Lepetit, Bernard. "Remarques sur la contribution de l'espace à l'analyse historique." *Paysages Découverts* 2 (1993): 79–90.

Liggett, Helen, and David C. Perry, eds. *Spatial Practices: Critical Explorations in Social/Spatial Theory.* London: Sage, 1995.

Lindley, Kenneth. *Seaside Architecture.* London: H. Evelyn, 1973.

Löfgren, Orvar. *On Holiday: A History of Vacationing.* Berkeley: University of California Press, 1999.

Loret, Alain. *Génération glisse; dans l'eau, l'air, la neige . . . la révolution du sport des années fun.* Paris: Autrement, 1995.

Lormier, Dominique. *Bordeaux Arcachon à la Belle Epoque.* Montreuil-Bellay: Editions C.M.D., 1998.

———. *Bordeaux pendant l'Occupation.* Bordeaux: Sud-Ouest, 1992.

Loti, Pierre. *Pêcheur d'Islande.* Paris: Bookking International, 1994 [1886].

Louis, Paul. *Histoire de la classe ouvrière en France de la Révolution à nos jours: La condition matérielle des travailleurs, les salaires et le coût de la vie* (Paris: Librairie des Sciences Politiques et Sociales, Marcel Rivière, 1927).

Lowe, Donald M. *History of Bourgeois Perception.* Brighton: Harvester Press, 1982.

Lunn, Joe. *Memoirs of the Maelstrom: A Senegalese Oral History of the First World War.* Portsmouth, N.H.: Heinemann, 1999.

Mackaman, Douglas Peter. "The Landscape of a Ville d'Eau: Public Space and Social Practice at the Spas of France, 1850–1890." *Proceedings of the Annual Meeting of the Western Society for French History* 20 (1993): 281–91.

———. *Leisure Settings: Bourgeois Culture, Medicine, and the Spa in Modern France.* Chicago: University of Chicago Press, 1998.

Magne de la Croix, Francis. "La Brigade Marine d'Extrême-Orient à Arcachon, 1945." *BSHAA,* no. 88 (1996): 40–52.

———. "La Brigade Marine d'Extrême-Orient à Arcachon, 1945 (Suite)." *BSHAA,* no. 89 (1996): 52–70.

Maguet, Frédéric. "De la série éditoriale dans l'imagerie: L'exemple des costumes régionaux," in "Usages de l'Image," special issue, *Ethnologie Française* 24, no. 2(1994): 226–41.

Mansuy, Michel. *Gaston Bachelard et les éléments.* Paris: José Corti, 1967.

Mareschal, Jules. *Compagnie d'exploitation et de colonisation des Landes de Bordeaux. 5e rapport à la Commission de surveillance, par l'inspecteur général de la Compagnie, 25 juillet 1835 [signé Jules Mareschal].* Paris: Impr. de Pillet Aîné, [1835].

———. "Journal du Voyage fait en Octobre 1833 dans les Landes de Bordeaux." In *Entreprise d'exploitation et colonisation des Landes de Bordeaux.* Bordeaux: n.p., 1834.

———. *De la mise en valeur des Landes de Gascogne.* Paris: Poussielgue, Masson et Cie, 1853.

———. *Note sur les landes du littoral du golfe de Gascogne, considérées dans leurs rapports avec le canal d'Arcachon et le chemin de fer de Bordeaux à La Teste.* Paris: Pillet Aîné, 1842.

Maret, Henry. *Arcachon: promenade à travers bois.* Paris: Le Chevalier, 1865.

Marié, Michel, and Christian Tamisier. "Le 'faire avec' ou le génie du lieu: Contribution à une histoire des ingénieurs et du rapport à l'espace dans le département du Var." *Annales de la Recherche Urbaine,* no. 10–11 (1981): 22–53.

Marrey, Bernard. "Arcachon ou le levier de l'idée." In *La Ville d'hiver d'Arcachon,* edited by Institut Français d'Architecture, 31–58. Paris: Institut Français d'Architecture, 1983.

Massey, Doreen. "Politics and Space/Time." *New Left Review,* no. 196 (1992): 65–84.

———. *Space, Place, and Gender.* Cambridge: Polity Press, 1994.

Maupassant, Guy de. *Pierre et Jean.* In *Œuvres complètes,* vol. 9, 193–401. Paris: Maurice Gonon and Albin Michel, 1969 [1888].

Mauriac, François. *Les préséances.* 2nd ed. Paris: Flammarion, 1928 [1921].

McPhee, Peter. *A Social History of France, 1780–1880.* London: Routledge, 1992.

"Mémoire des Marins du Quartier de Lateste [*sic*] Contre la mise en ferme de Lisle [*sic*] et Crassats du Bassin de Lateste, annoncée pour le 18 Juin 1806." La Teste, 1806. ADG S. Lotissements S 16 (Service Maritime).

Merger, Michèle. "La concurrence rail-navigation intérieure en France 1850–1914." *Histoire, Economie, Société* 9, no. 1 (1990): 65–94.

Mérimée, Prosper. *Notes d'un voyage dans l'Ouest de la France . . . Extrait d'un rapport adressé à M. le ministre de l'intérieur.* Paris : H. Fournier, 1836.

Merrifield, A. "Place and Space—A Lefebvrian Reconciliation." *Transactions of the Institute of British Geographers* 18, no. 4 (1993): 516–31.

Merriman, John M. *The Margins of City Life: Explorations on the French Urban Frontier, 1815–1851.* Oxford: Oxford University Press, 1991.

Michelet, Jules. *La mer.* Paris: Gallimard, 1983.

Mitchell-Lacroix, Annick. *Le Bassin d'Arcachon à la Belle-Epoque.* Bordeaux: Editions Eric Lacroix, 1992.

Mollat du Jourdin, Michel. *Europe and the Sea.* Translated by Teresa Lavender Fagan. Oxford: Blackwell, 1993.

———. "Le front de mer." In *Les lieux de mémoire,* edited by Pierre Nora, 616–71. Paris: Gallimard, 1992.

Monmonier, Mark. *How to Lie with Maps.* Chicago: Chicago University Press, 1991.

Montigaud, F. *Arcachon, statistique générale et notes historiques.* 2nd ed. Bordeaux: Gounouilhou, 1905.

Mortemart de Boisse, Baron de. *Voyage dans les Landes de Gascogne et rapport à la Société royale et centrale d'agriculture sur la colonie d'Arcachon.* Paris: L. Bouchard-Huzard, 1840.

Mouls, Abbé X. *Notre-Dame d'Arcachon.* Bordeaux: n.p., 1855.

Moureau, P. *Dictionnaire du patois de La Teste.* La Teste: Imprimerie Moureau, 1968.

Municipalité Gounouilhou. *Arcachon 1929–1935: Six années de progrès municipaux.* Bordeaux: Delmas, Chapon, Gounouilhou, 1935.

Musée des Beaux-Arts et d'Archéologie, and Musée des Beaux-Arts de Bordeaux. *Louis Valtat: Dans la baie: Arcachon 1895.* Besançon: Musée des Beaux-Arts et d'Archéologie, 1993.

O. D., *Guide du voyageur à La Teste et aux alentours du Bassin d'Arcachon.* Bordeaux: P. Chaumas-Gayet, 1845.

Pérotin, René. *Le chalutage à vapeur à Arcachon.* Bordeaux: Y. Cadoret, 1911.

Perrein, Paul. *Images d'autrefois de Bordeaux et de la Gironde.* Perigueux: P. Fanlac, 1980.

Peyrous, B. "La vie religieuse autour du bassin d'Arcachon durant l'épiscopat du Cardinal Donnet (1836–82)." In *Arcachon et le Val d'Eyre: Histoire, art, économie,* edited by Fédération Historique du Sud-Ouest, 117–30. Bordeaux: Biscaye Frères, 1977.

Picheral, Henri. *Espace et santé: Géographie médicale du Midi de la France.* Montpellier: Imprimerie du Paysan du Midi, 1976.

Pichois, Claude. *Le romantisme II: 1843–1869.* Paris: Arthaud, 1979.

Picon, Antoine. *L'invention de l'ingénieur moderne: L'Ecole des Ponts et Chaussées, 1747–1851.* Paris: Presses de L'Ecole Nationale des Ponts et Chaussées, 1992.

Pierrefeux, Guy de. "L'Arcachon d'autrefois." *Revue Historique de la Côte d'Argent* 1–2 (1908): 1–136.

Pinon, Pierre, and Annie Kriegel. "L'achèvement des canaux sous la Restauration et la Monarchie de Juillet." *Annales des Ponts et Chaussées* 19 (1981): 72–83.

Pollock, Griselda. " 'With my own eyes': Fetishism, the Labouring Body, and the Colour of Its Sex." *Art History* 17, no. 3 (1994): 342–82.

Price, Roger. *An Economic History of Modern France.* London: Macmillan, 1981.

Procès des prés-salés de La Teste (Notes pour les sieurs Oscar Moureau, François Mozas et Jean Cravey contre Harry-Scott Johnston étant instanciés dans la cause La comtesse d'Armailhé, le marquis de Castéja, l'Etat et la commune de La Teste. Bordeaux: Imprimerie Générale d'Emile Crugy, 1875.

Prochaska, David. "The Archive of *Algérie Imaginaire.*" *History and Anthropology* 4 (1990): 373–420.

Puig, A. "Un exemple d'ethnographie maritime: La pêche traditionnelle à la sardine sur le Bassin d'Arcachon." *BSHAA*, no. 40 (1984): 13–17.

Puig, Alberto. "De l'ethnologie comme matériau littéraire: L'exemple du Bassin d'Arcachon et des pratiques de pêche durant la première moitié du XXè siècle chez E. Barreyre et R. Rougerie." In *La littérature régionale en langue d'oc et en français à Bordeaux et dans la Gironde*, edited by Centre d'Etudes des Cultures Aquitaines et d'Europe du Sud and Université de Bordeaux III, 273–80. Bordeaux: Centre d'Etudes des Cultures Aquitaines et d'Europe du Sud and Université de Bordeaux III, 1989.

——. "Pêches du Bassin d'Arcachon, approche ethnologique." In *Le littoral gascon et son arrière-pays (Moyen-âge, économie, Arcachon et le Bassin): Actes du deuxième colloque de la Société Historique et Archéologique d'Arcachon et du Pays de Buch, Arcachon, 17–18 octobre, 1992*, edited by SHAA, 161–69. Arcachon: Graphica/SHAA, 1992.

Pujol, Alain, Jean-Pierre Moussaron, Alain Danvers, and Anne-Marie Garat. *Fous de Bassin.* Saucats: Editions Vivisques, 1988.

Pujol, Alain, and Alain Danvers. *Pinasses: Bassin d'Arcachon.* Bordeaux: Mollat, 1993.

Quennell, Peter, ed. *Memoirs of William Hickey.* London: Century Publishing, 1984.

Raban, Jonathan. "On the Waterfront [review article]." *New York Review of Books,* July 14 (1994): 37–42.

——. *Passage to Juneau: A Sea and Its Meanings.* London: Picador, 1999.

Ragot, Jacques. *Arcachon au temps des étrangers de distinction.* La Teste: Ragot, 1978.

——. "Le Bassin d'Arcachon en vers et en prose." In *Le littoral gascon et son arrière-pays (Moyen-âge, économie, Arcachon et le Bassin): Actes du deuxième colloque de la Société Historique et Archéologique d'Arcachon et du Pays de Buch, Arcachon, 17–18 octobre, 1992,* edited by SHAA, 219–30. Arcachon: Graphica/SHAA, 1993.

——. "Ces prés salés qui n'en sont pas." *BSHAA*, no. 63 (1990): 39–49.

——. *Le Cap-Ferret de Lège à la Pointe.* Arcachon: Imprimerie Graphica, 1982.

——. *De la Leyre au Cap-Ferret.* Arcachon: Imprimerie Graphica, 1980.

——. *Histoire de La Teste-de-Buch des origines à la fixation des dunes.* La Teste: J. Ragot, 1987.

——. *Pages d'histoire locale: Arcachon, La Teste, Le Mouleau, Pyla-sur-Mer.* La Teste: J. Ragot, 1986.

——. *Les pêcheurs du Bassin d'Arcachon au temps des chaloupes.* Bordeaux: Ulysse, 1983.

——. "Projets successifs d'amélioration des passes du Bassin d'Arcachon." In *Le littoral gascon et son arrière-pays (mer, dunes, forêt): Actes du premier colloque tenu à Arcachon les 27–28 octobre,* edited by SHAA, 91–104. Arcachon: Graphica, 1990.

——. "Rôle joué par les effluves 'térébenthines' des pins dans le développement d'Arcachon." In *Le corps et la santé: Actes du 110è Congrès National des Sociétés Savantes,* 57–65. Montpellier, 1985.

——. "La vie et les gens pendant les siècles où La Teste de Buch vécut sous la menace des sables." Paper presented at Cercle Universitaire d'Arcachon, 4 February 1970.

Ragot, Jacques, and Max Baumann. *La presqu'île Lège Cap-Ferret: Évocation historique.* Marguerittes, France: Equinoxe, c1992.

Rauch, André. *Crise de l'identité masculine, 1789–1914.* Paris: Hachette, 2000.

——. *Vacances en France de 1830 à nos jours.* Paris: Hachette, 1996.

Reclus, Elisée. "Les plages et le Bassin d'Arcachon." *Revue des Deux Mondes* 48 (15 November, 1863): n.p.

Revil, Claude. "Le pouvoir municipal à La Teste-de-Buch de la fin du Second Empire à la fin de la Troisième République." Honors thesis, Université de Bordeaux III, Faculté des Lettres et Sciences Humaines, 1987.

Ribadieu, Henry. *Un voyage au Bassin d'Arcachon.* Paris: J. Tardieu, 1859.

Ribereau-Gayon, Marie-Dominique. "Perceptions sensorielles et représentations des landes de Gascogne." In *Le littoral gascon et son arrière-pays (Moyen-âge, économie, Arcachon et le Bassin): Actes du deuxième colloque de la Société Historique et Archéologique d'Arcachon et du Pays de Buch, Arcachon, 17–18 octobre, 1992,* edited by SHAA, 145–60. Arcachon: Graphica/SHAA, 1993.

Ripert, Aline, and Claude Frère. *La carte postale: Son histoire, sa fonction sociale.* Paris: Editions du Centre National de la Recherche Scientifique, 1983.

Robert, Paul, and Alain Rey, eds. *Le grand Robert de la langue française: Dictionnaire alphabétique et analogique de la langue française.* 2nd ed. Paris: Le Robert, 1986.

Robert, Paul, A. Rey, and J. Rey-Debove, eds. *Le petit Robert: Dictionnaire alphabétique et analogique de la langue française.* Paris: Le Robert, 1985.

Robic, Marie-Claire, ed. *Du milieu à l'environnement: Pratiques et représentations du rapport homme/nature depuis la Renaissance.* Paris: Economica, 1992.

Robin, Claude. "Les transports sur rail à Arcachon." *BSHAA,* no. 112 (2002): 29–66.

Roger, Alain. *Court traité du paysage.* Paris: Editions Gallimard, 1997.

Rojek, Chris. *Decentring Leisure: Rethinking Leisure Theory.* London: Sage, 1995.

——. *Leisure for Leisure: Critical Essays.* London: MacMillan, 1989.

Rosenthal, Régine, and Charles Daney. *Bassin d'Arcachon: Baie sauvage.* Portet-sur-Garonne: Loubatières, 1988.

Ross, Kristin. *The Emergence of Social Space: Rimbaud and the Paris Commune.* Minneapolis: University of Minnesota Press, 1988.

Rouillard, Dominique. *Le site balnéaire.* Liège: P. Mardaga, 1984.

Roux, Anthelme. "Fanelly aux bains d'Arcachon." In *La poitrinaire de Nice, suivi de Fanelly aux bains d'Arcachon,* 1–77. Bordeaux: Imprimerie de Justin Dupuy et Cie, 1853.

Ryan, Simon. *The Cartographic Eye: How Explorers Saw Australia.* Cambridge: Cambridge University Press, 1996.

Sargos, Jacques. *Histoire de la forêt landaise: Du désert à l'âge d'or.* Bordeaux: L'Horizon Chimérique, 1997.

Sarraméa, Dr. Isidore. *Un regard sur Arcachon.* Bordeaux: Mme. Crugy, 1860.

Schivelbusch, Wolfgang. *The Railway Journey: The Industrialization of Time and Space in the Nineteenth Century.* Berkeley: University of California Press, 1986.

Schwartz, Vanessa R. *Spectacular Realities: Early Mass Culture in Fin-de-Siècle Paris.* Berkeley: University of California Press, 1998.

Scott, James C. *Seeing Like a State: How Certain Schemes to Improve the Human Condition Have Failed.* New Haven: Yale University Press, 1998.

Serpeille, Maxime. *Les petits trous pas chers: Guide des familles aux bains de mer, plages de la Manche et de l'Océan.* Paris: A. La Fare, 1900.

Sharp, Joanne P., ed. *Entanglements of Power: Geographies of Domination/Resistance.* London: Routledge, 2000.

Shields, Rob. *Lefebvre, Love and Struggle: Spatial Dialectics.* London: Routledge, 1998.

——. *Places on the Margin: Alternative Geographies of Modernity.* London: Routledge, 1991.

——. "The 'System of Pleasure': Liminality and the Carnivalesque at Brighton." *Theory, Culture and Society* 7 (1990): 39–72.

Simples notes sur les Réservoirs du Bassin d'Arcachon. Bordeaux: Gounouilhou, 1867.

Soboul, Albert. *Problèmes paysans de la Révolution 1789–1848: Etudes d'histoire révolutionnaire.* Paris: François Maspéro, 1983.

Société historique et archéologique d'Arcachon et du pays de Buch. "Dossier: Les passes du Bassin d'Arcachon dans les archives de Vincennes." *BSHAA,* no. 93 (1997): 39–57.

——, ed. *Le littoral gascon et son arrière-pays (mer, dunes, forêt): Actes du premier colloque tenu à Arcachon les 27–28 octobre.* Arcachon: Graphica, 1990.

——, ed. *Le littoral gascon et son arrière-pays (Moyen-âge, économie, Arcachon et le Bassin): Actes du deuxième colloque de la Société Historique et Archéologique d'Arcachon et du Pays de Buch, Arcachon, 17–18 octobre, 1992.* Arcachon: Graphica/SHAA, 1993.

——, ed. *L'ostréiculture arcachonnaise: Actes du colloque organisé par la Société Historique et Archéologique d'Arcachon, tenu à Gujan-Mestras les 15 et 16 octobre, 1994.* Arcachon: Graphica, 1994.

Soja, Edward, J. *Postmodern Geographies: The Reassertion of Space in Critical Social Theory.* London: Verso, 1989.

Soulignac, Bernard. "Aménagement agricole et évolution rurale de la Teste dans la première moitié du XIXe siècle." Honors thesis, Université de Bordeaux III, 1973.

Soultrait, Gibus de. *L'entente du mouvement.* Guéthary: Vent de Terre, 1995.

St.-L. *Un voyage à La Teste, ou Vade-mecum du voyageur sur toute la ligne du chemin de fer et sur le bassin d'Arcachon.* Bordeaux: Courrier de la Gironde, 1842.

Syndicat des Propriétaires. *Arcachon: Défense de la plage. Mémoire déposé à l'enquête de commodo et incommodo ouverte à la Mairie par arrêté du Préfet de la Gironde.* Bordeaux: G. Delmas, 1897.

Szelengowicz, Michel. *Le Bassin d'Arcachon vu par les peintres.* Angles-sur-l'Anglin: Editions de la Huche-Corne, 1994.

Taffard, Jules. "Mémoire sur la navigation du Bassin d'Arcachon." 1810. ADG 6 J 42.

Taffart, Jean-Baptiste. "Mémoire rédigé par M. Taffart sur les prés salés pour l'Administration des Domaines contre les Sieurs Fleury jeune, Oxéda et Sauvage." DM La Teste, 1832.

Tapie, Alain, Conservatoire de l'espace littoral, Alain Corbin, and Armand Frémont, eds. *Désir de rivage: De Granville à Dieppe: Le littoral normand vu par les peintres entre 1820 et 1945: Ville de Caen, Musée des beaux-arts, 1er juin-31 août 1994.* Caen: Réunion des Musées Nationaux, Seuil, 1994.

Tardis, P. M. *Organisation de la Compagnie Générale de Pêche et de Salaison du littoral d'Arcachon.* Bordeaux: Imprimerie de Lanefranque, successeur de Ragle, 1843.

Terret, Thierry. "A propos du Baigneur d'Ostende de G. Gerlier." In *Education et politique sportives, XIXe–XXe siècles,* edited by Arnaud and Terret, 381–89. Paris: Editions du Comité des Travaux Historiques et Scientifiques, 1995.

Terret, Thierry, Bertile Beunard, and Daniel Vailleau. "Pratiques et espaces balnéaires au XIXe siècle. Approche comparée de trois sites: Ostende, Marseille, La Rochelle." *Ethnologie Française* 1996, no. 3 (1996): 390–405.

Thompson, C. W. "French romantic travel and the quest for energy." *Modern Language Review* 87 (April 1994): 307–19.

Thrift, Nigel. *Spatial Formations.* London: Sage, 1996.

Tilly, Louise A., and Joan W. Scott. *Women, Work, and Family.* New York and London: Routledge, 1978.

Toulier, Bernard. "L'architecture des bains de mer: Un patrimoine marginalisé." *Revue de l'Art,* no. 101 (1993): 29–40.

Tuan, Yi-Fu. *Space and Place: The Perspective of Experience.* Minneapolis: University of Minnesota Press, 1977.

Turbet-Delof, Guy. "Paradis sur mer: Arcachon en 1825." *BSHAA,* no. 85 (1995): 37–47.

———. "Quelques aperçus de la presse périodique d'Arcachon au XIXe siècle." *BSHAA,* no. 49 (1986): 5–21.

Une Testerine. *La fête de la chapelle d'Arcachon, offert par une Testerine à Madame la Préfète et aux dames bordelaises.* Bordeaux: Chaumas-Gayet, libraire, 1849.

Urbain, Jean-Didier. *At the Beach.* Translated by Catherine Porter. Minneapolis: University of Minnesota Press, 2003.

———. *L'idiot du voyage: Histoires de touristes.* Paris: Plon, 1991.

———. *Sur la plage: Mœurs et coûtumes balnéaires (XIXe–XXe siècles).* Paris: Payot, 1994.

Urry, John. *Consuming Places.* London: Routledge, 1995.

———. *The Tourist Gaze: Leisure and Travel in Contemporary Societies.* London: Sage, 1990.

Vailleau, Daniel. "La vie balnéaire à La Rochelle de 1890 à 1914: entre plage et casino." In *Education et politique sportives, XIXe–XXe siècles,* edited by Arnaud and Terret, 391–407. Paris: Editions du Comité des Travaux Historiques et Scientifiques, 1995.

Valette, Jean. "Le culte catholique à Arcachon au XIXème siècle." In *Le littoral gascon et son arrière-pays (Moyen-âge, économie, Arcachon et le Bassin): Actes du deuxième colloque de la Société Historique et Archéologique d'Arcachon et du Pays de Buch, Arcachon, 17–18 octobre, 1992,* edited by SHAA, 203–18. Arcachon: Graphica/SHAA, 1993.

Véchambre, Abbé. *Bains maritimes d'Arcachon.* Bordeaux: Justin Dupuy et Cie, 1853.

Vigarello, Georges. *Concepts of Cleanliness: Changing Attitudes in France since the Middle Ages.* Translated by Jean Birrell. Cambridge: Cambridge University Press and Maison des Sciences de l'Homme, 1988.

Vivier, Nadine. "Le débat autour des communaux durant la crise du milieu du XIXe siècle." In *La Terre et la cité: Mélanges offerts à Philippe Vigier,* edited by Alain Faure, Alain Plessis, and Jean-Claude Farcy, 67–83. Paris: Créaphis, 1994.

———. *Propriété collective et identité communale: Les biens communaux en France, 1750–1914.* Paris: Publications de la Sorbonne, 1998.

———. "Une question délaissée: Les biens communaux aux XVIIIe et XIXe siècles." *Revue Historique,* no. 587 (1994): 143–60.

Vray, Nicole. *Les femmes dans l'Ouest au XIXe siècle.* Rennes: Editions Ouest-France, 1990.

Wagon, Bernard, and Conseil d'Architecture, d'Urbanisme et d'Environnements des Landes. *Le littoral aquitain: Paysage et architecture.* Libourne: Délégation régionale à l'architecture et à l'environnement d'Aquitaine, 1986.

Walton, John K. "Consuming the Beach: Seaside Resorts and Cultures of Tourism in England and Spain from the 1840s to the 1930s." In *Being Elsewhere: Tourism, Consumer Culture, and Identity in Modern Europe and North America,* edited by Shelley Baranowski and Ellen Furlough, 272–98. Ann Arbor: University of Michigan Press, 2001.

———. *The English Seaside Resort: A Social History, 1750–1914.* Leicester: Leicester University Press; New York: St. Martin's Press, 1983.

———. "Leisure Towns in Wartime: The Impact of the First World War in Blackpool and San Sebastian." *Journal of Contemporary History* 31, no. 4 (1996): 603–18.

Williams, Raymond. *The Country and the City.* London: Chatto and Windus, 1973.

Wilt, Alan. *The Atlantic Wall: Hitler's Defenses in the West, 1941–1944.* Ames: Iowa State University Press, 1975.

Wissocq, Paul-Emile. *Mémoire sur les travaux à exécuter pour améliorer l'entrée du Bassin d'Arcachon.* Paris: Imprimerie Porthmann, 1839.

Wood, Denis. *The Power of Maps.* London: Routledge, 1993.

Yvert, Benoit, ed. *Dictionnaire des ministres de 1789 à 1989.* Paris: Perrin, 1990.

Zonabend, Françoise. "Une perspective infinie: La mer, le rivage et la terre à La Hague (presqu'île du Cotentin)." *Etudes rurales,* no. 93–94 (1984): 163–78.

ACKNOWLEDGMENTS

It took me more than five years to research and write this book, and many people helped and encouraged me along the way. First, Charles (Chips) Sowerwine and Peter McPhee: Chips was incredibly generous with his time, advice, enthusiasm, and kindness, even while working on many other projects. He also employed me as a research assistant, making possible an ongoing intellectual exchange that was not confined to my preoccupation with Arcachon. Peter, who worked with me during Chips' absences, was always engaged, encouraging, and constructively critical. Both Chips and Peter were patient with my frequent leave-taking, smoothing the administrative path for me on many occasions. I feel blessed to have had the benefit of their combined wisdom, from my undergraduate years through to this, my first publication.

Jill Anderson guided my investigations into nineteenth-century literary representations of the sea, and Colin Nettelbeck encouraged me to apply for the Slezak travel scholarship, making possible an extended research trip to Arcachon,

Bordeaux, and Paris. The School of Graduate Studies and the Faculty of Arts (University of Melbourne) also contributed funds to this trip, as well as a conference trip in 1999, an Australian Postgraduate Award kept me alive for three and a half years, and the University of Melbourne also contributed to this book's publication costs. I thank Erica Mehrtens, Robin Harper, Antonia Finnane, and Joy Damousi from the Department of History at Melbourne for their help at various times and Jude Rossiter from the School of Graduate Studies for providing me with a work space for six months.

The Australian Film Institute unwittingly funded my first research trip when it gave me a grant to visit the Cannes Film Festival, where a film I was in was being screened; I used the opportunity to travel by train to Arcachon, and it was that first visit to the Bassin that confirmed my choice of research project.

I thank John Merriman, Alain Corbin, and the anonymous readers for Cornell University Press, for their encouragement, without which I would never have pursued publication. At Cornell University Press, Catherine Rice saw promise in my manuscript and guided me smoothly, with the help of Nancy Ferguson, through the submission process. John Ackerman and Karen Hwa took up the baton after Catherine's departure. I thank them for their enthusiasm and hard work.

I have many people to thank at the French end. In Arcachon, or rather in nearby La Hume, Jean and Colette Hourtané were my hosts. They fed me beautiful food (including a daily serving of oysters), lent me their bicycle and car, introduced me to oyster farmers, and kept me company during lonely research periods. This book would have been virtually imageless without the help of Caroline Hourtané, a dear friend (and daughter-in-law of Jean and Colette), who saved me the expense of ringing French archival services from Australia by making many local calls on my behalf and who facilitated the arduous process of seeking permissions for reproductions. My step-great-uncle, Albert-Jean Mignien, my generous host in Cap Ferret on numerous occasions, sought out useful contacts on the peninsula. In Bordeaux, Christine and Aurélie Raguet-Bouvart started out as my landladies and became my friends.

The Société Historique et Archéologique d'Arcachon (SHAA) is a wonderful local association of historians who publish regularly on the history of the Bassin and who maintain an impressive collection of local history materials in the Arcachon municipal library. Two members were especially helpful: Charles Daney and Michel Boyé. M. Daney and his wife welcomed me during my research trips, introduced me to other historians, and answered my endless questions with grace and humor. M. Boyé kindly brought me up to date with recent research during the period leading up to publication. I also thank the Society for inviting me to speak at their June 1999 conference on "Le littoral gascon et sa vocation balnéaire" (The Gascony Coast and its bathing vocation) and for publishing my paper, "Une forêt de piquets: Le désir de rivage à Arcachon" (upon which chapter 8 of this book is based) in their proceedings.

At the Archives Municipales de La Teste, Danièle Polèze and Marie-Christine Labouyrie were welcoming and allowed me to occupy the one reader's desk they had available. I also relied on the patient and generous Mme. Fernandez at the Bibliothèque Municipale d'Arcachon, who did extensive photocopying of material on an infuriatingly inefficient machine, as well as Louis Bergès, director of the Archives Départementales de la Gironde, and his staff, Pierre Astanières and colleagues at the Mériadeck library in Bordeaux, and the staff at the Archives Municipales d'Arcachon.

Jean-Louis Castaing deserves a special thank you. He facilitated interviews with elderly fishermen who were usually wary of journalist types. He provided free passes for the Bassin ferries and organized an outing on a fishing trawler with the gracious Michel Fourton and his crew. He introduced me to Richard and Cathy Lahaye, owners of an impressive postcard collection, many examples of which grace these pages. All in all, Jean-Louis made me feel welcome on the Bassin, among the people whose history I hoped to write.

Finally, I would never have written this book if my mother Helen had not taken me to France in 1978—planting the seed for a long connection with that country. She also housed my husband, daughter, and me—and our accompanying chaos—for two years while I finished this book. Bill Garner, my father, and Sue Gore supported and encouraged me through my under- and postgraduate years, morally and, at times, financially, and they actually read this book in its earliest stages. On my writing days, my parents, my mother-in-law, Pat Bowers, my aunt Sally Ford, the Melbourne University Family Club Co-op, and my friends, Nicole Tse, Clare Wright, Ange, and Emma-Kate Hitchcock, all helped to look after my daughter Olive. Clare also offered invaluable advice on publishing, and I could not have survived without my weekly campus lunch with Nicole.

Finally, I dedicate this book to my husband, David Bowers, whose love of the sea, surfing, and fishing inspired me to look more closely at the history of the beach. His commitment to our house and home, his total confidence in me, and his fortitude in enduring my frequent long absences made this book possible.

INDEX